HITCHHIKE THE WORLD

BOOK I

AMERICA, EUROPE, AFRICA

WILLIAM A. STOEVER

To Father John

Bill St~~~~ 2/25/13

D1417013

ISBN: 1461173973
ISBN-13: 9781461173977

Library of Congress Control Number: 2011908154
CreateSpace, North Charleston, SC

Cover: the author, Klein Karoo, South Africa, December 1962

SOUTH AFRICA, DECEMBER 1962.

I got a ride from Cape Town to Oudtshoorn, in the semi-desert region called the Klein Karoo, where I visited an ostrich farm and got a personal guided tour. My guide led me to a large corral with dozens of ostriches and asked, "Do you want to ride one?"

"I guess so. Is it safe?"

"Pretty safe. You're a young guy. You shouldn't get hurt if you fall off. But if you do fall off, watch out you don't get in the way of his legs. They kick forward and can kick pretty strong. They also bite, so keep your fingers away from his mouth."

Not real reassuring. But an ostrich ride seemed to be part of the package, so what the heck ...

He tossed a lasso cowboy-style over the neck of one of them and led it to a fenced-in run maybe a hundred yards long and three yards wide. He instructed, "You sit on his back and put your legs over his wings, sort of like sitting on a horse. Grab hold of his wings, right here, hands next to his body. Don't grab hold of his neck, though; their necks are vulnerable."

He helped me up onto my mount, about five feet above the ground, and jumped aside. The animal took off at a frantic clip down the fenced-in run. I bounced along on his back, holding on for dear life, for maybe ten seconds, and then fell off backwards. I hit the ground pretty hard on my rump and immediately tried to roll to one side, but the bird kept running ahead, so fortunately I didn't have to worry about getting kicked.

"Are you alright?" the guide asked.

"I guess so." But privately I doubted whether it was a good idea to invite people to ride on their backs like that – could've hurt myself pretty badly.

Excerpted from Chapter 13

TABLE OF CONTENTS

North American Travels

PREFACE: BEGINNINGS

One Saturday morning when I was twelve, a friend and I hiked three or four miles into the countryside. It was a beautiful sunny day, and we had a marvelous time passing through meadows and cornfields. Eventually we got tired and started walking along the gravel road back toward town. A farmer came along on a tractor pulling a wagonload of watermelons. I stuck out my thumb kind of tentatively, the first time ever to pull such a brazen act, and wonder-of-wonders, the man stopped and said, "Climb aboard!" We scrambled up on top of the watermelons, ten or twelve feet up, and were thrilled to ride into town on our high perches – conquerors returning home atop a triumphal float! A big adventure when you're twelve! The first hint of more to come ...

Ames, Iowa, my home town, has a downtown section and a university section separated by a river valley about a mile wide. One afternoon I missed the bus to get to my piano lesson, so I walked along the road toward the university and stuck out my thumb. Pretty soon somebody stopped and gave me a ride. After that I began hitching back and forth fairly regularly. I figured it was safe enough – the distances were short and the drivers almost all home-town people.

Once when I was seventeen and hitching home from an evening basketball game, a man picked me up and soon put his hand in my lap. It made me uncomfortable and bewildered, as if he'd violated some kind of boundary. I squirmed and edged away from him, and he removed his hand. I didn't know then that this was an invitation to homosexual sex. Nor did I know that I'd have worse experiences later.

Those were the days before interstate highways. One of the major cross-country highways, US 30, ran right through the middle of town, only two lanes wide. One night I went to a basketball game at the university which we unexpectedly won. The students celebrated by building a bonfire in the middle of the highway, which wreaked havoc for long-distance drivers passing through town. Heading home, I stuck out my thumb, and a big semi-trailer truck stopped. The driver asked, "Can you tell me how to get around this fire?"

"Sure, if you'll give me a ride a couple miles."

"Not allowed to do that – not covered by comp'ny insurance," he replied. Then, after some hesitation, "Well, come on up." I climbed into his cab – another new adventure, so high above the road! – and directed him through the residential streets and on to the downtown section. After the first mile he began to get agitated and announced, "You better get out now."

"Just two more stoplights," I pleaded, and he reluctantly agreed, but he looked visibly relieved when I told him, "This is my street."

These early experiences were a thrill for me: I discovered that I liked the sense of adventure that hitchhiking offered, of taking things as they came, of meeting new people who frequently had interesting stories to tell. It gave me a sense of exposure to a larger world, of more to experience *out there*. It provided a practical way of going new places that I might otherwise not have afforded. The destinations were important, sure, but the process of getting there was often more important.

─────

College Years

I did my undergraduate work at Amherst College in Amherst, Massachusetts, a small town about a hundred miles west of Boston. In those days it was a men's college [it's since gone co-ed]. There were two women's colleges, Smith and Mount Holyoke, each about eight miles from Amherst on different roads. That meant we usually didn't see women on campus during the week, but it was easy enough to get to the women's colleges for dates on the weekends. The college authorities actually encouraged us to hitchhike to the women's colleges: "Builds independence and self-reliance!"

The first Saturday evening of my freshman year the word went around that the residence houses at Smith were holding freshman mixers, so I put on my sport coat and tie and walked with a buddy to the corner of Rt. 9, which led to Smith College in Northampton. I was distressed to discover a hundred other sport-coat-clad freshmen standing on the same corner, but somebody assured me, "We'll all get rides," and sure enough, virtually every car that came by stopped, and a lordly upperclassman would call out, "We got room for two;" "Room for three," and so on. And when the evening was over, we all got rides back.

Hitching to the women's colleges rapidly became routine. Since I didn't own a car, I must have hitched back and forth more than a hundred times during my four years of college.

If you go to a single-sex college, you're likely to have a fair number of blind dates – a friend's girlfriend fixes you up, or you'd call up one of the women's residence houses and say, "We got three freshmen here who'd like to have dates tonight. Are there three women available?" Usually the answer was "yes," so you and your buddies would hitch over to the women's college to meet that evening's companions. Occasionally we'd even persuade the girls to hitch back to Amherst with us.

In those days the women's colleges had curfews (the men's colleges didn't): midnight on Fridays and Sundays, 1:00 a.m. Saturday night. If you were hitchhiking, you had to be sure to get out to the road within five or ten minutes after the curfew, or your chances of getting a ride home were greatly diminished. Most of us became quite adept at the timing, but I did miss the last student car a couple times and had to depend on the goodwill of the townspeople, which was chancier. Once I found myself wandering around Northampton at 2:00 a.m. with virtually no cars on the road. I passed a gas station that was still open, and the attendant saw my predicament and suggested I sleep in a nearby car, which he unlocked for me. Got six fine hours of sleep!

Mount Holyoke College was a more difficult story. That was down Rt. 116, a narrower and less-traveled road, and it was located in South Hadley, a much smaller town than Northampton. I never attempted to hitchhike there or back with a girl. There was no entertainment in South Hadley – no movies, no bars, hardly even a café – so you and your date were stuck unless there was some event at the college itself. The consequences of missing the last car back were more severe, so I always made a point of getting to the main road within five minutes after the witching hour.

————

My dad changed jobs and my parents moved to Albuquerque, New Mexico, when I was a freshman in college. My parents would have preferred to pay my airfare to the new city at the end of the school year, but I wanted to go overland. I found a ride with two upperclassmen who were driving to Denver to take summer courses. We drove straight through from Massachusetts to central Colorado, something over 48 hours, building up a sleep deficit. They dropped me in mid-morning on the road south of Denver, US 85 (no interstates yet).

I got a succession of rides after that, one town to the next – Colorado Springs, Pueblo, and some smaller towns in New Mexico. I had a heavy suitcase – most of my clothes and stuff from college – and sometimes I had to lug it for a considerable distance to find the road out of town. The time got later and later, and I got more and more tired. It was after midnight before I made it to Santa Fe, New Mexico, fifty miles north of Albuquerque. I was afraid I'd be stuck there for the night, so near to home and yet so far. But I was lucky: asked a driver in a gas station if he was going to Albuquerque, and he was. He wanted to converse, but I fell asleep almost as soon as I got in his car. An hour later he woke me: "You're home" – right in front of my parents' home!

"Thank you very much! But how'd you know the address?"

"You told me before you fell asleep."

I slept thirteen hours that night.

————

Amherst had a prom in early May. My junior year I happened not to have a date for it. The day of the prom a friend's date offered to fix me up with her friend. "I'd love that," I said, "but I don't think I can find anybody to drive me there at this time. She'd have to hitchhike back to Amherst with me." The girl's friend was willing to do that, so I put on my suit and tie, hitched to Smith, and met my blind date, who was dressed in a powder-blue ankle-length formal and looked absolutely stunning (notable cleavage!). "Wow!" I exclaimed. "You're *gorgeous!* And you do this for a guy you haven't even met! And you have to *hitchhike* with me!?" Why would such a beautiful creature consent to an adventure like this?! But she was game. We walked out to the main road, and she waited demurely on the sidewalk while I stuck out my thumb. Very quickly we got a ride from a local townsperson who seemed amused, maybe even startled, to see such formally-dressed hitchhikers.

Almost all the people who give you rides are men, but you do get an occasional ride with a woman. One afternoon in May on the road back to Amherst from Mt. Holyoke, I stuck out my thumb as per usual. Three women, probably in their early thirties and attending their class reunion, rode past and then suddenly hit the brake. They were laughing and talking animatedly as they gestured to me. I could almost read their minds: "There are three of us and only one of him, and he's a nice-looking boy, and we're on an adventure, so why not give him a ride?" As soon as I got in, I said, "Didn't your husbands tell you never to pick up hitchhikers?" They laughed uproariously at that, and we had a lively time for the fifteen-minute ride back to Amherst.

I hitched to Boston several times during my four years of college. The first time was with another freshman who had a friend living in a dorm room at Harvard. We challenged another couple of freshmen to a race: see who could get to that dorm room first. We set rules: couldn't pay for any transportation until we got to the Boston MTA, but then it was permissible to ride the buses and subways. The other two guys set out for the Massachusetts Turnpike ('Mass Pike'), while my friend and I tried to go on route 9. This latter route, although well-traveled, went through a series of cities and towns and was very slow going. We figured drivers might be more reluctant to pick up two hitchhikers than one, so we made up a sign on a piece of cardboard: "Amherst College students." We got a series of short rides, town-to-town, with delays between each ride, and it took us about four hours to reach the Boston MTA. The other guys, meanwhile, were lucky (in our opinion) and got a ride to an entrance to the Mass Pike and quickly thereafter another ride all the way into Boston. They beat us to Harvard by at least two hours.

On the return trip my friend and I found ourselves on what looked like a major road out of the city. We stood there with our thumbs outstretched for about an hour when a cop came along. Hitchhiking is technically illegal in Massachusetts, and we feared he might chase us away, but instead he said, "You won't have much luck here. This road ends at a T-junction a couple miles down the way. There's another road about a mile over that way [pointing]. You'll have better luck there. Be careful."

Appreciate those local police!

———

My parents weren't too happy with my determination to hitchhike everywhere possible, but they became resigned to my arriving home at odd hours, invariably bedraggled and tired. They wouldn't let me hitch away from home, however, always insisting on putting me on a plane or train to get back to college or wherever. I knew my mother was especially distressed, but I got the impression my father secretly admired my spirit of adventure.

CHAPTER 1.
FRESHMAN ON THE FREEWAY

North American Travels

March 1960.

Fingers numb with pain, arm about to drop out of its socket. Why the *hell* did I bring such a heavy suitcase!?

Steep embankment to struggle up, yellowish clumps of coarse grass, dust swirling at my feet. Without the suitcase I'd run right up this slope, but with it I'm pulled off balance and afraid I might fall back.

By the time I reach the top, my shoes, ankles and pant legs are covered with a grey film of dust. That's one of the things I hate about hitchhiking: you get so dirty.

At the top of the embankment, a broad expanse of concrete: the New Jersey Turnpike.

I hate standing beside turnpikes. The cars go by so fast they can't stop, and there's always the danger a cop will come along and haul me in. That's why I don't like New Jersey: the fuzz are so busy annoying 'hikers that they don't have any time to chase speeders. Too many times I've torn down some six-lane monstrosity, cringing in the front seat, the suicide seat, afraid to watch and afraid to take my eyes off the road, while some carburetor cowboy burns up the road at 90. Then you never see a cop, when you want one to save your life.

This is a good spot to stand because there's a broad shoulder where cars can stop after they see me. It's especially hard to catch a ride if there's no shoulder and the driver has to stop on the pavement itself. Also, there's a straight stretch as the drivers approach me, so they can see me in plenty of time. If there's a curve on the approaching road, they're on top of you before they see you, and they don't have time to look you over and stop. Sizing up a roadside for the best spot to stand comes automatically after a little experience 'hiking.

I usually carry on a sort of monologue toward the passing cars, mostly to entertain myself. It gets boring to stand for an hour or two when drivers are in an uncharitable mood. Here he comes now: "Hello, sir, why don't you stop..." and *zoom*!, he's past. And another one, "Let's see if you're a bastard too..." and *zoom*! "Yep, you qualify."

I have different grades of bastardness. Single men who ride by with suits and suitcases in the back seat, obviously going long distance and obviously with enough room for me in the front seat, are First-Class Bastards. Two or three men in a car are less likely to stop than a single guy, I guess because single men are more likely to want company. Two or three men in a car are usually Second-Class Bastards, unless they gesture obscenely as they pass by; then they're worse than First-Class Bastards. I guess it's amusing to a group of guys to jeer at a poor dope standing beside the road.

Another guy passes without even looking at me. But his wife is beside him: he's only a Third-Class Bastard. As a general rule, cars with women in them won't stop. I've even had men point toward their wives as they ride past, sort of blaming them for not being able to stop. I usually forgive them even though I suspect they're lying. I also forgive men with little kids in the car, although occasionally one of them will stop anyhow. Then the kids always stare at me, wide-eyed and silent.

Lots of traffic on the 'pike right here outside of New York City. But 'lots of traffic' doesn't do any good until one driver stops.

The sound of each car changes as it passes me: ZOOOO-oom. The pitch is higher as it approaches than after it has passed. We called that the 'Doppler Effect' in freshman physics and derived an algebraic formula to explain why the pitch is lower after the car passes.

Zoom! Third-Class Bastard, his wife in the car. I dislike him because he was deliberately ignoring me. I think many drivers like him are embarrassed by 'hikers. They have the feeling they should pick me up, but they don't want to take the risk or the trouble. So they ignore my existence. This guy was afraid to look at me and refuse me honestly. I don't forgive him, despite that plump little wife beside him. I've also observed that good-looking wives are more willing to pick up 'hikers than homely ones. I wonder if the good-looking ones are more confident of their ability to handle men. Or maybe they just enjoy male company more.

Next guy past waves to me and points downward. He's forgiven ... he's local, not going far. I like it when drivers signal to me, even though they don't actually help me out. At least they acknowledge my existence. There's a regular set of communications between driver and 'hiker. Pointing left or right indicates turning, pointing down indicates not going far, pointing backwards indicates short trip. Shrugging shoulders isn't such a friendly indication, almost like saying, "You've gotten yourself into this mess, now get yourself out of it."

More drivers. Most ignore me, a few signal turns. I glance at my watch: 10:00 a.m. – been beside the road for half an hour, getting tired of standing here. Automatically I curse myself for not getting out on the road sooner. But it takes willpower to drag yourself from a comfortable bed and go stand by the lonely roadside. Now I have no choice but to wait until somebody stops. That's my one article of faith: somebody will always stop. I read that in a book once, a lousy book about a juvenile delinquent, but it's helped get me through some pretty hopeless situations.

Right hand getting cold. New Jersey in late March, not unbearably cold but not yet spring. My light-weight topcoat isn't quite enough to keep me warm when the wind is blowing. But I don't want anything heavier when climbing in and out of cars with my heavy suitcase. I debated wearing a jacket and tie this morning, then decided against it. Now I wish I had it on – sometimes it does help in getting a ride. But clothes get dirty quickly when you're on the road, and I need clean shirts when I get to Washington.

Suddenly way down to my right a car is stopping. Most drivers don't start putting on the brakes until they're completely past me. Slow reaction time, thoughts wandering, wait-and-see-what-he-looks-like: I don't know what the reason is.

But right now I've gotta pick up the suitcase and carry it a good distance towards the fellow. Despite the heavy suitcase, I begin to run: running creates the impression of youthful eagerness, so the driver won't change his mind and take off before I get to him. Also, don't keep him waiting too long when you run towards him, which I think is good psychology. Besides these, I'm just so happy to finally have a ride that I'm glad to run fifty yards.

"I can lift you down the turnpike a short distance. Perhaps if I leave you at one of the restaurants, you will find another ride," he smiles across the front seat at me. A Chevy Tudor, six or seven years old, conservative blue-gray. My breath, slightly quickened by the run, clouds over a spot on the partly-opened window. "We can place your valise in the back seat. Please wait until I can make a place for it." He shifts a leather briefcase over to one side of the cushion. "Your valise must be quite heavy," he smiles. I like him.

"Yes, I should learn to limit myself to a sensible amount," I reply. I settle into the seat, slamming the door too loudly.

He peers carefully out his window, then engages the clutch – stick shift, I note – and accelerates slowly onto the pavement. "For which place are you heading?"

He speaks with a slight accent. It's warmish in the car, and I shift to take my topcoat off. "I hope to make it to Washington tonight. My economics class is having a seminar there starting tomorrow."

"In that case I am very sorry that I do not plan to return there today. I make my home in Washington, but tonight I shall visit my sister in New Brunswick."

"Oh, you live in D.C.? I might have guessed from your accent that you come from somewhere else." Foreigners are often quite decent about picking up hitchhikers. I guess they don't fear getting robbed and murdered and all those horrible things you read about in the papers. We're moving along at 55 now, in the right-hand lane. I can't help but check the speedometer of every driver I ride with. This fellow is almost too slow for my taste: I get impatient if we go less than 65.

"I am from France, but I have lived in Washington for seventeen years. I am with the World Bank."

World Bank ... World Bank ... what sensible question can I ask about the World Bank? "You provide loans to less-developed countries?"

"Yes, you are correct. You are doing economics then?"

"Maybe – not sure yet. Anyhow I'm going to an economics conference in Washington, if I make it by tomorrow."

"Have you started your journey from New York?"

"Started from New York this morning, but I go to school in Massachusetts. Got a ride with a classmate to New York and stayed in a sort of youth hostel in Greenwich Village last night. Got a ride this morning from the Holland Tunnel to where you picked me up." But I'm slightly embarrassed at discussing hitching and decide it's time to change the subject. "I guess your field must be macroeconomics, international investment and finance, with the World Bank?"

He takes the lead. "Professionally I have an interest in all branches of economics, but it is true that my specialty is foreign direct investment in developing countries."

I wrack my brain to ask an intelligent question about foreign investment. Might be a chance to learn something useful. Isn't that what a liberal education is made up of, smatterings of useful information from every discipline? I hit upon the problems of promoting economic growth in less-developed countries and am rewarded with a discussion of the political implications of investment by multinational corporations. I don't really have the background to understand everything he says, with only Samuelson's *Introductory Economics* behind me, but it's nice to hear the vocabulary tossed around.

Another fifteen minutes of foreign investment, and suddenly he says, "But I must leave you here, unless you desire to be left at the next exit." He turns carefully off into a restaurant area, traverses the vast asphalt no-man's-land parking area, and stops in front of the gas pumps.

I heft my suitcase from the car. "Thanks very much for the ride. You've taught me a lot. Maybe I'll be able to use some of it in my economics conference in Washington." I stand awkwardly for a moment, then, "Thanks again" and move on.

Another car right here by the gas pumps. I stick out my thumb as the driver starts up, but he ignores me. I'm ready to head for the restaurant when another car moves around the pumps. Once again my thumb out. This guy stops alright: *"Don't you guys know it's a felony to hitchhike on the turnpike?!"*

Lordy. Cop.

Unmarked car.

Experience has taught me to pick up my suitcase and start toward him. Try to look innocent and collegiate and first-time-I've-ever-hitchhiked-on-the-pike-Officer. "Get away from the pumps!" he bellows. "Stand on down there by the exit or I'll run you in." Obediently I move away toward the exit ramp, thankful there's no more unpleasantness. Suitcase feels heavy already. Probably have to stand there another half hour before somebody stops.

But the first guy by is a semi-trailer-truck, a big five-axle monster with a load of aluminum tubing on the trailer and a small sign on the cab: WILSON VAN LINES NEWARK NEW JERSEY. Air brakes, tsh, tsh, and the driver, a small wiry unshaven fellow with a dirty shirt, climbs out of the cab and walks around to inspect his load. Phooey, I thought he was stopping for me. But no harm in trying: "Are you heading south?"

After considering me for a moment, he replies, "I can give you a ride to the north edge of Philly."

That doesn't suit: it means he'll be turning off on the Pennsylvania Turnpike extension, and I really hoped to find a ride as far south as the Delaware Memorial Bridge. But it will get me away from that cop. "Can you take me just to the turnoff?"

"I s'pose." As I heft the suitcase into the cab, he adds, "If anybody stops me, tell 'em you're a relief driver. Insurance don't permit ta carry 'hikers."

That means he's running some risk to carry me. Amazing he'd do it for a complete stranger. I settle the suitcase beside me on the dirty seat. Glad now I only have my wash pants on. Semis are too warm, too rough, and too slow to be desirable rides in most cases, but right now I'm thankful for anything. At night they're a blessing too.

We move out into the road, engine roaring, transmission straining, and he grinds thru the gears to sixty before he says anything. "Yur headin' fer Florida?"

"Nah, I just want to get to D.C. Visiting a friend." Truck drivers aren't generally impressed with college economics conferences. (Educational snobbism?) After a moment I add, "I hope you don't get into trouble by giving me a ride."

"Oh, we'll be O.K. Police ain't likely to bother me on the pike. Not if I stay under 60."

"They're worse off the turnpikes?"

"Yeah, they'll hit you fer anything. Two miles over the limit, blooey! School bus anywhere in sight, blooey! Hundred pounds over the limit, blooey!"

"How much does your rig weigh?"

"Empty I weigh five tons, cab and trailer. Got eight tons load on me now."

"Will you get thru O.K. with such a heavy load?"

"I should make it O.K. I only got a little stretch of the city where I'm over the limit."

"What do you do if they catch you?"

"Unload, pay the fuckin' fine, and come back fer it."

"You got any money with you to pay fines like that?"

He glances at me for a moment, then chooses his answer carefully: "Most of us, we pay it on credit. They know they'll get it, or they can give us real shit whenever we drive in their fuckin' state. Sometimes ya do carry a little somethin' 'cause it's less bother. I usually don't, tho." Even truck drivers have to watch out for stick-ups." Maybe he thinks I'll pull a gun on him if he tells me he has lots of money.

"Does your rig run 24 hours a day?"

"Uhh, it usu'ly runs whenever there's a load for it. Like I'll get into our Philly warehouse 'bout 12:30, start unloadin' 'bout 1:00, an' there's another load waitin' ta go back ta Newark t'night. Should be back there 'bout 9:00.

"You'll drive it back to Newark?"

"Yeah, they usu'ly send a driver out for a complete run if it's a short one like this."

"Who unloads the truck, the warehousemen?"

"Oh, I'll unload 'er if I feel like it; otherwise I'll hire somebody ta do it."

"There are people waiting at the warehouse for unloading jobs?"

"Ya see, they give me money fer loadin' an' unloadin', an' if I ain't tired, maybe I'll unload 'er m'self an' keep the money, er maybe I'll get somebody ta do part of it."

"That'd make a long day, if you do it yourself."

"I git time-an'-a-half fer any drivin' over seven hours or 200 miles a day. Ain't bad money, an' now I'm on local runs, I get every second er third day off, an' I sleep at home 'most every night."

"You used to be on cross-country runs?"

"Buddy, I been drivin' fer eighteen years. I been on every kinda run ya c'n name. I don' like them cross-country runs, tho. Too fuckin' long away from home. I useta not mind it, but no more."

Good pay he gets. I wonder if I dare ask what he thinks of Jimmy Hoffa [President of the Teamsters Union; later murdered]. I imagine the union takes pretty good care of him.

Silence for a while, then he continues, "I quit school ta go inta the war. Lied, told 'em I was seventeen, an' I'd barely turned sixteen," with some pride. "Got decorated twice. Bravery beyond th' call a duty."

"Where'd you fight?"

"Guadalcanal. Them yellow sons-a-bitches kept ... Then I was wounded an' outa action after that. Still got a bad leg."

"But you keep driving O.K."

"Never went back ta school after I got outa the hospital. S'pose I shoulda," as he glances at me. "But I'm a good steady man, they don' have no trouble with me. Only been laid off once, '49, then the Korean War come along an' I never been outa work since. Never missed a day fer drunk, neither."

I have a shameful sense of economic snobbery: my father is a college teacher, and the idea of being out of work never occurs in our household.

Now I feel awkward, not knowing what to say. Finally I hit on: "Yeah, a good reliable man never has to worry about keeping his job." How'd that go over?

Apparently it didn't register. "I was on cross-country till '58. Been all over the fuckin' country. California, Texas, Alaska. Then I wanted offa cross-country, told 'em I deserved a break, but they wasn't gonna listen. So I found me this job with Wilson. I don't take no shit offa no company. Gave up a lot a seniority ta switch here, but I like drivin' fer Wilson."

"You've driven up the Alcan Highway to Alaska?"

"Yeah, that was a rough son-a-bitch trip. Skidded off the road twicet. They never made me do it again."

Silence for a while. A car gives a long blast on his horn, and then starts around us. "You see that son-a-bitch?" the driver says. "I could curve him offa the road so fuckin' easy."

"You ever curved anybody off?"

"Only oncet, he was drunk, I left him sittin' there in the ditch."

Silence again. The idea of this driver or any other deciding to curve me off the road doesn't have much appeal. I don't know how to change the subject without seeming awkward.

The truck makes a constant roar as it moves along, and the noise adds to my discomfort at the jerky ride. Cars constantly pass us, and I keep thinking how much nicer it would be to be moving along at 65 in one of them. I hope my wash pants haven't gotten too dirty in the cab.

These thoughts vanish abruptly, however, when the driver announces: "Wull, here's my turnoff. I'll drop ya beside the road."

By the time I've picked up my suitcase and coat, he's pulled onto the shoulder and stopped. I scramble down onto the gravel, coat in hand, and heft the suitcase down beside me. "Thanks for the ride."

"Shur thing, don' let the bed-bugs bite," and he's off, leaving me forlorn at the roadside. There's something harsh about suddenly being thrust from the warmth and drowsiness of a moving vehicle onto the hard road, like being born, moving from the secure womb into the cold world. Once again I'm on my own, alone, standing ... It's already 11:30, most of the morning gone, and I've still got a good ways to go.

First thing I'm faced with is getting downstream from this turnoff, finding a place where the cars will have plenty of space to stop for me.

Suitcase in hand, peer to the left, then cross the two-lane turnoff. Watch out for cars on this one … they really take these turnoffs fast. Then along the shoulder for a hundred feet, under an overpass, another hundred feet along the shoulder, and cross the feed-in from the Pennsylvania pike. I intensely dislike traversing these interchanges on foot because I have to walk too close to the moving traffic, carrying coat and suitcase over very rough gravel. At least I don't have to climb any embankments on this one.

And now I've got to wait until somebody chooses to slow down from 65 and stop for me. This hasn't been a very good morning: I've only gotten short rides and had to wait so long for the first. Mentally I figure: on the road for two and a half hours, and I've only made about sixty miles. Usually I hope to average 50 miles an hour on turnpikes or out west. Should've had the truck driver let me off at the last turnpike restaurant, wherever that was.

Not carrying on my private monologue with the passing drivers now. Getting tired of standing by the road and watching cars whiz by without deigning to notice me. But nothing I can do about it. Here I will stand until somebody picks me up.

Chevrolets, Cadillacs, Plymouths. I don't recognize a lot of them. Back in high school I had plenty of time and interest to follow the new car models, but I haven't bothered to keep up with them since starting college. Also, I don't recognize most of these little foreign jobs that go puttering past. There weren't many of those around in 1955, *my* year for cars, so I haven't learned them either. … Foreign cars are pretty good about stopping. I suppose the kind of person who will buy one of them is young-spirited and willing to try something new, the same sort of person who will pick up a hitchhiker. Convertibles stop too: anybody who'll take a chance on a rag-top will take a chance on a 'hiker. … Oddly enough, Cadillacs will often stop too, especially Caddies driven by the *nouveau riche*. … Actually, it's kind of hard to predict who will stop – there seems to be an exception to any generalization.

A driver in a medium-sized gleaming white car glances in my direction as he passes and immediately swerves off the road to wait for me. Marvelous, I've only been waiting maybe ten minutes, and now I'm away from this blasted intersection. He opens the door even before I've run up to the car. "Climb in," very welcoming.

"Hi, I'm heading towards Washington," I pant as I lift the suitcase over into the back seat. I settle into the seat, and zoom! he accelerates so hard it throws me back in the seat.

He chuckles a bit in my direction. "I'm very pleased to have you with me," with a sort of welcoming smile.

"Are you going all the way to Washington?"

"Oh, I'm going much farther than that. I can take you a long way."

I wait for him to say where, but he doesn't volunteer anything further, so I change the subject. "I should know what kind of car this is, but I can't recognize it."

"It's a Thunderbird. Do you get many rides in them?"

"Oh, are they this large? I thought they were much smaller. This one has a back seat."

"This is the largest T-bird. It has power windows, power brakes, power steering, power seat."

"Isn't all that unusual in a sports car? I thought all those power appliances cut down on the speed of the car."

"Well, it seems to be moving along alright, doesn't it?" He's right, we're doing 70, and it hardly feels like it's moving. "I like my cars luxurious." Again that smile, sort of self-satisfied, sort of like ... like he was getting ready to reveal a secret ...? Then: "Would you like to drive?"

"Me? Now?!" I'm startled, because he doesn't seem like the sort of person to have a 'hiker take over the wheel, especially after two minutes' conversation. Middle-aged, medium-heavy build, well dressed, glasses, fleshy features. Odd.

With no reply, he swerves immediately onto the shoulder and stops. I get out and walk around the car, while he lifts himself slowly across the center fixture into the right-hand seat. I settle into the driver's seat, then look at him expectantly. "Ready?"

"Go ahead."

I start carefully onto the pavement and accelerate slowly up to 60. Glad I brought my driver's license along. "It's sure beautiful to drive."

"You like the power steering? You can adjust the seat so it's comfortable. Feel the little button down on your left."

Power seats – boy, what a snow-job car! "Power seats are nice for long trips, aren't they? ... You've come a long way?"

"Yes, down from Troy, New York. Driven almost four hours, couple hundred miles. It's good to have somebody to relieve me for a while." Well, that's not so unusual. I've driven for other tired drivers before. He continues, "You're only doing 60. Take her up to 75 if you want. Don't worry about the fine; I can pay for it if they stop us."

O.K., 75 it is. "You must be in a hurry. Are you down here on business?"

"No, just a pleasure trip. I'm travelling a long distance, that's all. Besides, I know how you young fellows are. You like to drive fast."

He's right about the driving, purring along steadily at 75, breezing effortlessly around cars and trucks in the slower lane. "You're not going to Washington?"

"No, I'd planned to go south of it. I can take you farther west if you'd like."

"Oh, it's kind of you to offer, but I'm going to a college economics conference in D.C. Where are you heading, California?"

"Yes, I thought I'd go out to San Diego. I have a friend there."

"When is he expecting you?"

"Oh, he's not really expecting me. I just thought I'd go out and see him. I'm always welcome when I go to his house."

"I envy you being so free. If I didn't have this conference in Washington, I'd go out there with you."

"I could take you farther along if you wanted. Maybe your parents live somewhere along the way." He sounds almost hopeful. Probably wants someone to help with driving on the long trip.

"It happens my folks live in Albuquerque [New Mexico, only two states removed from California]. It's a very tempting offer."

"See, there you are. If you ride with me, I'll leave you right on your doorstep."

"Would we drive straight thru?"

"Oh, no, I'm too old for that. I mean, you're younger and probably don't have as much money. But I could put us up in motels along the way."

"Actually I don't think I have enough time for it. And I should go to this conference anyhow."

"Well, we'll see. Anyhow, the offer remains open, if you want to take advantage of it. I know how you young fellows are."

At one point I notice a lonesome figure with a suitcase off to the right. We flash past so fast I don't get a chance to inspect him. Another hitchhiker? Does my host want to stop? I glance at him: obviously he didn't even notice the guy. That's O.K. with me ... I'm too comfortable to want to stop and pick up another 'hiker. Besides, he's a half-mile behind by now. Next guy can pick him up. Does that make me a First Class Bastard?

Not knowing what else to say, I ask, "Are you on vacation now?"

"I can take a vacation whenever I want. I'm in business for myself. I'm prosperous enough that I can afford to leave whenever I want."

"You leave your business to your staff?"

"Yes, um, yes, my staff ... um ... yes ...."

"How long will you be in California?"

"Oh, a month or two." Funny he wouldn't have more definite plans.

Something about this conversation is rather odd, disconcerting. I can't quite figure this guy out. But that's not unusual; I can't figure most people out. So I respond, "I suppose after I've graduated I'll be able to make long trips like yours. But this spring vacation, I've gotta get back to college and write a term paper after the conference is over."

"Where do you go to college?"

"It's up in Massachusetts. It's called Amherst ...." Does that ring a bell?

"Yes, I've heard of it. It's a men's college, isn't it?"

"Yeah, that's right. We've got two girls' colleges right near us, Smith and Mt. Holyoke."

"I think conditions would be rather ... difficult ... in a men's college. What do you do to ... relax?"

"Oh, we can have dates most Saturday nights. And we have sports, and there's a movie theater, and some of the guys drink pretty hard."

"I didn't really mean that kind of relaxing. I mean, when you're a man, well, you have to have a release of tension every so often. ... I don't suppose you've ... slept ... with ... a girl?" He rubs his thumb hard across the dashboard, leaving a streak where it presses against the metallic surface.

"No, I haven't, not for any real moral conviction, but just that, well .... it doesn't seem ...."

"But you wouldn't hesitate if you felt right about it ... about ... the girl!" A statement, almost an assertion. He lets out a long breath and settles back into his seat, relaxed and smiling. Patronizingly, "I know how you young fellows are. I'm more experienced now, but when I was a little younger, I always wanted the person ... the girl ... to know I loved her, I mean even though I had as high morals as anybody, of course."

"The thing is, I'm not always attracted to the girls I could do it with, and the ones I'd like to have relations with aren't the sort who'd let me."

"Yes, sexual relations have to be a gesture of true devotion. They can mean that in some pretty unusual circumstances, though." Glances at me. "I mean, you could take an example a time when I was visiting a couple of friends, a man and his wife. They wanted to have children, but he was impotent. We used to sleep in the same room, and one time the husband said to me, 'Bernie, I wish I was a man like you.' That's my name, Bernie, and he wanted me to start a child for them, and I did it because I loved them both."

????? ... strange ...? But I go on, "Yeah, I suppose it's the circumstances which make it right or wrong. Otherwise you can be hurt by it."

"Yes, especially the woman can be hurt. I mean she can be hurt physically too. Take me, for example. I have to be careful that I don't penetrate a small woman too deeply. I'm a big man, eight inches long."

How the hell did I get into this conversation anyhow? Plenty of conversations in the college dorm are about sex, but this is a little too explicit for comfort. "Your T-bird is a beautiful car to drive ..."

"I don't suppose you've ever measured yourself?"

God Almighty! "No, I never bothered to."

He hears the irritation in my voice. "Of course, that's the sort of thing men don't talk about unless they're on quite intimate terms."

We're silent for a while. I like to talk with people who give me rides ... I feel I owe it to them to be pleasant when they're kind enough to pick me up, but I've never encountered anybody so insistent on this topic before. Not that it's not an absorbing topic, but somehow ....

He smiles his smile .... something about that smile seems kind of strange ... like the disembodied Cheshire cat in *Alice in Wonderland*, not quite here, not quite real, like there's something undisclosed underneath ...

Then he goes on, "I'm very glad you enjoy driving my Thunderbird. A sports car like this one is really nice for men who are young at heart, isn't it? I could've brought my Continental, but I thought I'd prefer to have a livelier and sportier car for this trip. Just the sort of car to appeal to a young fellow like you."

"You certainly have a nice choice, if you have a Continental too."

"Yes, I like cars. I had three cars until recently, but I sold my convertible. I've been thinking of buying one of these foreign sports cars. Which one of them would you suggest?"

"Gee, I don't know enough about any of them, really. Actually I'm not much of an authority on cars, I just enjoy driving them, just like covering distance."

"You have a real sense of adventure," he pronounces "You enjoy travel and excitement and cars and youthful things like that."

"Well, I.... there's a bridge ahead. That's the Delaware Memorial, isn't it?" I'm flattered that he thinks I have a sense of adventure. Except my folks don't call it 'sense of adventure'; they say 'foolhardiness'.

"Yes, you're right. Ah, I see an open booth in the second lane. Over there." He takes the toll card from the glove compartment as I roll down my window. He rolls his down too.

The routine at these toll booths. "Hullo, nice day," into my window, the toll collector, completely expressionless.

My host smiles. "I'm afraid I don't have any change." He takes out a fat wallet and produces a hundred-dollar-bill. One hundred smackers. He smiles apologetically at me, "That's a fault of mine, I suppose. I never carry enough change."

The toll collector reaches into his booth and takes out a clip-board. "I'll have to take your license number," he says matter-of-factly. He walks to the front of the car and writes on the board. Then he takes the c-note and counts out ninety-seven dollars and some change to my host.

Accelerating from the toll booth. Motionless, then suddenly moving, like being shot from a launching block. Then I ask, "Why did he take our number?"

"Oh, it's routine on all bills over twenty dollars. It protects against counterfeiters. I'm afraid driving won't be so agreeable on this next stretch. We're off turnpikes when we cross Delaware and Maryland."

"Delaware will be my 45th state."

"It seems you've traveled a lot. You enjoy going new places and trying new things. So do I. I think we're very compatible. I think we should call each other by name. It's much more relaxed that way. I've already told you my name is Bernie...."

"My name's Bill." He reaches over and shakes my hand, which turns out to be an awkward maneuver when I'm driving.

"I am very pleased to have you with me, Bill.

'Let's see, we turn here, onto route 40, I think?" He nods. We curve off to the right and back through an underpass, following signs to US 40.

He resumes the conversation: "I think you do most of your learning about *life* outside of class. Girls, love, sex, the most important things."

Well, that's a pretty large order. "College seems to be a pretty isolated existence. Particularly Amherst, it's in a very small town, and I don't get into a city very often. It's a very one-sided life, I think."

"Yes, you need more ... *experience* ... than you can gain in your .... inhibited atmosphere. I used to feel the same way when I was studying. But now I've .... learned something .... about ... the world .... I feel that I can .... give a lot to a young fellow like yourself. Of course, I get a great deal of satisfaction in return."

"Actually, the existence in a college world isn't any narrower than the existence in any other environment. You can broaden your range by taking a variety of courses in different subjects."

The smile narrows perceptibility. "Yes, all this intellectual learning is all right, but you want to gain experience in love and life too. That's where a person with deep emotional experience can help you. You can learn about the different aspects of love without being hurt in the process if you have a proper teacher. Most young men don't have the proper outlook on sex."

That topic again. We always seem to return to sex. "Yeah, I used to think that sex was something you could just do naturally, you know, wedding night and that sort of thing. But I've begun to think it must take practice, like everything else. I've read marriage manuals that say that a man and wife have to learn to obtain satisfaction together."

The smile returns. "Ahhhh. Yes, you are exactly right. Exactly right. You do have to get experience in order to have a successful sexual relationship with your partner. You need a good teacher. Otherwise your partner may be disappointed and hurt. I had to learn the hard way."

"Well, I suppose you're right. There's some guy at the University of Illinois who talks about 'mature couples who know what they're doing'. But, um, he got fired."

"Yes, many people in the United States try to impose their own conservative views about what is and is not proper in one's personal conduct on others. You must know what I mean: legislation against homosexuality ... against prostitution, for example. It only means that they drive homosexuality and prostitution underground where it's shameful rather than keeping it in the open, where it's respectable and clean."

"Yeah, I suppose ... I don't know much about it ... about those things."

"I think a young fellow should be given the opportunity to learn in the most honest and open fashion possible. But with me, for example, I had to have my first experience with animals on a farm."

"With *animals*?"

"Yes, it's a common enough way for boys who have access to cows or sheep. It's really a very pleasant way to obtain relief."

I am mentally puzzling over the geometry of such an operation: with cows? and *sheep*?? "It strikes me as rather unnatural, really."

"Ah, yes, but who is to say what is natural for every individual in every circumstance? I'm sure you could conceive of situations where it would be natural for you to have relations with some rather unexpected .... ah ... in some unconventional circumstances."

"Yeah, I suppose. I'm not much of an authority on that sort of thing."

"You could take for example that time that I was driving the daughter of a good friend of mine home from a high school girls' government convention of some sort. I happened to be going to the town somehow, so I told my friend that I'd bring his daughter home. It was a hundred-mile trip, and he had no reason to drive all that way when I was going anyhow. So I picked her up in the afternoon, but we took so long packing and having an afternoon snack that we couldn't make it back before night-fall. So I decided we should stop somewhere along the way."

What a ghastly tale this is going to be. "Say, do you know whether...."

"We of course stayed in separate rooms in the motel, but just before bedtime we were just talking ... about things in general. I think she was very interested by some of the things I told her. She recognized that I was wiser and had had more experience that she. Then I got up to leave for my cabin, and she said, 'Don't go yet.' I of course didn't know what she meant, but she came over to where I was sitting on the bed and took my hand.

She put it on herself over her nightgown. I didn't want to do it, but she wouldn't let me leave until I did."

Motel, sitting on bed, nightgown. How 'innocent' you were .... but in spite of my disgust I begin to feel a warm intenseness, the beginnings of an erection, and I shift the seat until I'm comfortable. The smile grows broader: "You can see that this was a case of her showing respect and affection for me in the most natural and expressive way she knew how."

Gad, what a repulsive tale!! *If* it's true. And if he really did have sex with her, how consensual was it, really? My excitement is gone as quickly as it came. "Unh, um, does this road go through Baltimore?"

"Yes, no, there's a good four-lane out-off which goes around the city. It feeds into US 301. You realize that I wouldn't have had relations with her if it hadn't been for the right reasons."

Is there something wrong with me? I find this guy suddenly one of the most repulsive people I've ever run into. I can't think of anything to say. I don't *want* to say *anything* to him.

Maybe I should be impressed at his story, but ... but ... but it's not the sort of thing *I* would brag about ... All he can talk about is sex. It's an absorbing topic and all that, but with a perfect stranger ... and somehow especially with a hitchhiker .... maybe he really does think he can help me ...

The Baltimore cut-off... Breezing along at 55, I can feel my heart racing just the least little bit. Driving on these bypasses is a challenge, like roller-skating too fast on a crowded floor. But in this Thunderbird it's a pleasure to fold through the pattern of weaving and darting traffic. I suppose little old ladies would be terrified by it.

"Here's our turn," he says suddenly. "US 301." Obediently I head onto the exit ramp. Brake sharply as we enter the curve – they always build these exit ramps sharper than you expect. Around under the overpass. There's more traffic down here, and we have to go more slowly.

A mile at 30; then traffic begins to thin out and move faster. Getting through cities is a pleasure with these new cut-offs and overpasses. It's better than the times I remember fighting slowly through crowded downtown streets on auto trips with my folks. My God, am I already saying, "Back when I was a boy ..."?!

US 301 turns out to be four lanes, but not restricted access. We can move along between 55 and 60, but it's no longer the elated magic glide of the turnpike. I have to slow for turning cars and take special care as I pass semis.

We've been silent since leaving the city, but now my host suggests, "Bill, are you hungry? I'd like to stop in a restaurant along the way, if you would."

"Fine. You pick one; you'll probably guess better than I." Besides, I don't know what his taste will be, hamburger or escargot. I hadn't thought about being hungry, but now I remember I didn't have much breakfast, and it's almost 2:00. On the road I tend to forget about food.

"Yes, there are plenty to choose from, aren't there? Up ahead there, I see one, JOHNNY AND KATE'S, I think it says, right there on the right. Does that look all right to you?"

I have to brake sharply in order to turn onto the asphalt parking area in front of Johnny and Kate's. "Anything's O.K with me. After some of the places I've eaten, this'll be a feast, I'm sure." Looks like steak. Hope it won't set me back too much. Probably have to get the fish dinner, or 'Today's Special', whatever that might be. Of course, there's always the chance he'll pay for it.

We sit at a cloth-covered table near the front of the room. The waitress comes to us immediately – not much business at this hour. "How are ya? Nice day for travellin'." She puts a couple of menus on the table and gives it a perfunctory brushing with a cloth. My eyes light on a white square of paper clipped on the menu saying: LUNCHEON SPECIAL: CHIPPED BEEF ON TOAST, VEGETABLE, ROLL AND BUTTER, and COFFEE ***$1.55.

My host glances up at the waitress, "Can you please tell me how long it would take to prepare your sirloin steak?" I look inside to find that: $4.50. Lot of money to a penurious student.

"Oh, we'll have it in a jiffy. The grill's clean right now."

"Yes, I'll take that, then. Does that sound good to you, Bill?"

"Sure, I love it, but..." Careful to protest just enough to sound genuine but not enough to discourage him.

"Very good. We'll both have the steak, miss." That's clearly an offer to treat me.

"Thanks a lot. I hadn't thought..."

"Oh, that's alright. I know how you young fellows are," he smiles. He certainly tries to be agreeable. "This place isn't as good as I'm accustomed to, but it doesn't look bad for a roadside restaurant."

Rolls and butter appear, and conversation stops as we tear into them. Soon the steaks follow, sizzling and tender. I polish mine off completely before turning to the French fries and salad.

After the meal, my host asks, "Would you like to continue driving?"

"Love to!"

He unlocks his door and gets in before he hands me the keys. "If you come west with me, I'll let you do as much driving as you like," as we take off.

"You're sure tempting me, but I really don't think it'd work out very well. And I really should attend this conference. I told them I would."

"Alright, but it seems foolish for you to pass up such a good opportunity. I could teach you a lot. Of course, maybe you don't like the car. Or my company."

"Oh, not at all. It's very beautiful. And you're very kind. Nice to travel with. But I really can't." He doesn't make any reply, and after a couple minutes I start on something different: "Have you made this trip to California often?"

"Mmmm." He doesn't seem eager to carry on any more conversation. Have I offended him or something?

Now every five or ten miles there's another turnoff to the right, with signs indicating WASHINGTON DC 28 MILES and then 22 MILES. Finally a sign announces US 5 NORTH ONE MILE. As soon as I see it, I start to slow down: "That's my turnoff ahead?"

"Yes, if you've definitely decided to pass up this chance to be with me," my host replies.

"Well, as I said, I'd love to go with you, but I really can't."

"But don't you think … that is, you know of course most young fellows would jump at the chance. You know it won't cost you anything. I have plenty of money."

I slow the car down to 30 before pulling off onto the shoulder. I wait a few seconds before opening the car door, and my host looks questioningly at me. I guess with his money he's never had this from-the-womb-into-the-cold-world experience. I want to prolong this pleasurable command-of-the-road feeling for just another moment before once again becoming the poor plaintive figure at the roadside. But one must face reality sometime.

After we stop I open the door and step out, foot grating on gravel, and reach into the back seat for my suitcase and coat. "Well, I sure appreciate all the help you've given me. The dinner and the ride and everything. Thanks an awful lot," with my biggest smile.

"Are you sure you won't change your mind? I thought for a moment...."

"No, I wish I could, but thanks an awful lot," and I pick up the suitcase to leave. He moves over into the driver's seat, and the car starts to move. I always wait for my hosts to pull out so that I can wave to them. I think it gives that last little warm glow which makes them say, "I'm glad I picked him up." This time my host looks more unhappy than warm-glowish, but he manages a small wave as the car pulls away. Somehow I feel a sense of relief as he leaves.

Well, here it is, ten after five, close to the city but nonetheless dependent on another ride. For that matter, when I get to Washington, where will I go then? This thought hadn't occurred to me until just now. Oh, well, something will work out.

US 5 appears to be four lanes all the way into Washington. There's a lot of traffic on it, making it slow going. I understand they're going to replace it with an interstate highway sometime – they're constructing so-called interstates all over the country now.

Will anybody stop? They all look like commuters, hurrying home and not in the mood to help out a lonely figure by the roadside. I lug my suitcase maybe ten yards down the road, away from the congestion at the intersection but close enough that the cars won't be going too fast.

Then the monologue begins: How are you, sir? .... Zoom! I'm not very happy about having to stand here again, but there's-nothing-I can-do-but-wait. It's always especially hard to get back to the roadside after the security of a nice long ride.

And then suddenly there's a car already stopped on the shoulder ten yards down, honking to attract my attention. I hadn't even seen him pass by, I was so lost in my own thoughts. How long has he been sitting there? I pick up the suitcase and start running towards him.

An old Chevy sedan, 1951 maybe, nondescript brown and grey two-tone. The whole family sitting inside – Momma in the front seat with the baby, Grandma and two or three kids piled on the junk in the back seat. Papa steps out from behind the wheel, a wiry black-haired man, saying, "We oughta be able ta squeeze ya in here someplace. I'll put your case in the trunk." He lays it on top of some dirty machinery parts in the rear end, and they move a couple kids to the front seat so that I can sit in the back comfortably. Looks like the whole family's been out for a visit or a picnic someplace. Ironic, how all those single men in their roomy cars pass me by, and then these people, crowded in their old clunker, with cares of their own, take the trouble to stop and help me out.

Conversation isn't much: "You headin' fer Washington?" and my reply, "Yeah, just drop me wherever's convenient, and I'll find a phone," and after a few minutes, "You like some beer?" as he produces a bottle from a red cooler in the front seat.

We get into the city, and he says, "You can come to our house to phone if ya want." After weaving through some side streets, we arrive at an anonymous house somewhere on an anonymous street. I help carry sleepy kids and leftover food through the back door into the kitchen.

"The phone's in the front room, and if yur hungry, come an' have a bite to eat first."

I'm overwhelmed by their kindness, but I'd feel rotten if I imposed on them any further. "Gosh, thanks an awful lot, but my friend is expecting me to call as soon as I get here."

"Well, if ya change yur mind, don't be afraid to come an' have a bite.

Let's see, I'll call Al, a friend from school ... told me to call him ... lives somewhere near here ... and he's going to the conference. ...

Al invites me to stay in his parents' place. After writing down the directions to his home, I return to the kitchen and tell these wonderful people I'm leaving.

"Listen, jest stay an' have a bite, I'm awful hungry, an' then I'll drive ya ta where yur goin'."

"Gee, that's awfully kind of you, but I just can't. He really is expecting me."

"Well, dinner won't be ready for a little while. I'll drive ya up there now."

Boy, it just overwhelms me. But how awful it would be of me to accept. "No, he's waiting to meet the bus."

"Well, I'll take ya out to the bus station."

"Oh, I can't trouble you. I can....."

"Oh, come on. If ya walk, it's a long way, but it's short if ya drive." So back to the car we go, and he takes me about a mile to a bus stop. I'm really struck by it: my family is much better educated and much better off than he is, but the thought of taking in a stranger and feeding and helping him like this just wouldn't occur to us.

Half an hour on the bus puts me at the Chevy Chase terminal station, and I phone Al again. In five minutes he's here in his father's new Buick RoadMaster. "How'd you get down to D.C.?" with a big welcoming smile.

"Oh, I got a ride to New York with some guys from my fraternity, and I hitched this morning from there."

"Take you a long time to get rides?"

"Yeah, it was fairly slow going. I had to get, let's see, five different rides. Could've gone all the way to New Mexico with one of them, though. In a Thunderbird, no less."

"Oh, really? Was he driving straight through?"

"No, He didn't seem to be in any particular hurry. He had lots of money and said he'd pay my way too. I think he wanted me to help drive."

Al gives me a look. "He had a nice car, had lots of money, was in no particular hurry, had no particular destination, and he wanted your company. Did he ask you about your sex life?"

"Yeah, how'd you know?"

"Probably a homosexual. They often go out cruising for young guys."

The light finally dawns: homosexual, cruising. Explains a lot. "Yeah, that's probably it." Oh, well, I'm no worse off for riding with him. You meet all kinds out on the road.

"Did he touch you?"

"No. He tried to persuade me to go to California with him, but I give him credit: he respected my privacy, didn't try to molest me." But I wonder what might have happened if I had accepted his invitation to drive across the country.

———

I guess the economics conference was worth the trip. We heard a couple lectures by government economists who quoted lots of statistics at us, and we met a couple of Congressmen who were impatient at having to be polite to yet another collection of junketing college kids. I couldn't keep my eyes open during some of the sessions. The professor who had organized the whole thing spoke to me about it on the last day, and I apologized, and he sort of acknowledged that some of the sessions had been boring.

————

After the conference is over, I hang around Washington for a couple more days, staying in the YMCA, but don't find the excitement I'd dreamed of while hitching down. After a bit of sightseeing I decide to head back to Amherst and get back to studying. Funny: the hitching trip down here was really more memorable than the time in Washington itself.

Maybe I'll stop over in Baltimore and look up that Smith College girl John Leonard introduced me to just before vacation. John said she was quick to get passionate .... might as well see if I can get anything ...

Fortunately there's a nearby bus stop, and the bus line runs to the north edge of the city.

Not looking forward to Sunday hitchhiking. Sundays are lousy because of all the pleasure drivers. Short distances, leisurely speeds, and it would *never* do to pick up a *hitchhiker*: a profane deed on the sacred day! But I'm only going to Baltimore, 40 miles, so it doesn't really matter if it's slow.

Well, here's the bus, finally. Been waiting twenty-five minutes for it. "Can you tell me when we get to that last stop along Route 1?" I ask the driver as I lift my suitcase onto the bus. I'm embarrassed that I'm so obviously a hitch-hiker. I give him fifteen cents, leaving me with only a dime in change.

But he's pretty understanding. "I know the best spot for you to find a ride. I'll tell you when we get there." I smile gratefully at him, then ignore the disapproving glances of the other few passengers on the bus.

After the houses have thinned out a little, the driver turns to me and says, "This is as far out as I go. You'll have your best luck up the street a piece." I thank him and lug my suitcase out to the roadside.

There's a fair amount of traffic, but nobody seems anxious to stop. It's always easier to hitch into cities than out of them because so much traffic within the city is local. But today I don't mind standing, half-sleepy in the warm spring sun, occasionally carrying on my little monologue with the pass-ing drivers. Some of them signal they're turning or only going short distances. It gives me a pleasant feeling to communicate with them in our silent way.

A woman in an expensive fur coat walks past on the sidewalk, her little daughter following a step or two behind. When the mother sees me, she takes her daughter's hand and walks faster. The child looks curiously at me, but her mother hurries her along and speaks sharply to her in a low voice. I feel a chasm between myself and the woman, a much greater separation than from the sympathetic drivers who wave as they ride past. The drivers and I are voyagers, going someplace, understanding each other, while to her I'm an unfamiliar being intruding into her world, alien and unwelcome and maybe dangerous. To me her town, her street corner, are only a spot to stand between rides, while to her they're home, the center of the universe, and she resents my intrusion for even the brief minutes I must stand there.

Then one of my fellow-voyagers takes mercy on her: offers me a ride and thus removes this blot from her corner of the world. I can imagine her turning to look at me from a safe distance and muttering to herself, "They oughta keep bums like him off the streets."

The guy who stopped for me is mid-thirties. "I'm going only half way to Baltimore, but it'll get you out of the city," he says.

"Anything's a help," I reply as I lift my suitcase into the back seat. After we start of, I try a familiar conversation-opener: "Do you live in Washington?"

"Yeah, in a suburb farther in." He doesn't volunteer anything more, and we ride in silence for a while. I speculate idly about whether I'll be able to get a date with what's-her-name from Smith College tonight, where could we go in her town, what sort of person she'll be. This is a familiar routine at a men's college, the pre-date jitters. However, hope springs eternal: maybe this will be 'the girl'.

My host interrupts my reverie: "This is where I turn off. Hope you get another ride." He heads off to the right fifteen or twenty yards on a gravel road, then stops and helps me lift the suitcase out. I have to carry it back to the highway. Why couldn't he have left me right beside the main road?

Then I'm standing again. Hardly different from when I was sitting in the car .... my daydream goes on just as before. Cars fly past at 60 or 70 and I'm hardly conscious of them, until another single fellow stops: "Goin' into Baltimore?"

I blink for a moment to come back to the present, then, "Yeah, I sure appreciate your help." It's a newish convertible with the top down. Convertibles almost always stop – drivers of convertibles are intrepid types.

I lift my suitcase over the side into the back seat, saying, "Nice day for a ride in a convertible." I sit in the front.

He grins, "Hope my girl thinks so. She's not expecting me until this evening." He accelerates fast, and the car lurches forward, throwing me hard against the seat back. He winds it up to 55 before shifting from second to high. "Smoke?" as he picks up a pack of cigarettes from the padded dashboard.

"Oh, no thanks," the old embarrassment at refusing. Non-smokers are insipid types. "I'm sure she'll be glad to see you." The thought occurs to me he might like to double-date this evening. Solve my transportation problem. "You been dating her long?"

"Oh, yeah, we're gonna be married in June. She's already making arrangements for the wedding."

"Sounds like it'll be a big event." The wind buffets around my face and hair, and we have to lean close and speak loudly to hear each other. Convertibles aren't really practical.

"Oh, her ma's making the biggest fuss about it. Her ma's a real bitch. She doesn't like me much, but she likes the idea of having a wedding."

"She's kind of taking over it from you, eh?"

"Well, I'm not gonna let her ruin it. She can do what she wants with it until Jeannie or I don't like it, an' then I'm puttin' my foot down. But trouble is, Jeannie don't dare cross here too much, or then she'll get mad about me. She's a real bitch."

"I guess you must make this run pretty often, with your fiancée over in Baltimore."

"Yeah. Jeannie works in D.C., an' she stays there during the week, stays at a friend's house. Lately she's been stayin' at my place, but her ma don't know it. I'm goin' over to take her back."

"You often give guys rides on this road?"

"Oh, goin' over I always do, every time I see somebody. I sure don't goin' back when I got her in the car, you betcha."

"Well, um, yeah, that's understandable." So much for doubling.

"I always like to give hitchers rides. I hitched around a lot when I was a private, an' I know what it's like to stand by the road and watch them big turds in their big fat-ass cars ride past. Now I got my own car I don't like to pass up other guys. Might always be a serviceman."

"Yeah, I s'pose," I murmur.

"You ain't in the service, are ya? What are you, college kid?" I nod, and he continues, "I was in college for a while. A whole year. I coulda gone back, but I just got sick of it."

"Well, I can sure see how that'd be possible. I'm in my first year, and I'm debating whether to return next fall. I don't know what to study if I do go back." Actually I have no intention of dropping out, but might as well try to find some common ground with my host.

"Sometimes I wish I'd stayed there. But the army's been purty good ta me since I quit and joined up. I've had a chance ta travel around, and now I'm due for a promotion and c'n get married."

"I understand in the service you can get rides on planes all around the world?"

"Well, I had some buddies done it, but I never did. I hitched mostly. We wasn't s'posed to, but I hitched around anyhow."

"Let's see, I believe you guys can stand beneath the road with signs, but you're not supposed to stick out your thumbs. Isn't that it?"

He grins broadly. "Yeah, I remember the first time I hitched home, from Leonard Wood. The C.O. [Commanding Officer] found me on the road and bitched me out, and then I got home, an' Ma bitched me out again. She was worse than the C.O., can you imagine? She's glad I got a car, she didn't cotton much to my hitchin'."

I'm grinning too. "Sounds like me. My folks know I hitch around college, but they live in New Mexico, 2000 miles away, and it doesn't bother 'em much. But if they knew I'd hitched to D.C., they'd be pretty unhappy about it."

"Your ma'd bitch you out good too?"

"She'd be mostly silent, but you c'd tell she wouldn' approve."

"Well, you get the silent treatment at least. Ma sure tore into me. She useta do it all the time. She don't so much now I'm gone away most a the time."

"That sounds familiar too. My folks never were too hard on me, but nowadays I'm real king every time I go home, they see me so seldom."

"Hunh! They don't appreciate their kids until they ain't got 'em around anymore."

"Friends of mine at college say the same thing. It's funny, we all get along better with our folks now that we're gone away."

"You got a girl? See, I'm worst off than most guys, 'cause I got her parents as well as my own to bitch at me. I get it comin' and goin'."

"Oh, I'm sort of dating a girl who lives at home and goes to the nearby women's college. I've only met her mother once. She seemed to like me, though."

"Well, I suppose you'd say you're lucky. People's parents never seem to like me. They think I'll lead their dear little ones down the path to delinquency. I ain't the clean-cut kind," he leers at me.

"Well, I think you just got to smile at the right times." I don't suppose I should say that I've always found it easy to get along with other people's parents.

"Sure you don't want one?" as he reaches for another cigarette.

"Hm-mm." Shake my head. Guess that makes me 'the clean-cut kind,' not smoking.

After a few minutes of silence, he starts in again. "Yeah, it's sure nice havin' snappy wheels. I didn't get engaged to Jeannie till after I got this buggy."

"Yeah, underclassmen in my college aren't permitted to have cars, and I have to depend on the upperclassmen for rides. The worst part of it is the never-ending routine. Every week you gotta go 'round asking everybody if he's driving to the right place at the right time, and then you gotta arrange you date to fit his schedule."

"I useta borrow a car when I had a date with a real sharp chick. Sometimes I took taxis. They think that's real class. And you can sit in the back seat and the cabbie don't mind what ya do. Unless you want ta get real deep, then you gotta have your own wheels."

"Yeah, that's one nice thing about not having a car at school. I always end up in the back seat when I'm taking my date back to her school. I don't have to drive."

"Ah-ha, you ain't so clean-cut as all you look. It's just a pose, I get it, until you get her away from mama into that back seat," in a bantering tone.

"I never said I was clean-cut. I think it's only natural for a guy to want to .... neck ..... with some girl he thinks is nice."

"That's the diff between you and me. You do it with nice girls. I never made a nice girl in my life. Till I met Jeannie, that is."

"I don't exactly *make* them. Believe it or not, I'm .... a virgin. I don't date the .... um .... kind ...." Boy, foot-in-mouth. I don't exactly feel like telling him I'd be scared stiff if I ever did have the chance.

"Yeah, I know, the kind'll let you do it. I've laid plenty of them. But you'd be surprised at some of your 'nice' girls. Plenty of them'll give it to you too, if you're the right guy."

Right guy. Harvey, one of my roommates, used to say that. I continue, "Yeah, I don't think you can always tell by appearances what a girl's gonna be like."

"Appearances, hell! I can tell by the way she wears her make-up, the way she sits in a chair, the way she says 'hello'. Fine clothes and rootsie-tootsie accent don't cover up no ginch if ya know the signs. A ginch is a ginch."

Well, he *sounds* confident enough. When I was in high school, I would have dismissed his talk as braggadocio, but after a year of college, I'm inclined to believe a lot of it.

Somehow I get the feeling this guy is putting on his crudest front just for my benefit. I really kind of like him, in spite of it. But he must think I'm a real nerd. *Virgin!*

We're getting into Baltimore now. The increasing traffic and the 40 MPH signs don't slow him down the least, until suddenly he hits the brakes and swerves around a corner. "Well, be seein' ya. Jeannie lives up this way. My name's Sanson, by the way. Bob Sanson." He sticks out his hand, and I'm so startled that I can't grab it until I put down the suitcase. "Bill Stoever," I say.

"Please-ta-meetcha," we both murmur. Then I add, "You smile nice at her mother, now. Maybe she'll decide you're clean-cut after all."

"Shit chance of that. Have a good trip back to yer college, wherever that is." And he's off: vrrrooom!, tires spinning, gravel spewing out behind

– peeling rubber, we call it in my home town. Entertaining character, although I'm still sort of half frightened by people like him.

Now what do I do? Here I am lost in a strange city, burdened by the suitcase, with nothing but a phone number to give me a reason to be here ... I came all the way to Baltimore for *this*?! ..... always nervous before I call a new girl .... but nothin' to lose. ... I find the number in my suitcase ... there's a drug store on the corner ... maybe a pay phone inside ... insert the dime, my last bit of change ... always nervous ... *RING!* ... *RING!* ...

A man's voice answers: "Hello?"

"Hello. Can I talk to Ellen Chapman?" Heart thumping ...

Pause. Is he gonna ask who I am? What'll he think about some strange guy from out of town calling his daughter? And how should I explain myself if he asks? But then he says, "Well, yeah, I suppose. Just a minute."

Half a minute later a girl's voice: "Hello?"

"Hi, is this Ellen Chapman? This is Bill Stoever, from Amherst. I met you a couple weeks ago with John Leonard. He gave me your name and phone number. I wonder if you'd like to go to a movie or something tonight?"

"Ahhhh ... yes, I think I remember you. ... um, ... we're going out this evening, but not too late. ... Um, I'll ask Mummy. Hold on ... unnh ..."

"Sure, I'll wait." If you're going to dinner, any chance you'd like to include me? But not likely for an unexpected call from a virtual stranger.

A minute or so later she's back on the line: "Hello?"

"Hello. Did you find out?"

"Yes, Mummy said we'll be done here by nine. Is it O.K. if we wait until then?" Clatter, clatter, noise farther down the soda-fountain counter, making it hard to hear her.

"Yeah, that's just fine. How do I get out to where you live?"

"Where are you now?"

"I don' know. In a drugstore someplace."

"Well, I s'pose the easiest way to get out here would be by taxi .... but maybe that's .... ah .... a waste of money. It's rather far out to where I live. Do you want to take the streetcar?"

"Yeah, that's just fine."

"Well, can you find the center of town?"

"Sure." I hope.

"Well, you just find a streetcar number 43. Number 43. Then you just ride it north until you cross over the city limits, over into Parkville. Get off at the Old Mansion Hotel. Everybody knows where that is. Then just across the street you walk down Green Lane, to the next-to-last house on the right. It's a big green house. You won't have any trouble. Think you can find it?"

"Yeah, I got that," as I scribble down #43, Old Mansion Hotel, Green Lane, big green house.

"Well. I'll see you here about 9:00 then?"

"O.K., yes, I'll be...yes, around 9:00."

"Well, um, 'bye, till then."

"Yes, 'bye."

"Bye." Click!

Boy, every time! What an ass I make out of myself over the phone! But at least I've now got a reason for having come to Baltimore. Boy, I'm glad that call is over! That's the worst part of the date, the phone call beforehand. That and the last ten minutes before you meet her in the evening. My hands feel sweaty.

Now what to do? Four and a half hours until 9:00. Might as well see if I can find Johns Hopkins. I ask the guy behind the counter, "Could you tell me how to get out to Johns Hopkins? I, um, want to see a friend."

"Why, surely. You catch the bus right out front here. Runs straight past ol' Hopkins. You just ask the conductor. He'll be glad to help you."

"Sure thing, thanks a lot." Heft the suitcase, and out to the bus stop.

After ten minutes, a bus arrives. I lift my suitcase on, and we start off. "Does this bus go past Johns Hopkins University?" I ask the driver.

"Yep."

"Could you tell me when we get there?"

"Alright, I'll call it out."

"Thanks. How much is the fare?"

"Fifteen cents. You must be new in town."

"Actually, I'm just passing through. Goin' out to Hopkins to visit a friend." I grope my pocket for change, then remember that I've used it all up. Billfold from left rear pocket...but it's empty! Oh, hell. How stupid of me....I've got $50 worth of travelers' checks but no cash.

"Say, I'm sorry to cause you trouble, but I've used up all my bills. I've got travelers' checks in my suitcase. You can't wait while I cash one of them?" Does he think I'm trying to get a free ride?

"Sonny, I'm runnin' three minutes behind now, otherwise I'd do it."

"Well, where can I get one of them cashed? You can't do it, can you?"

"Sorry, son, I'd be glad to do it for you, but comp'ny reg'lations don't allow. I'll let ya get off here without no trouble, tho." He brings the bus to a halt on a street corner.

Well, he seems sympathetic enough. "I'm sorry for the trouble I caused you," I murmur. What else can I say, really? I carry the suitcase down to the pavement below, and the bus moves away from the corner.

Well, better see about cashing one of the travelers' checks. There're a few stores along here, although they show very little activity on this lazy Sunday afternoon. But there I see an open candy store, and I lug the case towards it and inside.

The proprietress is a fat disapproving woman in a slovenly pink dress. She eyes my suitcase and doesn't offer any greeting until I ask, "Good afternoon. Can you give me some help? I need to cash a travelers' check."

She starts frowning. "Can't cash no checks for no transients." Obviously a dirty word, *transients*.

"But these are travelers' checks. You know they'll honor these." Can't she tell I'm a college student? Does she think *transient* is synonymous with *bum*?

"You heard what I said." Just get outa here, her manner says. The candy in the counter window reminds me that I'm hungry, but now I wouldn't buy anything off this bitchy .... well, might as well try the next store. I'm tempted to flip the bird at her as I leave.

The next two stores are closed, and then there's a small grocery.

"Can you cash a ten-dollar travelers' check for me?" I ask, leaning inside the door.

"Sorry, don't have enough cash on hand," the proprietor says from somewhere inside.

Liar. But at least he was pleasant about it. I'd rather have him lie than snarl.

No more open doors on this side of the street. Across the street, I try a small place which looks like an agency of some sort. "The boss won't let anybody but himself O.K. checks," I am told.

Hell, how stupid this is – plenty of money with me, and nobody will let me spend it. Well, I can only keep trying, but there are only a couple more stores open along here. The next place I see is a Dairy-Dreme shop. I'll try a different tactic this time. I'm hungry anyhow. "Hello," bright smile, "I'd like a small cone."

Another fat unpleasant woman. She takes her time about getting up from her chair to serve me. Rrrnnnnnnn! The machine, and she methodically winds the white confection into a curl and hands it to me.

"How much? I'll have to give you a travelers' check." Really working on that bright smile.

"Sorry, cain't accept no check. Specially not for a ten-cent purchase. Just gimme a dime."

"Golly, all I've got is the travelers' check. But you know they'll honor these." This is really for shit.

"Either gimme a dime or gimme the cone back."

The bitch! O.K., here's your damn cone, and you know where you can stick it. I stand it on the counter. She starts eating it as I walk silently away.

One more store left. Looks like a kind of bar. Surprised it's open on Sunday. Might as well try my luck, but I'm getting sick of this.

Inside it's dim and welcoming. I lean on the bar, and the bartender walks over to me: "What'dja like?" He's a pleasant-looking fellow, nor more than 26 or 28.

"Look, I know it's risky to you, but I need to cash a traveler's check. I'll show 'em to you …. they're perfectly good. And it's only ten dollars I want."

He looks me over. "You got any identification on you?"

"Oh, yes, all kinds of it. What do you want, driver's license? draft card? college ID?" A ray of hope!

"Oh, just anything. Just a moment." He goes to serve a customer, and while he's gone I reach in the suitcase for the packet of checks. I also spread out the contents of my billfold on the counter: college ID, draft card, student newspaper press card, a card with my name on it saying USE TETANUS TOXOID IN CASE OF INJURY, a recent receipt from a dry cleaner in Amherst.

Soon the bartender comes back. "Sorry to keep you waiting." He picks up several of the cards and examines them minutely, then looks at the signature on the check. "O.K., I'll cash one of them for you."

"O.K., thanks, whom shall I sign it over to?"

"Oh, just put your signature on it. The bank'll cash it for me."

I sign carefully, and he hands me a ten from the register till. "Thanks a lot, I don't know what I would have done if you hadn't cashed it for me. It's funny people won't cash them, 'cause I think the company will always make them good."

"Oh, they're afraid they might be stolen. If the bank has a notice out that these checks with your name on them are stolen, then I'm just out ten dollars."

"Well, I'm glad I look honest." Although he seems to be the first person who thought so.

"Well, I know what it's like to be alone in a strange town. Glad to help you out. Well, good luck. There's a customer."

"Yeah, so long, thanks a lot." I go back to the bus stop, thankful that there are at least a few decent people left in the world.

I pace impatiently up and down the sidewalk waiting for the bus to come. Time 5:05. I've got no real reason to be impatient .... still four hours to kill .... but I can't help pacing. Another person comes to wait on the street corner too, a pleasant-looking Negro, and I nod sort of tentatively to him. He doesn't return the nod.

Finally the bus comes. As soon as we get inside, the driver jerks it forward, and I almost lose my balance. After setting the suitcase down, I hand him my ten-spot.

"Ain't got enough change. Ain't you got 15 cents?" he growls at me.

"No, I'm sorry, I haven't got anything but this bill. Can't you give me change? I'll take anything – coins, dimes, nickels." Why didn't I ask the bartender for small bills and change?!

"Can't give up all my change so early on the run. You people should bring change with you."

Boy, what a shit he's making of himself! "Couldn't I wait for a while, until you've gotten some more change, and then pay you when I get off?"

"Pay up or get off, buddy."

"Look, I've got money ...." The old anger rising in me again. It's not as if I'm trying to bum a ride off him. "A t-t-t-ten isn't so r-r-r-ridiculously l-l-large," stuttering with frustration. The old turd, anyhow. For a moment I want to kick something. Does all Baltimore take special delight in irritating visitors?

"Sit down, kid." He gestures impatiently at me.

"Sit down ….?"

"Siddown! You heard me ! You ain't supposed ta be standin' when th' vehicle's in motion."

"Well, O.K., I …." What the heck ….?

"He paid your fare," gesturing in the direction of the Negro who got on with me.

"Uh, thanks, um, I'll, um, thanks…." I'm so surprised I can't think of what to say to my benefactor.

" 'T's O.K. Forget it," the guy seems almost embarrassed.

"Thanks. I'll get change and pay you back."

"Forget it." He starts looking out the window.

"Well, gosh, thanks a lot." I sit down and start looking carefully out of my window. I'm utterly … what can I say….?

The bus moves into the downtown area, and a few more people get on. Through the window it doesn't look like a very attractive town. The sidewalks are dirty and the buildings gloomy. I have the impression I'm riding down a brown-grey canyon. Glad I don't live in Baltimore.

> Large areas of Baltimore have been renovated in recent years, and the city looks quite attractive now.

We may be getting to Johns Hopkins soon. I ask the person sitting next to me if he'll point it out to me. Shortly after leaving the business center he indicates some red brick buildings: "That's the place."

After I get off the bus, I lug the suitcase in the general direction of the buildings. I spot a quadrangle of buildings, obviously dormitories, and walk into one of them. It seems quite deserted. How come there aren't all sorts of people running around looking collegiate? It must be vacation; that's why it's so deserted.

Well, my date's in three hours; I might as well get ready for it (shower, shave and shit: that's what we say at Amherst). I find a large room with

books and comfortable chairs in it, a lounge of some sort, and open the
suitcase and start selecting clothes to wear for the evening.

Here's a men's room with a shower, very welcome. ... Dope, didn't put
a towel in my suitcase .... got all these clothes I've never worn, and then no
towel. ... Oh, well, I'll remember one next time. Meanwhile, gotta figure
out some way to dry myself off tonight. ... On the wash basin I find a reasonably clean washcloth; I'll use it for a towel.

Back in the lounge I dress myself. Feels weird, using the facilities of the
dormitory without anybody else around, like I'm an intruder in a haunted
house.

Finally I'm ready. 7:15.... takes time for all these preparations. What
to do with the suitcase? Can't haul it all the way out to her place and back.
Might as well just leave it here.... not likely to be disturbed in a college
dormitory. I sort of hide it behind one of the chairs and then walk out of the
dorm. Hope it's there when I come back.

I follow the girl's directions and eventually find myself riding a streetcar out into the suburbs, Baltimore County. Get off at the Old Madison
Hotel. 8:10, a long trip across town. Go into the Old Madison through a
side door and find myself in the kitchen. Forgot how hungry I was, but the
smells sure awaken my appetite. Maybe I can get a free meal by coming to
the back door.

One of the girls come over and asks me what she can do for me, and I
ask whether I can eat.

"Here?! In this room?"

"Well, yeah, why not?"

"Well, most of our patrons eat in the dining room ... but I suppose you
can eat here if you like ... what d'ya want?"

"Well, it has to be in a hurry. Can you make me a sandwich?"

"I can cut you a roast beef sandwich right here."

"Wonderful!" I watch while she slices off several thick juicy chunks of
beef and places them on a sliced roll, with a couple pieces of spicy pickle.

"Would you like something to drink with them?" she smiles.

A glass of milk? .... no, I'll save the 10 cents. "No. thanks." I stand
while I eat it. The hard crust crunches in my teeth, and the juice soaks into
the bread, and the beef is nice and chewy. When I'm finished I'm hungrier
than I was before. But it's already 8:45, and I'd better get on down there.

Or should I forget the date entirely? My stomach suddenly feels queasy. But I've come this far – shouldn't quit now.

"How much is it, please?" I ask the girl. Maybe she won't charge me ...?

"That'll be 65 cents."

"*How* much?"

"Sixty-five."

Wow, I was expecting 30 or 35 cents. It was good and all that, but 65 *cents* for a *sandwich*?! – hamburgers cost a quarter. I hand her my ten, and she hands me $9.35. Well, hotel price.

Too late I remember: should have given her a travelers check; a hotel would have accepted a travelers' check.

Back outside, across the street, down Green Lane about a quarter mile, till, hidden in some trees, I see a big green house. One final glance at the piece of paper .... name is ... Ellen Chapman ... wonder how many times I'll forget it tonight ... and I knock on the door.

A plumpish girl in a blue dress answers. "Hello .... Ellen?" I murmur.

"Yes, hello .... Bill," she replies. "Do come in."

"Thank you. You look nice," as I follow her into the living room.

She turns to a man sitting in a chair reading a paper. "Daddy, this is Bill ... Stoever. He goes to Amherst. Bill, this is my father...."

"How do you do, Mr. .... Chapman?" We shake hands.

"Well, we'll be going, Daddy. 'Bye."

"Yes, goodbye, Ellen .... and .... have a good time." Does he look a little nervous?

"Yes, we will, sir, goodbye," I reply, and whoosh, we're back out the door. That was quick.

"We can take our car, if you'd like," Ellen says helpfully.

"Oh, marvelous. I was sort of worried how I'd get you downtown to the .... downtown, to wherever we're going."

"You can drive if you'd like." She offers me the keys.

Wow! "Very nice of your father to loan us his car. Trusting of *you*." Really shows Mr. Chapman's confidence in his daughter – never met me, but he lets me take his car because she'll be along. Or maybe he's so glad she has a date – she's more than a little plumpish – that he'll risk his car to make it a success. Or maybe he didn't realize she was going to give me the keys.

Feels like I'm back in the plutocracy. First time I've ridden in a car without first flagging it down for at least a month.

Ellen carefully positions herself halfway between her door and me, leaving about eight inches between us.

"I'll have to follow your directions into town," I say. "Which movie are we going to, anyhow?"

"Well, there's a movie from Brazil at The Modern Arts Theatre, and I've heard it's really good. It's called *Black Orpheus*." She indicates that I should turn left with a quick little flutter of her hand.

"Have you lived all your life in Baltimore?" I ask, making conversation.

"Baltimore County, yes, um ...."

"Nice suburb where you live."

"Um, yes, thank you...."

"I'm staying in town. At Johns Hopkins."

"Oh....do you have friends there?"

"Well, sort of .... do you?"

"No.... I don't know many .... um ... boys ...."

After this there isn't much more conversation, and I find the silence embarrassing. John Leonard warned I might have trouble conversing with her. But it's not conversation I'm after.

Black Orpheus turns out to be an excellent movie, and I quite enjoy sitting beside Ellen to watch it, although she carefully avoids letting her arm touch mine on the armrest. It's a long movie, more than three hours.

Afterwards, walking back to the car, we're silent again, but now it's not an awkward silence. The movie cast a certain spell over us, and it would seem to break it if we spoke.

Back at the car I hold her hand as I open the door for her, but she again positions herself carefully eight inches away from me on the front seat. Well, alright, it's her decision whether she wants to sit closer. Doesn't look like we're gonna go park someplace ... despite what John Leonard said about her ....

"Would you like something to eat before we go back?" I ask.

"Oh, gosh, it's after midnight, I better get back or Daddy will be worried."

That's just as well with me....this evening's cost enough already, without paying for a meal on top of it.

On the drive back out to Parkville, conversation starts on the movie, then moves on to travel, and then we're back in front of her house before I realize it.

"Well, here we are....?" I look at her questioningly. Obviously there's going to be no romance tonight.

But she surprises me by suggesting that I should come in for a coke. I hesitate, but she sounds quite eager to have me come in, so I accept.

Out in the kitchen she asks, "Do you want a large or small one?"

"Well, I don't really want much," I murmur. "Split one with you?"

"O.K." After she pours it, we move back into the living room. I sit on the sofa and glance hopefully at her, but she selects the chair opposite me. We continue our conversation, first on travel and then on school life. I soon finish my coke, and I stand up to leave, but she remains sitting, so I sit back down. Conversation continues on school life, and she seems genuinely interested as I talk about the fraternity I joined, the blind dates I've had as a freshman, the academic successes and failures I've had. I'm really curious ... I know my prattling can't be so entrancing as all that. Talk ....

Finally at 2:00 am our conversation marathon is beginning to lag, and I stand up again. This time she does too. "Well, gosh, Ellen, I've sure enjoyed talking with you. Thanks for the show and everything."

"Oh, thank you, Bill. I enjoyed it very much." We walk to the door, and she asks, "By the way, how will you get back into town? You said you're staying at Johns Hopkins, didn't you?"

"Oh, I assume there's a streetcar or something. I'll get back somehow or other." Such blithe confidence; I hope I really will get along O.K. "Goodnight. See you in Massachusetts sometime."

"Yes, goodnight," she says. She makes no move closer to me, so I turn and step out the door. When I'm outside she smiles, says, "Goodnight" again, and closes the door.

Well, heck, didn't *get* anything. All that long conversation, and not even a good-night kiss. I'd gotten the impression from John that she was pretty quick to get, shall we say, 'affectionate,' but tonight was sure nothing.

Well, heck, some dates you win, some you lose. The movie was good. Maybe I actually will look her up sometime back at school.

Well, here I am, 2:00 in the morning, and I have to get back to my suitcase at Johns Hopkins. And then I have to figure out where to sleep tonight. I walk back to the main road and stand in the middle of the deserted street. Maybe I should have had her drive me back to town. The Old Mansion looks pretty dark. Hope they're enjoying my $0.65. It's pleasant enough, warm night air, street lamp glowing on the pavement. Might as well start walking. Towards town.

After 15 minutes a car comes along behind me. I turn and stick out my thumb. It stops. Uh-oh, cop car. But might as well ask: "Hello, can you give me a ride into town?" I'll bet that's the first time anybody ever tried to hitch in a police car.

Two officers in the front seat. They actually smile(!), and the driver says, "We're county sheriffs and can't cross over into the city proper." Then the other one says, "Oh, hell, let's give the kid a ride down to the trolley line." So I climb in.

We ride in silence. Soon we cross the border into the city. I'm beginning to hope they'll take me all the way to Hopkins when they pull over and stop. "A trolley should be along soon. They run all night," the driver explains.

Out I get. "Thanks for the help." When they're gone. I stand for a couple of minutes. Warm night air, magic at 2:30 am. But I get impatient and start walking again.

Soon a streetcar comes along, and I get on board. There is one person besides the driver. "Can you tell me how to get to Johns Hopkins University?"

A discussion ensues about where would be the best place to let me off. The other passenger disagrees with the driver, and I don't know which to believe. "Aren't you a student at ol' Hopkins?" the driver asks me.

"No, I'm visiting a friend," I reply. Better that than to admit what I'm really doing. "I don't imagine you see many travelers at this hour of the night, do you?"

"Oh, you'd be surprised at who rides trolleys at night. Here's Ol' Charley now." The car stops, and a small blond-haired old man steps carefully aboard. He makes a great show of drawing out his billfold, extracting a dollar, and presenting it to the driver. "Here is your blood money, you … lecherous … vulturous … culturous … lecher, you," he enunciates each word with emphasis. He takes his change and says, "Major … Johnson … came … in … tonight."

"Ha, ha, ha!" the driver laughs. "Good ol' Charley. ... Okay, Charley, you sit down now. I don't want you lurching all over the place when we start up." Ol' Charley sits down, and we start off.

"Ol' Charley is the bartender at the VFW," the driver explains. "Major Johnson buys drinks all around." He goes on to talk about some of the interesting characters who ride streetcars late at night and says he prefers to drive at night because there's no traffic and fewer passengers to fight. It's true: we're flying down the street at 30 mph, metal wheels grinding against metal tracks, with hardly an interruption until the driver stops to let me off: "Straight up this road about six blocks, there's ol' Hopkins."

I thank him and set off into the moist dark side-street. Hope he's right – I'm a little worried after the disagreement they had about where I should get off. But in no time I've arrived at 'ol' Hopkins.' It takes a few minutes to locate the building where I left my suitcase. Thank heaven the building isn't locked: once in Boston I left a suitcase inside a building and was locked away from it for 36 hours. The lounge is dark, but here's my suitcase, just where I left it behind the chair eight hours ago. Now where to sleep?

There are no large couches, or I'd just pitch myself onto one of them. I did that one night at Brown University, up in Providence, and the janitor woke me up at 6:00 the next morning.

I hear some music from somewhere upstairs (music? at 3:00 a.m.?!) and decide to investigate. I lug the suitcase up two flights and find a door with the music coming from behind it.

Now, if a perfect stranger knocked on my door at 3:00 a.m., what would I think? ... I'm nervous: if I knock, will anybody answer? Maybe it's a bunch of guys throwing a drunk, and they'll razz me. ... No, it's classical music; people usually don't throw drunken parties to that. ... Maybe some guy's trying to seduce a girl: he'd *really* appreciate my interruption! ... Oh, well, what the heck, it's college life. So I knock.

The door opens, and a startled face looks at me. "Hullo, I'm from Amherst College, can I have a bed?"

"Uh, well, unh, um, I suppose. My roommate's bed. He's gone for the vacation. His bed. In there. Uh, sure. His bed. In there."

"Thanks very much. I appreciate your help."

"Uh, sure, in there. My roommate's bed. There are some clean sheets."

"Gosh, thanks." We make up the bed together.

"Uh, is this O.K.? I hope the music won't bother you?" he asks.

"Sure, this is fine, thanks a lot. No, the music won't bother."

"Uh, O.K., uh, goodnight," he says, as he goes out and closes the door.

"Goodnight," I say after him. Within seconds I'm sinking ....

The next morning – the next noon – when I wake up, there in the next room is the same fellow, sitting at a desk writing something. "Good morning," he says. "You've certainly had a good sleep."

"Yeah, thanks, I guess I was pretty tired. My name's Bill Stoever." I hold out my hand.

"Gerald Wittig. How do you do?" We grasp each other's hands tentatively.

"How d'you do? Do they call you Jerry? I bet you were surprised to see me last night, this morning."

"No, Gerald. I don't like nicknames. Yes, we don't get many complete strangers knocking on the door at 3:00 a.m., but you said you were from Amherst College, so I figured it was all right."

"Up at Amherst we get all kinds of guys from Williams and Dartmouth staying over Saturday night after dating at Smith or Mount Holyoke. So I figured I'd try the same thing here."

The door opens, and a heavy fellow strides in saying, "Did that guy ever wake up?" He sees me and says, "Oh, sorry. You're the guy down from where-was-it?"

"Yes, from Amherst. Do you live in this room too?"

"Am-hurst, that's up in Connecticut someplace, isn't it? How'd you get all the way down here?"

"Yes, Massachusetts. I've been down to Washington for an economics conference. My name's Bill."

"Well, how do you do? Emmanuel Mfff." He takes my hand and manages his first smile. "Do you always go knocking on strangers' doors at 3:00 a.m. in the morning? I think Gerald was surprised to see you."

"Yeah, I don't blame him. But I figured the direct approach was the best. I was tired."

"You must have been. You slept till noon. Now you're awake, we can go get something to eat." Emmanuel stands up.

"Yes." Addressing my host: "Gerald, you must have slept late too. You were up as late as I was."

"Oh, I always stay up late," Gerald replies. "Fewer people around after midnight. I think better then."

"Aren't all the university facilities closed now, with the vacation?" I ask. "I always try to get away from Amherst during the holidays. It's so depressing when the place is deserted."

"Oh, I like it to be here when all the students are gone," Gerald replies. "Most of them are so crude. Especially the engineers. I think best when the place is deserted."

"We can eat at Rexall's," suggests Emmanuel. "Ninety percent of the student body of this university – or any other – are animals. Just animals. Crude."

"I always eat at Rexall's, even when school is in session," Gerald says.

That afternoon we go back to see Black Orpheus – second time for me. When Emmanuel first suggests it, I protest that I saw it just the night before, but he replies that he always sees good films twice. At Amherst I hardly have time to see most films once, but I let them talk me into it, because after all it is vacation time.

In the evening, Emmanuel brings out a bottle of cheap whiskey, and he and I get into a philosophical discussion, with contributory comment by Gerald. Emmanuel states strong opinions on philosophical writers throughout the history of thought, and feeling myself challenged, I respond with the best I can recall from my one semester of History of Modern Philosophy. The evening is his, undeniably, because he certainly knows more than I do and expresses his views more emphatically, but nonetheless it is an entertaining conversation, in its own way.

"We read John Stuart Mill," I say, "and I thought it was pretty sensible, although most everyone else called his arguments trivial."

"Well, you're a utilitarian, then," Emmanuel replies. "Of course, if you think a person can assign numerical values to the amount of pleasure he gets from each activity, then you're welcome to him."

"Oh, I don't agree with his calculus of numerical values of pleasure, but I agree with the enlightened self-interest idea. It seems to me that modern economic theory would find its philosophical basis in enlightened self-interest."

"*If* you agree with modern economic theory," Gerald volunteers.

"Well, yes, Keynes and all. *If* you agree," says Emmanuel. "But now you take Kant, for example. What this modern age needs is some sort of absolute to tie itself to, like Kant's 'categorical imperative'. *There's* a real philosophical system." He pours himself a half-inch of whiskey.

"Yes, I once read a book called *The Decline and Fall of the Absolute*, I reply. "Seems to sort of characterize the twentieth century."

"Which is a good reason for rejecting the twentieth century," asserts Emmanuel. "I find this century the most debased that mankind has ever brought upon himself. Plato, now, he had a vision of purity which could stand us in good stead today."

"Well, I hardly think you can reject the times in which you live. I like to think I *embrace* the twentieth century," I venture.

"The twentieth century is adrift in a rudderless philosophical void. Once your absolutes are gone, you're left with nihilism."

"Or existentialism," inserts Gerald.

"I think I must be an existentialist," I reply, "although I don't know much about it."

"Existentialism is only a name for a blind groping out of nihilism. You could hardly call it a philosophy," Emmanuel says. "In this age Man has found himself thrust into a philosophical mess of his own making, and in his frantic search to extricate himself he grasps at straws like existentialism. Or else he turns completely cynical. That's why this is such a cynical century. Mankind has lost its absolutes." A swallow of whiskey.

"Well, I lost my absolutes when I became an atheist," I say. "I can't believe in Christianity any more, but without it I feel very lost. Maybe that's what makes me cynical."

"Nobody believes in the Judeo-Christian tradition anymore," Emmanuel states. "No intelligent person with a mind of his own, at least. The only sensible answer to any religion is agnosticism. It's as much a religion to say God doesn't exist as to say he does. It's like Hegel: he rejects God, and then he makes a god out of a system of history. The answer for our century is to reject all these fallacies and find inspiration from people who started our traditions in the first place. The pre-Socratics, now, there you can find systems both rigorous and satisfying."

"Agnosticism seems sort of fence-sitting to me. I took the whole plunge and became an atheist," I reply. "It was a real sort of blow to me when I first lost my belief on God. No reasons for anything, I thought. But now I don't see why anybody follows such teachings. I feel so free without it."

"The Roman Catholic Church is the worst pile of superstition of all," Gerald suggests.

"Of course you can turn to monsters like Schopenhauer and Nietzsche for another answer to nihilism, although they're just as cynical in their own way," Emmanuel asserts. "Worship of the State, Hitler and Mussolini, that's what comes from 'the will to power,' if you take it literally." Gulp! more whiskey...

This goes on for three hours. They clearly outpoint me, but it's been entertaining and, in a way, enlightening. I wouldn't exactly call it sophomoric, but ...

Around midnight, Emmanuel decides he has had too much to drink, and Gerald and I help him to his room and bed.

I spend the next day at Hopkins, and again in the afternoon we go to a movie, and in the evening we have another philosophical argument. These guys sure are good at a kind of pseudo-erudition. But today's symposium is rather repetitious of yesterday's, and I decide to move on the next day.

9:00 a.m. Wednesday morning. Heck of a late time to wake up. Once again the fine resolve for an early start shot to hell.

Packing takes three minutes. Emmanuel comes in, and I take leave of him and Gerald: "Well, so long, you guys. Thanks for the bed and all. Come up and see me at Amherst sometime. We'll have us another discussion."

The walk to Rexall's sets me to swearing at the heavy suitcase again. After a quick breakfast it's on to the streetcar stop again.

While I'm waiting for the streetcar, I stick out my thumb on the idle chance that somebody will give me a lift, and lo-and-behold, an old geezer in a rattly old car pulls over for me. "Hi, ya, Johnny, where ya headin'?" with a broad friendly grin.

"Hello, there! I'm trying to get to the edge of town on U.S. 40."

"Well, hop in! I'm headin' over that way m'self."

"Well, thanks a lot. Appreciate the help." So I pile in, and off we go at 20 mph toward the center of town.

The old man pays a good deal more attention to his talking than his driving, and it takes quite a while to maneuver through the city. En route I learn quite a bit about the hazards of motoring when he was young and adventuresome. It seems the youth of today just haven't got the gumption of his time.

A couple of kids in a hot-rod swing around us and swerve narrowly back into line. "Gol-durn kids. High-school-harrys. Didn't drive like that when I was a boy," the old man mutters. He pulls over in front of a shop on a side street and announces, "Jest have to check in here for a minit, then I'll be right with ye and we'll get right to the highway."

"Wait!" I call as he gets out. "If you'll be any time, perhaps it would be better if I took a streetcar."

"Oh, no, you jes' wait right there, Johnny, I won't be a minute." He goes into the shop.

Well, maybe he will only take a moment. Although some people don't seem to realize how long their 'little-minute' errands take.

. . . . .

It will be helpful if he can take me past the bulk of the city traffic. Maybe he lives a few miles out of town on US 40.

. . . .

Nice of him to be helpful. People are generally helpful, if they're not afraid of you. Not often somebody will pick up a hitchhiker in the middle of town and carry him all the way out of town.

. . . . .

Wish the heck he'd hurry. He's already been in that shop fifteen minutes.

. . . . .

Lots of interesting people entering and leaving the shop. Appears to be an agency of some sort. Maybe it's a bookie. But my host doesn't seem the type to patronize a bookie ...?

. . . . . .

WHERE THE HELL IS THE OLD GOAT!? TWENTY GOD-DAMN MINUTES!

. . . . .

After five minutes more the old man finally returns. "Sorry to be so long, Johnny. Hope I didn't keep ya waitin'." He's just as cheerful as ever.

We set off on some quiet side streets, then soon turn onto a main road and go tearing down it at 20 mph, with cars giving long irritated honks before they zip around us.

After a while traffic begins to thin out, and the houses are more widely spaced. The road surface becomes narrower and rougher. Then the old man stops and announces, "Here ye be, Johnny. I'm a-turnin' in here. You jes' stand right here, you'll get a ride in no time."

"But this doesn't seem to be US 40," I protest.

"Aw, it's the best way out of town. You go right down this road two miles and turn left for two more, then you're on the main road. Lots of people come this way, quickest way out of town, avoids all the traffic."

The old bastard can't figure out that I want to be in the middle of all that traffic. "But … you couldn't help me a little farther along, could you? There doesn't seem to be many cars along here," I plead.

"Well, I suppose I could. Hop in." So I get back in, and he gets out. "Jes' have to tell Maw where I'm goin'. So she won't be worried."

He goes into the house, and after a moment Maw comes back with him.

"So you're the young man Paw's takin' down the road a piece. Where ya headin'?"

"I'm heading for Massachusetts, the time is late, and I really would like to be on the road," I reply. I don't care if my impatience shows through.

"Paw tells me your name is Johnny. Well, have a good trip, Johnny. Come back an' see us sometime when ya got more time," she beams.

"Yeah, sure, thanks a lot," I mutter.

Paw finally gets back into the car, and down the road we go again. He takes me two miles to the turnoff, which turns out to be another gravel road. "I'll set ye down right here, ye just go two miles down this road here, and ye'll be on the main road again."

"Yes, but… thanks a lot, I appreciate your help, but I wonder if you could get me down there," I plead, once again. Two miles away, easy in your car, but impossible on foot.

"Oh, no need for that, Johnny, lots of traffic on this road. Well, be seein' ya. Have a good trip to wherever you was headin'."

So I climb reluctantly out, and he potters away.

The old bastard.

What a shit of a fix this is. 11:30 in the morning, I'm getting hungry, I'm two miles off the main road, and there's no cars anywhere in sight. Shit.

I can't walk to the main road because the suitcase is too heavy. So I'm stuck until somebody comes along.

The old bastard meant to be helpful. But he killed a half-hour of my time in town and then left me in a hell of a situation on this pissing, deserted side road.

Fuck.

. . . .

Finally after twenty minutes somebody gives me a lift to the main road.

Then wonder of wonders, just as I'm climbing out of the first car, I wave at a passing car on US 40, and the driver hits the brake and skids to a stop halfway off the pavement. Looks like an old clunker, a huge old '52-or-so eight-cylinder Buick with rusty beat-up fenders and a dirty faded paint job – but a ride is a ride.

Turns out to be two guys. "Am I glad to see you guys!" I exclaim.

"Yeah, sure, get in th' car, we'll give ya a ride, I useta hitch a lot" says the driver as the passenger opens the rear door. I'm not even settled into the back seat when the driver guns the engine, shifts into first, drops his foot off the clutch and peels out, spewing gravel out behind. The tires *squeeeeeeeal* as they hit the concrete. Eight cylinders give you awful fast acceleration.

My hosts are both probably early twenties, with longish stringy hair, ratty old shirts and dirty jeans. They aren't much for conversation, occasionally muttering together as they reconnoiter the road. I watch in horror as the driver swerves into the passing lane and kicks it up to 60 ... 65 ... 70, way too fast for the crowded four-lane roadway – speed limit's 50.

We charge down the road, alternately accelerating and braking as the driver weaves around the cars traveling at sensible speeds, a high-speed steeplechase. We pull up behind a slower-moving car, and the driver mutters, "Fuckin' bastard." He sees an opening in the right lane and swings into it, zips around the slower car and swerves back into the fast lane. At another point we're hemmed into the right lane by a big semi-trailer-truck on our left, and the driver is forced to brake hard and slow down to 25 behind a car preparing to turn off to the right. "Fuckin' bastard," the passenger mutters. We pass two more "fuckin' bastards" and an "ass-hole" in the next fifteen minutes. One of them wasn't even blocking our way, just driving down the right lane as we barreled past him on the left.

Boy, I read about free-floating hostility in a psychology article, but these guys sure embody it, glaring out at the other drivers and privately calling them scatological terms. I debate whether to ask them to stop and let me out – the driving style and excessive speeds and antisocial attitudes frighten me. They'd probably call me a "fuckin' bastard" too, but so what? – better safe than sorry.

This bobbing and weaving goes on for about half an hour, and then the driver hits the brakes, skids off the road, and says, "We're turnin' here. We'll letcha out."

"Thanks for the ride," I murmur weakly as I get out. "Yeah, sure," the driver replies, and guns the car down the side road.

Glad that's over.

Not too long a wait until the next ride. Surprisingly, it's a man and his wife. "We're going as far as Trenton. Will that be of any help to you?"

Would it! "Oh, yeah, that'd be wonderful, thanks!" I exclaim.

We set off at a comfortable 62, neither too fast nor too slow. The man and his wife are both very pleasant. He tells me a tale about another hitch-hiker he picked up.

"It was just after the War, when times were wilder and I was younger. One night I was driving along the old 40 right through this area right here. They hadn't started building all these new superhighways then. And the road was narrow and winding, and there wasn't much traffic. It was late and it was raining, and when I saw this poor fellow standing beside the road, I just couldn't pass him by. When he got in, I noticed he had a kind of furtive look about him, like he didn't want me to look at him too closely. He was a young fellow, about your size and build, and he had a dirty grey coat on, which he kept pretty tightly wrapped around himself.

"He didn't seem to want to talk much, so I switched on the radio. They were playing music, and I wasn't listening too closely, but then suddenly there was an interruption, and they announced, Flash!: Somebody had broken out of the State Penitentiary and was heading for this area here. I listened pretty carefully, and I noticed that the young fellow was listening pretty carefully too. They warned everybody to stay indoors and lock up their house. The escaped man was desperate, they said. They described him as medium height, wearing prison clothes. And you know, I got to thinking maybe my young rider was that escaped convict. He just might have stolen that grey coat someplace, and he kept it on tight, like he was trying to hide the clothes underneath."

We cross the Delaware Memorial bridge and continue onto the NJ Turnpike. The driver resumes his story: "I was having a hard time with the driving, what with the rain on the windshield, but I was still keeping watch on this fellow. You see, in those days I carried a pistol under the dash in my car. Times were wilder then, and I thought a little protection couldn't hurt anything. You can bet I was glad I had it that particular night."

"Yeah, I'll bet!" I agree. His wife shifts in the front seat and looks bored. But I think it's a pretty good story.

"Well, we were driving down some pretty winding roads, and I was having a hard time with the driving. Then suddenly I felt his hand behind me but I couldn't look, like he was trying to take my billfold. Sure enough, when I looked back at him, he had put his hand back inside that grey coat, and he wouldn't let me see what he was holding.

"Well, that settled things in my mind. I was pretty sure this must be that escaped convict. Why else would somebody be out on a night like that? I couldn't feel my wallet in my pocket any more, and so I decided he must have stolen it. Where else could it have been?

"I had to think hard what to do next. I thought I couldn't do much while I was driving down that dangerous road, and so I had to wait until I could stop someplace without arousing his suspicions. Then luck played into my hands: a small animal of some sort ran across the road in front of us, and I hit the brakes hard to avoid hitting it. Only, you see, that's what the fellow thought. I pretended to be thrown forward too by the sudden braking, just like he was, and I thrust my hand under the dash. Then as soon as the car was stopped dead, I yanked the pistol from its hiding place and turned it on him. 'Gimme that wallet, and no funny business,' I shouted. I was pretty scared too. 'Yes, sir!' he said. And he reached in his pocket and handed me the wallet, and then I told him to open the door and get out, and I made him keep his hands in the air and walk away and then when he was a safe distance, I let out the clutch and took off fast. You can bet I was glad to have him out of the car!"

"Boy, I'll bet!" I exclaim. "What an experience! I'm surprised you ever pick up hitchhikers again."

"Now wait, that's not all," he replied. "You'll see. When I got home, my heart was still beating fast, but I finally looked at that wallet he handed me, and you know, it wasn't mine! So I looked around in the car, and I found my own wallet on the floor, right where it had fallen from my pocket! Now what do you think of that?"

"You mean you ... the billfold he gave you was his ... gosh, what he must have thought ... no wonder he was scared!" I respond. I can see he is enjoying my astonishment.

"Yes, so when you go hitchhiking, you be care who you ride with. Just hope nobody makes a mistake with you like I did with him," he says. "And don't give him any reason to be scared of you."

"Gosh, what'd you do with the wallet?"

"Well, let's see. Oh, I guess I drove back along the same road, but of course I didn't find him again. So I advertised in the paper, but he never came forth to claim it. I've kept that wallet ever since as a reminder to myself not to jump to conclusions."

"And you didn't see his name and address in the wallet?"

"Ummm ... no .... didn't have his driver's license in it or anything."

"Oh, boy, you're lucky he didn't report you to the police. You'd had had trouble explaining it to them!"

"Well, I suppose I could have," he replies. After a pause, he continues, "Of course, that's not a true story. I just thought you might enjoy it if I told it."

Not a true story! NOT A TRUE STORY!!? "Wow, you sure had me believing it!"

"It was fun telling it to you. I made it up for you."

I suppose I can believe him this time ...?

We go on to swap more tales about hitchhiking and about travel in general, and the time passes quickly. Later we stop for a snack in one of the turnpike restaurants, and they treat me to a full meal. It tastes very good since I haven't had any food since breakfast.

I finally have to leave these people about 3:00 p.m., before they turn off for Trenton. They drop me in a turnpike restaurant, and after waving good-bye to them, I wander around the parking area looking for a ride. Every few minutes another driver emerges from the restaurant, and I approach him and ask if he might be heading north, by any chance.

Three women in tailored suits come out of the restaurant laughing together, apparently on an outing. Might as well give it a try, I figure, so I straighten down my hair and try to look as youthful and presentable as possible. "Pardon me, but I wonder if you might be able to give me a ride a little ways north?"

One of them looks at me rather startled, but she smiles and calls to her companions, "Oh, girls, here's a young man who wants a ride. I wonder if we might have room for him."

The other two 'girls' gather around to look at me, and then one giggles and says, "Yes, why shouldn't we? After all, we're on vacation this afternoon."

So it's agreed that I should ride in the back seat and all three of them will protect each other in the front seat. After we get settled in the car and take off, I say, "Don't you know you should never pick up hitchhikers?"

"Yes," one giggles, "they told us never to pick up people on the highways. But you spoke to us in person, and politely."

"We thought you were a nice-looking boy," the second contributes.

"And we wanted to help," the third.

"We're just coming back from Bryn Mawr [college]. We've been to the Spring Tea," the first.

"It used to be called the Daisy Tea, but there weren't any daisies yet, so they changed the name," the second.

"We might as well tell him 'daisy tea' sounds too much like 'daisy chain,' which has another meaning, not nice. I think that's the real reason they changed it," the third contributes.

Daisy chain, daisy chain – isn't that where homosexuals get in a circle and each performs a sex act on the person next to him, or to her? I'd better keep quiet about this one.

Fortunately the first woman steers the conversation back in an acceptable direction. "It's a chance for all the alumnae to meet the students," she says. "We're the class of '47."

"Hush, you shouldn't admit that," the second giggles.

"Where are you from?" the third asks.

"I'm from Amherst College, up in Massachusetts," I reply. "I've been down to an economics conference in Washington D.C."

"Oh, how interesting," they chorus. "Are you majoring in economics?" the first asks.

"No, I haven't made up my mind, but I'll probably pick either history or physics."

"Physics!" the second squeals. "I had trouble getting through freshman geology when I was in college."

"You must be very brilliant," the third.

"No, in fact I think I'd probably be stupid to sign up for a hard major like physics," I answer, and they all giggle.

"Are you going to be an atom smasher?" the first asks.

"No, they don't offer nuclear physics at the undergraduate level. I might like to study something like that in graduate school."

"Oooo, a nuclear physicist," the second thrills.

"I'll bet all the girls at Am-hurst College really fall in love with nuclear physicists," the third.

"No, in the first place Amherst is a men's college, and in the second place, the girls seem frightened when I mention it. That's why maybe I should major in history," I reply, and they all giggle.

"Oh, no, you become a physicist," the first says. "All the girls admire a man with brilliancy."

"Don't you think historians have 'brilliancy'?" I ask.

"Well, I majored in history, and I'm not very bright," the second says.

"I'll bet he went to Washington just to see his girlfriend," the third accuses.

"I haven't got any girlfriends. We physicists don't have time for women," I reply, and they all giggle again.

Conversation goes on in this vain for an hour, and they continue to laugh at everything I say. I suppose their trip back to their old college made them feel like girls again. It's funny how even long-married women seem to enjoy making fun with a young kid like me.

Eventually the banter wears thin, and we ride in silence until we get to the Elizabeth (NJ) turnoff, where they leave me.

The traffic seems to be all local, and the afternoon is wearing on, and very few drivers pay any attention as they tear past. In an hour and a half, I only get one short ride. It's a single man who says, "I'm only heading home, a few miles down the road."

I respond, "I'm heading for western Massachusetts. Can you tell me the best route to follow?"

"I don't know," he says, "but I suppose you might as well stay on the NJ Turnpike up to the New York border and then follow the New York Thruway up to the Mass Pike feed-in."

I'm 'flying blind,' don't have a map to check his suggestions, but I can frame a mental picture of the route, and it seems sensible enough.

This guy lets me out just at the New York border. On all sides there is a dense wilderness, and there seems to be very little traffic on the road. I'm a bit surprised to find the area so deserted, since I know I'm only a few miles from New York City. But without a map I can't figure out exactly where I am, and in the oncoming darkness I begin to feel a bit uneasy. I keep telling myself that there must be some traffic along here ..... it is a turnpike, after all ... but it's unnerving how helpless and alone I feel in the gathering gloom.

In fits and starts I lug the heavy suitcase down the road a mile or so. Very few cars pass during the whole time. But now it's pitch black and there is no light to make it easier to see the road. Finally in complete darkness I come onto some sort of overpass. Underneath it there is another turnpike which seems to stretch off on either side, east and west. It must be the New York Thruway, but why doesn't it run north and south? I don't know which direction would take me upstate.

From the overpass it's quite a struggle to climb down the steep embankment to the other road. I'm feeling my way down along the top of a concrete retaining wall, and there's no moonlight to make it easier to pick my footings. Over the edge of the concrete wall there's nothing but a deep gloom, and I know it must be quite a fall if I slip. Dangerous situation, but I've gotten myself into it and have to get myself back out. I put on my topcoat in order to free up one hand. I have to lean against the weight of the suitcase and lift my feet carefully from one scraggly tuft of grass of the next. It's a long and steep descent, all the more frightening because I can't see where I'm going.

Finally I reach the bottom, thankful to be on safe ground again, underneath the overpass. I put down the suitcase, glad for the chance to rest my tired right arm and fingers. ... tired ... hungry ... lost ... scared ... what should I do now ...?

At least there are occasional cars passing on this highway. Hopefully if I stick my thumb out somebody will take me away from this scary place. One direction must lead to The City, and the other upstate. But which is which? I arbitrarily decide to stand on the westbound lane: I hope it's the one that winds around north and heads upstate. But I could be wrong.

I'm cold; wrap the topcoat tightly around myself. I stick my thumb out as cars pass, but they all whiz rapidly by. It's pitch dark, and I can't see anything but the glare of the headlights as each car hurtles past. No monologue with these drivers.

Until this situation, I've always taken it as an article of faith that *somebody* will eventually stop. But here, for the first time, my hopes are pretty much lost. I can't even tell if these drivers can see me in the brief instant when their lights fall on me as they roar past.

But what can I do? Should I give up and hide in the bush and sleep until daylight? Could try that if it gets too late. But it would be awful cold. I mean, sure, it's spring, but it hasn't gotten very warm yet. And I'm uncomfortably hungry.

Can't even read my watch to tell the time.

Meanwhile nothing to do but stick out my thumb and hope.

An hour or so goes by. Nobody even slows down from a comfortable 70 to pick up a dangerous-looking vagrant like me. Who else would be on the road at this hour but an escaped convict or a stick-up man? Better to protect themselves and fly on by.

What a hell of a fix this is! My own stupid, damn fault. Should have better sense than to get myself into no-way-out situations like this.

Then way past me a car slows and pulls onto the shoulder. He's a good hundred yards further along ... must have been well past me before he decided to stop. But heavens be blessed – I'm saved! I pick up my suitcase and start to run towards him.

Atop the car a flashing red light comes on. Next a powerful searchlight is aimed directly at me.

Shit! State Trooper!!!

I stop running and put down the suitcase.

And stand......

And wait........

The powerful light in my eyes makes it hard to see, but eventually I make out a figure advancing toward me. He's a big, big man. And in the holster at his side he's got a big, big gun – probably a .44 – snub-nosed police revolver, reputedly the most powerful pistol on the market ....

He isn't actually holding the gun, but he's all ready to draw it if necessary ... right hand poised an inch above the pistol grip ... he paces towards me, feet digging into the gravel: crunch ... crunch ... crunch ... just like some western movie, Gary Cooper in *High Noon*. Draw, podner! and shoot to kill!

Wild thoughts race through my mind: should I run? but where: be an awful struggle to go back up that embankment ... or on the level? – impossible with the suitcase.

And I don't want to leave the suitcase, don't want to abandon my stuff. And anyhow he'd find some identification in it and trace me.

Instinctively I put my hands out at my sides, 45 degree angle away from my body – palms open, facing him – want him to be darn sure I'm not holding a knife or a gun – no danger to him ...

I may not have *much* sense ... pretty young and inexperienced ... but I know if he feels threatened, he'll shoot first and ascertain the facts later ... don't make any sudden moves ... makes me feel silly, standing there with my arms splayed out at my sides, but I want to be damn sure he doesn't aim that ... *cannon* ... at me ...

The most frightening minute of my life ...

... crunch ... crunch ... crunch ... his footsteps on the gravel as he comes closer and closer. The hair on the back of neck rises ... ka-THUMP, ka-THUMP, ka-THUMP ... my heart races. I feel sweat breaking out on my forehead.

... crunch ... crunch ... he paces right up to me ... never says a word ... pats me up and down with his left hand while carefully keeping his right side away from me ... out of my reach ...

Feels under my arms with his left hand ... right hand still poised within an inch of that gun ...

After patting my coat several times, he appears satisfied I don't have a gun. He finally speaks, or rather, growls: "Alright, Sonny, you can put your hands down now."

I lower my arms and breathe out a big sigh. My heart still racing, thump-thump-thump-thump ...

"Whatcher name?"

"William Alfred Stoever." My voice sounds frightened.

"Got any identification?"

I take out my wallet and take my college ID card – at least I have the presence of mind to select that one. Maybe he'll be lenient when he sees that.

He inspects it carefully, then demands, "Whatcha got in that bag?"

"Dirty clothes." Hope he takes that humorously, isn't angered by it.

"Start walkin' towards the car. Walk slow, keep your hands where I can see 'em. Bring your bag."

So I start pacing towards the flashing red light, carrying the suitcase, and he follows twenty feet behind. It's a long walk to his car, and I have to shift the bag between my right and left arms several times, and my arms and fingers start to hurt again ...

The flashing red light and the searchlight hurt my eyes as we get closer. Don't know what's gonna happen when we get to his car ...?

"Open the door and put your bag in the back seat. Get in there." He gestures towards the front door. Obediently I get in and sit down.

He closes the door and walks around the car.

He gets in the driver's seat and reaches for a radio microphone. "Car number 613 calling headquarters. Car 613 calling headquarters. Over."

Squawk, wheeeooo, "This is headquarters. Come in, car 613. Come in, 613. Over," the radio loud speaker replies in a nasal metallic whine.

"I've picked up a hitchhiker on the Thruway, position northbound, two miles east of Suffern exit. Name William Alfred Stoever," he reads from the ID card. "That's William .... Alfred ... Sto-ever ... S-T-O-E-V-E-R."

"I read you, car 613. S-T-O-E-V-E-R. Hold on. We'll check on that name," the radio says.

An interminable wait. Three or four minutes.

I can hear police signals going back and forth on the radio, but most of it is pretty confusing. Lots of static. Finally the metallic whine says, "Car 613? Over."

"Car 613. I read you," replies my trooper.

"No record on William Alfred Stoever," the whine says.

"Thank you, I read you, over and out," replies my trooper. He puts the microphone down and turns to me, "You could be in serious trouble, Sonny. It's a felony to hitchhike on the New York State Thruway. Whatcha doin' out on the road this time of night?"

"I'm trying to hitch back up to my college. You've got my ID card."

"Yeah, I know you're a college kid. You got any money?"

"A little bit. Enough. Some travelers' checks." Don't want him to think I'm a bum.

"If you got money, Sonny, the best thing I can advise you is to get into the nearest town and take the bus back home. You can kill yourself walkin' along this Thruway at night." He starts the car engine and pulls carefully onto the pavement.

"Where ... where ... are you taking me?" I ask, scared again.

"You'll see."

We ride in silence for a few minutes; then I ask, "How did you happen to see me there?"

"We got a report there was a girl on the road. They couldn't see too well underneath your overcoat."

"Do you always stop so far away as you did with me?"

He sort of growls, then decides to answer. "Standard procedure. You'd be surprised the people we pick up hitchin' on this Thruway. Some of 'em are college kids, like you, but the rest of 'em, most of 'em, are runaways and small-timers."

"You don't get any stick-up men?"

"Nah, they know this Thruway is too closely patrolled. We don't get any of the big-timers hitching here. It's too easy to pick them up when they expose themselves. But we get lots of petty criminals and runaways."

"Is that why you called in to ask about me?"

"Huh? Oh, yeah, wanted to find out if you was a runaway or anything like that. It's a felony to hitchhike on this Thruway, and that would give us a good reason to book you."

To book me? Is that where we're going? I fall silent, considering this possibility. I don't want to go to jail.

We turn off the Thruway at a special exit marked FOR POLICE USE ONLY. Soon we're in a small town. We drive several miles thru its quiet streets, and then we pull up in front of a store.

"Here you are, Sonny," the trooper growls. "Now if you got any sense at all, you'll go find the nearest bus and pay your way back to your college." He hands me my ID card.

"Yes, sir, thank you, sir," I reply. After getting out, I turn to ask, "If there's no bus and you find me back on the road again, what will happen?"

"Back on the road again!?" he looks startled. "I must remind you that it is a felony to hitchhike in this state, an' especially on the Thruway. Next time you get picked up, they won't be so easy on ya."

"Well, thank you, sir," I say after him, as he pulls away. Thank God nothing more came of that encounter. Did he really think I might have a police record? Pays to be safe, I guess. He might have called in just to frighten me a bit. If so, he succeeded.

Now what to do? Should I try to find the bus station? It's late ... time is .... 10:30. Town is very quiet. Can I get anything to eat? Haven't had any supper.

Down the street I see a light. It's an old streetcar made into a diner. I walk in and am reminded of a Van Gogh painting of a night café. The light is bare and unpleasant, and there is the same air of desperation. A high-school boy and girl are sitting in the corner poking each other and giggling. A solitary man is sitting on one of the corner stools, disapproving of everyone around him.

"Can I have a hamburger?" I ask the counterman. No reply, but he turns and starts to cook it for me.

I eat in silence, pay in silence, and walk out.

Now where?

"Where is the turnpike?" I ask a passerby, and he points silently down the street. So I set off walking. I can't go more than a block at a time because of the heavy suitcase.

Soon I'm in the residential district, and I ask a man sitting on a front porch, "Which way to the turnpike?" He too points silently down the same road, and I continue walking.

After a while the houses thin out and the road turns to gravel. I spot another front-porch-sitter and ask, "Which way to the turnpike?" He too gestures silently down the road. Can't anybody in this lousy little town *speak* to me? I continue walking.

I'm going on blind faith, stumbling along in the dark. It's a rough rocky road, and walking hurts my feet and legs. The trees are thick on either side of the road, and I can't see a thing in front of my face.

This uncomfortable hike goes on for an hour. I have to stop walking and put the suitcase down every few minutes to rest my arms and fingers. Did all those people deliberately send me on the wrong road?

Then in the far distance I see a faint blue-greenish glow. Streetlights?

More tiring, uncomfortable, miserable stumbling walking brings me into an open field, no road at all here, but I can finally see the distant lights of the Thruway, and there like a desert oasis is a toll booth. Oh blessed sight!

It takes another half-hour to reach the toll gate, and en route I have to climb over an eight-foot-high National Steel fence. Lifting my suitcase over is easy enough, but finding a foothold and lifting myself over the bastardly thing is tough. The way they put up this Great Wall around it, you'd think they wanted to keep people off their damn highway.

I approach the toll collector and ask, "Is this the northbound road? Can I stand here to hitch a ride?"

He looks me over and then gestures down the approach pavement: "Ya can stand way down there beyond the last streetlight. I ain't even supposed to letcha do that."

"Thanks," I reply. I carry the suitcase a ways down the paving and stand directly underneath one of the streetlights .... maybe somebody will stop if he can see me. Not that I have much hope at 2:00 a.m. I feel sleepy .....
....

"Hey, buddy, d'you want a ride or doncha?"

I wake up with a start, and I see a truck driver parked down the pavement. Semis are a blessing at night. "Yes, sir, thanks a lot," I shout, and run towards him. Climb up in the cab with him, and he grins, "Figger ya was catchin' a little shut-eye back there. Standin' up."

"Yeah, it's late. Maybe not for you, but for me." I glance at my watch: 3:00 a.m. "I been standing there for an hour."

We're barely through the tollgate when I'm asleep again.

Later I awake again when he pulls into a turnpike restaurant. "Ya want some coffee?" he asks.

"Oh, no, no coffee, but I could use somethin' to eat," I reply. He doesn't make any move to buy me a snack.

I notice a number of semis like ours parked outside, and inside there's a big confab of truck drivers. "You know these drivers?" I ask my driver.

"Two or three of 'em by name, but most of 'em run this route purty reg'lar, and I seen 'em around." He nods to the men, and they greet him. The conversation concerns axle loads and who's driving the longest run and whose children are cutting teeth and where can you get laid in Albany. I have another hamburger while listening to the talk, which is interesting in its own way.

A puffy little highway patrolman with a high voice comes in, and everybody greets him. Pays to stay on his good side, I guess. He orders a piece of cake, and the waitress smiles and slices off a chunk of cake three inches across. He digs in with gusto. I figure that's a pretty good bargain for a quarter, so I order me one too. The waitress smiles just as sweetly and cuts me a piece one-half inch across. I'm about to protest, but then murmur to myself, "Of course, stupid!" and eat my trifle in silence.

My driver asks me, "Where you goin'?"

"I want to turn off on the Mass Pike extension," I reply. "Would it be better for me to wait in a restaurant until I get a ride turning that way, or should I ride with you all the way to the turnoff, what do you think?"

"Well, you c'n do as you like."

Not much help .... I decide I might as well ride to the turnoff. Better than sitting still.

The first morning light is appearing when he drops me off, and I immediately wonder whether I would have done better to wait in the restaurant until I got a ride. Once again I'm thrust beside the road with nothing but fast moving traffic. But too late to reconsider now.

Across the road I see the Mass Pike feed-in. There's a huge bridge directly ahead of it: Hudson River. I cross the road and walk onto the metal flooring of the bridge. The only place to walk is on the center dividing strip, but cars are whizzing by close on either side, and I find it quite uncomfortable.

But I keep moving forward, until I can see through the metal grating to the river far below. It's a huge gosh-darn bridge, high in the air and a good quarter-mile long. I don't have much hope that anybody will stop until I've gotten across this metal monsterpiece. The old complaint: the heavy god-damn suitcase. Fingers hurt, et cetera.

Then in front of me a car pulls onto the center stripping. That's nice, hadn't even stuck my thumb out for him. I walk up to him, and I'm very close before I notice: another cop!

Oh, Lordy, here we go again. What do you suppose that radio voice at headquarters will think when they receive a second call in one night about the criminal record of William Alfred Stoever?

"Get in," the patrolman says. I get in.

We move carefully back into the roadway and drive silently across the bridge. After several miles we pull into a restaurant, and the cop says, "You'll have better luck here. Better stay off bridges next time."

Relief floods over me. "Yes, sir, thank you, sir."

Within five minutes I find a ride in the restaurant with a young guy who promises to wake me up when we get to the West Springfield interchange. It'll be nice to be back in Massachusetts, I muse, as I drift off to sleep. Been enough of a struggle to get here.

West Springfield interchange at about 8:00. This is familiar territory. Only twenty miles from Amherst. And it feels good to be so close. So friggin' tired ....

Couple of short rides to Northampton, home of Smith College. Then the last familiar nine miles to Amherst, nine miles faithfully traversed every other Saturday night to the women's college.

Finally back at Amherst. The place is deserted, there's no food to be had, there's hard study to be done. But when I unlock my room, I feel I'm home. Boy, am I glad to be here!

I am so tired ......

———

Late in the evening I wake up. Outside my window the streetlights down on route 116 are already coming on. I've slept all day. Boy, I was tired! These trips always wear me out.

A snack of peanut butter sandwiches, and then I open Hobbes' *Leviathan*. Not very exciting reading, but sure to be on the next philosophy test.

I glance out my window .... see a bus passing down route 116. It casts a greenish light on the paving as it passes, and I can see a couple faces through its windows.

It's going someplace. Anyplace.

How soon can I get out on the road again?

CHAPTER 2.
HOME FROM MEXICO: A MENACE?

After my sophomore year in college I planned a summer trip to Mexico with a college acquaintance and his brother. Their parents bought them a new station wagon for the trip(!). I hitched to their home in Westchester County, just above New York City. Their parents disapproved of my mode of transportation but graciously put me up for a night before our trip.

We had a pleasant voyage along scenic highways in the southern U.S., then headed on through Texas into Mexico. It turned out, however, that their idea for the trip was quite different from mine. They wanted to stay in first-class hotels and spend a lot of time shopping for souvenirs and crafts, whereas I was much more budget-conscious. I had brought a backpack and sleeping bag, for example, but never had a chance to use them.

We got along OK down through Mexico City and indeed drove all the way to the Yucatan Peninsula. The road to the Yucatan was rough and unpaved – slow going, with very little traffic. We happened to come to a bridge under repair on a Sunday. The workmen had simply closed the bridge to all traffic, so we had no choice but to wait until they reopened the bridge late that evening. The only food available was at a tiny roadside stand that sold packages of cookies and unrefrigerated soft drinks. There was also an unlimited supply of bananas from the plantations on either side of the road, so we survived for a day on cookies, warm soft drinks and all the bananas we could eat.

Unfortunately on the way back we grew out-of-sorts with one other. Little things about our personalities began to irritate each other. For example, we disagreed about how often to play the radio and what kind of music to listen to. They began to criticize my driving. One brother grew silent, which made it uncomfortable to ride along in the car with him. I wanted to spend some evenings in local bars, not to drink, but to listen to the music and hopefully interact with the locals, while they continued to haunt souvenir shops. Influenced by their constant shopping, I did buy a pair of heavy stone bookends, but I found the shopping boring and wasteful of time. These irritations are natural enough for three people in constant company, but I found it increasingly uncomfortable to ride with them.

When we reached Monterey in northern Mexico, I decided to strike out on my own. My father had changed jobs again, to a university in Carbondale, southern Illinois, so that was my objective. I had some trepidation about hitchhiking in Mexico – tales of deserted roads and *banditos* haunted my mind – but I resolved to brave it. I loaded my stuff into my backpack – it was awfully heavy with the bookends and other junk – and set out to hitch to my parents' new home.

I got a quick ride to Nuevo Laredo with a local farmer who didn't speak any English but plied me with pieces of guava and mango, a most hospitable host.

From Nuevo Laredo I carried my backpack across the bridge to Laredo, Texas. The customs officials offered to help me find a ride and very quickly found a Mexican fellow driving to Chicago who wanted help reading the street signs. He spoke some English and I had a little Spanish, so we stammered along in Spanglish for twenty-four hours. He drove straight through – Texas, Arkansas, and into Missouri. We arrived in some town in southern Missouri in late evening. He was continuing north toward Chicago, whereas I wanted to turn east toward Carbondale, so I thanked him and got out.

It was late, and I was hungry and tired. I got a hamburger in some roadside restaurant, but then the question: where to sleep? Well, what the heck, I had a sleeping bag, the weather was warm, and here was a vacant lot under a billboard. So I moved back into a corner of the lot where the grass was fairly high, affording me some protection from possible molesters. I spread out my sleeping bag and got a pretty good night's rest.

Next morning I awoke, rolled up my sleeping bag, and headed back to the highway. A woman with two small children saw me emerging from the vacant lot and hastened to the other side of the street, gesturing to her children, obviously warning them to keep away from me. I vaguely considered hollering, "Don't be afraid! I'm a college student!" but then decided, "Why bother?" Maybe I even enjoyed being a Menace for a few moments.

It took most of the day to work my way along back roads across Missouri and southern Illinois. By early evening I'd made it to about 25 miles from Carbondale but was worried about covering that last crucial distance. Fortunately a kindly elderly couple picked me up. They lived in a nearby town, but they seemed interested in hearing about my trip and drove me all the way to my parents' doorstep in Carbondale. At that hour I tremendously appreciated their generosity.

My parents were glad to see me safe at home, but they weren't overjoyed when I told them I'd hitchhiked from Mexico. Little did they, or I, know that this was just a harbinger of greater adventures to come.

CHAPTER 3.
ADVENTURE ...

... is another word for *discomfort,* which describes lots of things about hitching. You have to lug your suitcase or backpack out to the edge of town to a suitable place to start looking for rides; you may have to wait a long time for the next ride; you can get caught in a cold rain or a sweltering unshaded sun; your meals tend to be catch-as-catch-can and sometimes you go hungry; you may not know where you're going to sleep that night, and when you do find a place, it may be a hard floor or a lumpy mattress, or it might be dirty or crowded or all the above. I once ended up in a hippy crash pad in New York City, squeezed together with a dozen unwashed wayfarers on the filthy floor of a decaying apartment on Manhattan's lower east side, trying to sleep but worrying I'd wake up covered with bedbug bites. If you're on an extended trip, especially in foreign countries, you could very well experience culture shock and homesickness. There can be health hazards – intestinal disorders, diarrhea, weird diseases – and maybe even occasional personal dangers.

Still, I wanted the excitement of going new places, seeing new things, meeting new people, having new experiences – what I considered the essence of adventure. I also wanted to experience a broad swath of life, Gorky's 'lower depths,' people different from my comfortable middle-class upbringing, and I figured hitchhiking would be a pretty good way to do it.

I was drawn by the lure of faraway places and strange-sounding names: the more exotic, the better. So as I gained more confidence at hitching, I focused more and more of my travels on developing countries, clearly the most exotic. (They're also called less-developed countries or LDCs or the Third World.). I wanted to go overland (or by boat) as much as possible – no airplanes for me if I could avoid them. I don't know what it was about riding across the countryside that appealed to me, especially since a lot of the terrain was flat and featureless, but I still felt I learned something just from traversing those barren landscapes.

Travel in the less-developed countries of Africa, Asia and Latin America tended to be particularly rugged and uncomfortable, especially my kind of low-end travel. Some of my rides were on the backs of trucks or crowded into buses with local peasants and their luggage and assorted animals and produce they were taking to market. A lot of my meals were in open-air bazaars or mud-brick restaurants, and the quality and cleanliness of the food were often suspect. And I spent more nights than I can count in cheap, crummy, often lonely lodgings.

Some of the countries in Asia and Latin America that would have been called 'less-developed' when I was traveling there in the 1960s have made significant progress and would no longer be described that way. .

There are some distinct disadvantages to hitching. It's time-consuming, especially when you have to wait a long time before some driver takes pity on you. When I was young and had more time and less money, I didn't mind the waiting too much, but you can get feelings of frustration and rejection after a hundred cars speed past and nobody gives you so much as a glance. And when you finally do get a ride, you have to go when and where your host-driver wants to go, which means you may have to pass up visiting some place you'd really like to see.

So I'm glad I did my hitching when I was young – I'd never put myself through that much discomfort after I reached middle age. [Still, it gets in your blood – even in late middle age I remain a backpacker at heart.]

By contrast, as a middle-aged adult almost all my travel has to be planned so much in advance – air tickets, fixed itinerary, hotel and rental car reservations, etc. – utterly lacking in spontaneity.

I virtually never took taxis in those days, although I was willing to take shared taxis (called publicos, jitneys, dolmu 's or other terms, depending on which country you're in) that ran along established routes and were cheap. However, it became kind of a badge of pride with me not to pay for trips outside of cities. It's part of the hitchhikers' ethic.

Tricks of the Trade (U.S.A.)

You soon learn some tricks of the trade. One of the most important is to pick the right spot to stick out your thumb. If you're in the middle of a city or town, most of the traffic will be local, and even if they aren't, they won't know where you're going; in either case they won't pick you up. You have to get to the edge of town, but it has to be a spot where traffic isn't yet moving too fast. If you want to hitch on an interstate highway (which is illegal anyhow), you should stand by an entry ramp, preferably one with a fair amount of traffic. If you're already on an interstate and the driver wants to drop you off, ask him/her to leave you at a service area.

It may help if you have a sign, and it should have only a couple words on it: COLLEGE STUDENT or FOREIGN STUDENT. Another possibility is to name the city you're heading for: BOSTON or DENVER. Your sign should be in large, heavy black characters on a light background so drivers can read it in an instant.

If cars aren't going too fast, you can probably make eye contact with some of the drivers as they pass. It can be comforting if a driver gestures that he would pick you up except that he's local or his wife is in the car and won't let him stop. It indicates some kind of human bond, some sympathy for your predicament. I often felt closer to drivers who acknowledged me as they drove past than to pedestrians who hurried past me refusing to speak or smile – trying to pretend I wasn't there.

Then there's the one about stopping a few feet away, looking over the hitcher and quickly driving on if you don't like his looks. That happened to me twice: some guy (or his wife) must have thought I didn't look acceptable – despite my being youthfully slender, clean-cut, appropriately dressed, and glasses-wearing.

I have a soft spot in my heart for truckers, particularly long-haul over-the-road drivers, the guys who drive the big semi-trailer trucks, who were often willing to give me a ride when nobody else would. How welcome to climb up in some warm comfortable cab after a cold lonely vigil beside the road!

Many drivers simply wanted company. I've had truckers tell me their job is boring and stupid. But even though it's monotonous, they have to keep alert, so they welcome the opportunity for a little conversation. I was always glad to ask them about their experiences, and I learned quite a bit about the trucking industry and the highway life. Some drivers told me their insurance didn't cover riders, so if we were stopped by a cop or a company official, I should say I was a replacement driver. If we rode any distance together, sooner or later we'd stop at a roadside restaurant, and often enough the driver would treat me to a meal. I think many of them actually did feel like *hosts*. In retrospect, I shouldn't have let them pay – I was on a student budget, but I wasn't poverty-stricken – and in fact if I were a trucker and gave a 'hiker a ride, I'd make clear to him before we entered a restaurant that he'd have to buy his own meal ("I'm gonna stop for a bite of food. You're welcome to join me, but unfortunately I won't be able to treat you").

The problems were different in the less-developed countries, where there were many fewer cars and trucks on the roads. In many remote regions of Africa and Asia I frequently waited beside the road as long as four hours for a vehicle to come along. I once waited nine hours on the outskirts of a town in Africa (as described in Chapter 13, about my trip to southern Africa). However, when a vehicle did finally approach, the driver would almost always stop for me.

The World Traveler Circuit

When you travel in the more out-of-the-way places – say, east of Istanbul, Turkey, or anywhere in Africa or Latin America – you can get on the World Traveler Circuit and pick up information from other student travelers. (People swap information in European youth hostels too, but those hostels are heavily populated by teenagers traveling in organized groups, and there are fewer knowledgeable W.T.s.) You learn where to eat and stay: in those days the Circuit included the youth hostels in Beirut and the Old City of Jerusalem (then part of Jordan, now part of Israel), the YMCA in Baghdad, the Red Cross hostels in Bombay (now Mumbai) and Calcutta (Kolkata), the youth hostel in Tokyo, and so on. I never picked up the name of a place to stay in Bangkok, but all the way back in Beirut I heard about a restaurant in the old part of town called Thai Song Greet; when I got to Bangkok nine months later, I discovered it was a little hole-in-the-wall joint with a guy stirring up Chinese food over a wok and a few hippies hunched over the tables. An anticlimax, but nonetheless a friendly oasis for a lonely hitchhiker.

I stayed in plenty of youth hostels and cheap hotels. Some were pretty crummy, but the majority were clean enough. Hanging out in these places, I met, not surprisingly, a lot of other W.T.s. You get to thinking that everybody is a sightseer of the world, that adventure travel is normal, routine. It was a reality shock when I returned to the U.S. after four years and rediscovered that the large bulk of people would never dream of doing what I did, could never conceive of traveling when and where I did, or in the style that I spent so many months of my life doing.

I managed to get into the Peace Corps hostels in several cities: Addis Ababa, Ethiopia; Lahore, Pakistan; New Delhi; and Bangkok; and the International Voluntary Service hostel in Saigon (now Ho Chi Minh City), Vietnam. These weren't part of the Circuit and normally weren't open to W.T.s, even Americans, but since I'd been on a similar U.S. government aid program in Africa for 2½ years, the people running those hostels seemed willing to let me stay. Here too I could get lots of first-hand information from Peace Corps volunteers about where to go and what to eat.

I also stayed in a few fine old hotels whose time had passed, that had been supplanted by larger, newer, fancier, more modern competitors. One disadvantage was that I seldom found other World Travelers staying in these old hotels, so they were lonelier than cheapy places on the Circuit.

I got quite used to the sensation of waking up in some strange room, glancing around at the mud-brick walls and thinking, literally, "Where in the world am I?" Then I would remember, oh, yes, I hitched into such-and-such town in XYZ country last night, and I'm in the small hotel I found, or the youth hostel, or the home of somebody who'd invited me in, or even a room in a vacant building I'd sneaked into.

Self-education

My objective for hitching in foreign countries was somewhat different from my objective in the U.S. My earlier travels in the U.S. were intended mostly to get someplace – to the women's colleges, to visit friends in some distant college, to get home – while hitchhiking in foreign countries became an end in itself. I viewed these latter trips as educational opportunities: one of my major motivations was to learn as much as I could about the places I visited.

Part of my self-education in both the U.S. and foreign countries was the exposure to a wide variety of people, especially the drivers who gave me rides, but surprisingly often people who invited me to meals and even to stay in their homes as a guest. I came to appreciate people from different nationalities, religions, ethnic groups, socio-economic classes, racial backgrounds and life styles. Some of the most generous people I met were quite poor by customary standards. These encounters dispelled any lingering prejudices I may have acquired in my comfortable middle-class upbringing in a small Midwestern town.

I tried to read about the people, culture, history, politics, economy and so on of the countries I visited. I devoured guidebooks when I could find them, although these were surprisingly hard to come by in many countries, and even when I did find them, they varied in the quality and quantity of information provided. Also, because of my extremely limited budget I was reluctant to spend much money on them, especially since the only practical thing was to throw them away as soon as I moved on to the next country.

Even where I couldn't find reading materials, however, I felt that I still learned a lot simply by traveling through a country and just keeping my eyes and ears open. I had visited 86 countries by the time I was thirty (and I've added 21 more since then). Some of these visits were a year or two (Tanzania, Turkey and Uganda); some were a month or more (Germany, India, Pakistan, Egypt, Great Britain, Thailand, Brazil, Philippines, Mexico, Japan and South Africa in roughly descending order); while others were necessarily shorter. Obviously the longer I stayed in any given country, the more I could learn, but even a brief visit was enough to give me some flavor of the country, and it gave me a framework and an incentive to learn more as I found reading materials about that country later.

Companionship

There's a distinct trade-off between companionship and loneliness. If you travel with a buddy, you have to have similar ideas about a lot of things. First and foremost, of course, is that you both have to want to go to the same places and spend roughly the same amount of time there. (This is true whether you're hitchhiking or going first class.) But you also have to have similar ideas about how much money you want to spend, what time you're going to go to bed and get up, where you're going to eat meals, and so on. If you're a budget traveler and your companion wants to pay for elegance and comfort, you're bound to have clashes. It also helps if you have similar ideas about how you want to spend your time in each place: if you like to go to bed and get up early while your companion likes to stay up late drinking, this is an obvious source of conflicts. If you're a fanatic sightseer and your companion wants to lie on a beach, you're going to have clashes. Sometimes it's possible to separate during the days – you visit the historic site and the museum while your companion goes to the theater and the shopping trip – and then get together in the evening for supper and a recounting of your respective experiences. But it's not always possible to split up this way, especially if you're frequently moving from place to place.

Another possible source of conflicts involves planning and decision-making: if you want to make most of the major decisions and your partner does too, you may end up in a power struggle or a state of constant disgruntlement. And if neither of you wants to make the decisions, you can end up dithering away time and not taking advantage of the available opportunities.

In my experience any two people who spend a lot of time together may begin to grate on each other. It can be just the small things: you get tired of how much time he or she spends in the bathroom every morning when you want to get going, or he/she begins to find your habit of gulping your meals irritating, or you run out of things to talk about after eating so many meals together.

At times I joined up with one or more companions, usually male, occasionally female. The large majority of World Travelers are guys, usually in
their twenties, and so the companions I met were usually other young men.
A few times, however, when I was really lucky, I met a girl – one advantage of traveling alone is you'll probably have better luck 'hunting' than if
you've with another guy. I soon learned, however, that joining up with a
girl could lead to incompatibilities and conflicts too.

There were plenty of times I couldn't find somebody who wanted to go
when and where I wanted. In these cases I decided I'd rather go alone than
not go. And I guess I was independent-minded enough that I ended up
making quite a few trips on my own.

Not surprisingly, one of the problems with traveling alone is the loneliness. Sometimes I would go two or three days without really having a conversation with anybody. Even if I got a ride with a truck driver in a foreign
country who spoke some English, we couldn't really carry on a meaningful
discussion. The proprietors of the cheap local lodging places where I often
slept seldom spoke much English, and in the low-end restaurants and stalls
where I ate most of my meals, communication was usually limited to pan-
tomime and pointing.

I frequently tried to strike up a conversation with somebody at a tourist site or restaurant or theater or wherever. Sometimes these attempts
would lead to meaningful interchanges, but all too often they elicited
only polite-but-brief replies. So I came to appreciate every opportunity for
having any conversation at all: with a German hitchhiker in a youth hostel, an American hippy in a bar, an African government worker in a city
park, a Haitian schoolboy on a hike to a historic fort, a Chinese student in
Xi'an who wanted to practice his English, and so on. And other voyagers:
undeniably the easiest persons to strike up conversations with were other
World Travelers; non-adventurous types frequently can't relate to my kind
of experiences.

I've never been much of a drinker, but I learned to seek out bars in
unfamiliar cities. It had to be the right kind of bar, not an elegant hotel
lobby or upscale eatery, but rather one with ordinary people and an informal atmosphere. Some nights in bars were quite memorable. I spent an evening in a sort-of-nightclub in Nairobi, Kenya, with an American doctor, an
African-American. The civil-rights movement was just getting started in

those days, and relations between black and white Americans were somewhat fluid and uncomfortable. But he and I had a marvelous conversation; we started out talking about civil rights but ended up comparing our experiences in Africa and discussing our personal lives and philosophies. I also spent some pleasant evenings in bars in Mogadishu, Somalia; Lahore, Pakistan; Colombo, Sri Lanka; Bangkok, Thailand; various towns in the Philippines and Russia, and others, which I've described in later chapters.

One of the problems of an extended hitchhiking trip, or any trip where you're traveling alone and frequently moving to new locations, is the rootlessness, the feeling that you're always an outsider. You get feelings of alienation, of not being part of society, almost an anti-social attitude: why not sneak into the tourist site or the theater without paying if you can get away with it? why bother to be civil to some vaguely annoying host citizen? why respect somebody else's property if you know you'll never come back there again? why worry about respecting local customs or persons in authority? By the time I'd been hitching for a year, I could understand why hobos and gypsies and social dropouts felt they could rip off wealthier members of society without guilt pangs.

In India, for example, I attended a party in the Peace Corps hostel in New Delhi. I hadn't had much contact with women for a while, and I started kind of harassing a young American secretary from the local Peace Corps office, sitting close beside her and trying to put my arm around her shoulders. The PC director chided me: "Your conduct is out of place. She doesn't want your attention." He was right, and I knew it, but I was tempted to give a smart-aleck reply ("What are you, a missionary or something?"). Fortunately I retained enough sense of civility that I only said, "Yes, sir."

I knew when I set off on my eighteen-month odyssey around the Middle East and Asia that sooner or later I'd get homesick and discouraged, that the loneliness and unsettled lifestyle and feelings of semi-alienation would get to me, that I'd get tired of constantly having to orient myself in new cities, that I'd get weary of living out of a suitcase and hand-washing my laundry twice a week, that I'd get saturated with filling up my days with sightseeing and catch-as-catch-can reading. (You also get to thinking: why bother to visit the church / temple / famous building / historic sight – you'll see it next time you come back, as if there *will be* a next time.)

The first time it hit me was in Tehran, Iran, five or six months after I'd left the city in Africa where I'd lived for eighteen months and had worked and had friends. Several months later I had similar feelings of weariness in Malaysia and Bangkok and the Philippines, but the next time it really hit me was my first couple weeks in Japan. It wasn't exactly homesickness, but rather just getting tired of the loneliness and the constant movement. If I could have joined a study-abroad group or a work camp or a kibbutz – any source of companionship and belongingness, even just temporary – it could have alleviated the unhappiness, but sometimes I had to endure several weeks of feeling isolated before finding a haven of friendliness and belongingness. Each time it happened I said to myself: you can end this misery, you can get on a plane and go home. But I knew I didn't really want to do that; if I had surrendered to the feelings and gone home, I would have gotten itchy and bored within a few days and would have wanted to be back on the road.

Whenever I got these feelings of dissatisfaction, my response was to Keep Moving On, to head for the outskirts of town and stick out my thumb. Maybe the next ride would provide some real companionship; maybe the next city would produce a group of instant friends. But one of the problems with Moving On is that you're continually having to reorient yourself to a new place: new city, new country, new culture, new language, new currency, and so on. (This is true on any do-it-yourself trip, of course, whether low-end or luxury.) And of course you're an outsider all over again each time you land in some new place.

Mail from home

One thing that gave me an anchor, a sense of stability and belongingness when I was moving from place to place was letters to and from my parents. In these days of the Internet, faxes, multi-country cell phones and inexpensive international phone calls, you can usually maintain communications with people back home without too much trouble. But reliable, instantaneous, inexpensive communication facilities weren't available when I was budget-traveling, and during my longer trips I had to work out ways to receive mail from my parents and from the few business contacts I had.

Sending letters was no problem, of course. It was important to me to keep writing to my parents in the U.S.: they provided a home base, a place of reference, which helped overcome the sense of rootlessness. I wrote regular letters and aerograms, both to reassure them I was still breathing and as a way of keeping a diary of my adventures. The correspondence gave me a sense of sharing my experiences, even if separated by distance and time. My parents kept the letters and eventually returned them to me, and I have them to this day.

Receiving communications was more of a problem. During my trip to southern Africa (Chapter 13) I was largely cut off from receiving mail, but that trip was only seven weeks, so I didn't mind being incommunicado. The big problem was on my eighteen-month Odyssey from East Africa to the Middle East and around Asia (Book II). I wanted to be able to receive communications from my family and from the law schools I'd applied to. Fortunately I'd discovered that American embassies would receive and hold mail for American citizens (and I even met a few Germans who received mail at U.S. embassies). I didn't have an exact time schedule, but I was able to estimate approximately when I would arrive in the capital city of some country three or four weeks ahead – "I expect to be in Bangkok about March 1" – and there would usually be a letter or two from my parents waiting for me when I got there. These letters were extremely important to me: they provided a sense of stability and belongingness, a welcome psychological reassurance.

My parents also helped with the few business dealings I had. Specifically, they served as intermediaries with the law schools and when I needed money from my bank account.

Communicating

Friends sometimes ask how I could get along in so many countries when I couldn't speak the languages. My answer is that it's amazing how much you can communicate through gestures and pointing even if you don't speak the language. You can learn the standard greeting in most countries – *merhaba* in Turkey, *jambo* in East Africa, *salaam aleikum* in the Arab countries, *namaste* in India, *sawadi* in Thailand, *konuchiwa* in Japan, and so on. That plus a friendly smile will often elicit a friendly response and willingness to be helpful.

In the first few countries I visited on my Middle East-Asia trip I tried to learn to count to ten in the local languages, but after a while it became

confusing and too much to absorb, so I gave it up. I couldn't remember
which set of numbers matched which country: was the word for 'five' *pyat*
in Russian and *panj* in Farsi, or vice-versa?

Many people speak at least a little English – it's become the most
commonly-spoken foreign language, the *lingua franca* of travel and commerce in most countries around the world today. Educated people, especially the younger generation, almost always seem to speak some English,
as do taxi drivers, tourist-shop merchants and hotel personnel in the larger
cities.

You also learn whom to approach when you want to ask directions or
strike up a conversation. In some cultures (such as the Muslim countries)
you should be very cautious about speaking to a woman. Manual laborers
and peasants aren't likely to speak much English or to know the answers
to your questions. You pick somebody who looks alert and intelligent,
probably somebody fairly well-dressed. You walk up close to him (or her)
– don't shout from a distance. If you ask, "Do you speak English?" the
individual may respond, "No" unless he is really fluent, but if you ask,
"Where is the church/ the government building/ the road to .../ etc.?" he
may understand the question and point the right direction even if he isn't
really fluent.

In some countries it's considered rude to contradict another person, so
you have to be careful not to ask the question in a way that suggests a particular answer. One trick I learned is to point in the opposite direction from
what you think is the right road – point east if you think the right direction
is west – and ask, "Is this the road to ....?" Then you can probably be more
confident if the person responds, "No, it's that way," pointing west.

You also have to be careful about hand gestures: a gesture that's perfectly polite in your home country may be rude in another culture. For
example, Americans often wiggle the index finger to indicate, "Come here,"
but that gesture is quite rude in some countries. If you have a guidebook,
it should warn you about these and similar local customs and taboos. And
again, the low-end traveler can pick up lots of helpful hints from other
World Travelers.

On the other hand, the gesture of sticking out your thumb to passing
vehicles seems to be recognized and accepted the world over: it's gotten me
rides on five continents.

Information

Organizing papers when you're traveling is nowhere near as much hassle as when you're living at home and managing your business and personal affairs, but in some ways it's equally crucial. Obviously it's extremely important to keep track of your passport, money and any documents you might have (tickets, vouchers, currency exchange receipts in some countries, etc.), but you also want to have information about the places you're traveling. (Again true whether you're a low-end or first-class traveler.)

To me the single most helpful piece of information is a map, or better yet, several different maps with different kinds of information: streets, government offices, place of interest, transportation networks, etc. (You don't need a map if you're on a guided tour, but I've always wanted to see where I'm going even on the few guided tours I've taken.) You may also want tourist information – where to go, what to see, where to eat and sleep, what kinds of things to buy if you're a souvenir collector (I'm not), and even short descriptions of the culture, history, languages, geography, economy and so on of the places you're visiting. But one of the troubles with hitchhiking, especially when you're crossing borders of Third-World countries, is that you can't always find a map or a guidebook of the country you're coming to. As a result I sometimes took roundabout routes or failed to learn about some interesting place until I'd passed it.

Then you have the problem of where to store whatever information you do collect: maps and tourist brochures can get lost or crumpled in a backpack. And you have some 'housekeeping': a given piece of paper may be extremely important for a while, and then when you've moved on, suddenly it's just extra weight to carry. So you periodically have to sort through your papers and throw away things that are no longer useful, which can be surprisingly difficult.

Traveling light

The longer I traveled, the less luggage I learned to get along with. In my early trips around the U.S. I didn't do a very good a job of estimating my actual needs and invariably ended up taking too many clothes: two or three changes of slacks, several shirts and changes of underwear, a spare pair of shoes, and the usual toiletries. This stuff usually filled a good-sized suitcase. Early on I almost always ended up carrying 30 pounds or more, which may not sound like much, but it rapidly gets heavy if you have to lug it a half-mile down the road (and suitcases didn't have wheels in those days). On those early trips I sometimes felt like my right arm was going to drop off.

On my summer work-camping in Europe (Chapters 4-6) I had to have a variety of clothes: work clothes and shoes for the work camps, a sport jacket and permanent-press slacks for occasional dress-up activities, and the usual jeans and stuff for ordinary wear. I also carried a small packet of detergent since I knew I'd have to do laundry frequently. I crammed all this stuff into a backpack that weighed a little over 30 pounds. Carrying it on my back was certainly easier than lugging it by hand, but it still got heavy whenever I had to walk any distance. I also discovered that a backpack wasn't entirely satisfactory: it was awkward to get on and off, crumpled the dress-up clothes in spite of the permanent press, didn't prevent dirt from leaking in, and jumbled the clothes together, making it hard to find anything.

So my next approach was to try a soft-sided suitcase, which I used on my trips around Africa. Firmly resolved to hold my packing to a minimum, I eliminated the spare pair of shoes and some changes of slacks and shirts. I ended up carrying about 25 pounds, more manageable than 30 but still a burden.

When I was preparing for my extended Middle East-Asia jaunt (Book II), I thought I'd lighten up still more. I took only a light sweater for warmth since I would be mostly in tropical regions. I wanted to rig up a way to carry the suitcase on my back, so I got a local leather craftsman in Dar-es-Salaam to make two straps about five feet long and a couple inches wide, with belt buckles at one end and belt holes at the other, with the idea of strapping on the soft-sided suitcase sort of like a backpack. And I did strap it onto my back and wear it a few times, but it proved to be very uncomfortable. It sank down onto my back lower than a regular backpack, and the straps cut into my shoulders. So I ended up tossing the straps and carrying the suitcase by hand.

By the time I got to India I realized that I had never worn half the stuff in the suitcase. Instead I simply washed clothes every three or four days and recycled them. I was tired of the heavy weight and the strain on my arms and hands every time I carried the suitcase, so I resolved to cut down to bare essentials. I found a canvas worker in Madras [now Chennai] to make a small shoulder bag for me, approximately 15" long by 8" high and 8" wide. It could be zipped closed and sort of locked with a tiny padlock. Into it I put one change of slacks (permanent-press), a pair of shorts (which doubled as a swimming suit), three supposedly wrinkle-proof shirts (one white and two colored), three changes of underpants, five pairs of socks, a couple T-shirts, a pair of pajamas, a light sweater, a towel, a necktie for those few occasions when I wanted to dress up, a small packet of detergent, a few toiletries and a couple rolls of film. These plus the clothes on my back were all that I had for the last six months of the trip. The rest of my stuff I put into the suitcase and shipped home.

I felt liberated with the light luggage and, for the first time in my hitchhiking experience, didn't mind having to walk. I figured if anything wore out, I could always buy replacements in the local shops. And indeed I bought towel in Egypt, a sweater in Darjeeling (northern India), and a pair of shoes in Malaysia (for $8) when my old pair was about to crumble off my feet. [The Malaysian shoes nearly disintegrated by the time I got home.] I never bought a single souvenir.

When you travel light, you learn to make to 'make do,' to get along without many things that you would consider necessities at home. You learn to improvise: it's amazing what you can do with a finger-nail clipper and a penknife if you have to. On the few occasions when I needed to dress up, I put on the white shirt (which hopefully didn't look *too* dingy), the necktie and my most-recently-washed pair of permanent-press slacks; I hoped people wouldn't notice how wrinkled I was. The few times when I hit cool weather, usually in some mountainous region, I had to pile on almost all my available cotton slacks and shirts, and even then I wasn't always warm enough.

I didn't carry very much food, although there were times when I wished I had something edible with me. Occasionally I carried sandwiches or cookies, although these added to the weight and took up room and weren't really nutritious anyhow. There were times when it would have been nice to have brought my own bottle of water, especially in hot sweaty tropical countries where it wasn't safe to drink the tap water, but that would have added quite a bit of weight.

I wanted to have some kind of reading material for those times when I had to wait for an office or store to open or for a ride to pick me up, and sometimes I got weary of the routine and just wanted to relax and chill out and read, so I usually carried a paperback book or two. When I finished one, I would look for another traveler to trade with, which meant I sometimes ended up with some weird things I would never have chosen for myself. I once got a copy of Albert Camus' *L'Etranger* in French, which I struggled partway through, relying on my one year of college French. But hey, that's part of the Experience.

The mechanics of living are different when you're traveling, especially if you're on a budget and traveling light. You don't spend time on things like cleaning house or grocery-shopping or commuting to and from your job, but you do have a bit of housekeeping. Your backpack or suitcase can get pretty dirty and messy, so you have to clean it out every so often. I washed my clothes by hand every few days. Sometimes when I washed my slacks or underwear in the evening, they weren't completely dry in the morning. Well, so what – I just put them on damp, and they'd dry within an hour or two.

One problem I never satisfactorily solved was shaving. During my summer in Europe I carried an electric razor, a Norelco (Phillips) that could be switched between 110 and 220 volts. It had an adapter plug that could fit into some 220-volt outlets, but not all, so it could be used in some countries, but not all. And when I began traveling in Third World countries, sometimes I didn't have access to any electric outlet.

Eventually I switched over to a blade, but that wasn't completely satisfactory either. I didn't always have access to hot water: I once went two months without ever shaving in hot water. I usually carried a can of shaving cream, but that added to the weight of my suitcase and took up a disproportionate amount of room when I switched to the shoulder bag. And when it ran out, I couldn't buy more in some countries and had to use plain toilet soap, which didn't protect my face very well. And blades: in some countries (notably India) you could only buy locally-manufactured blades, which were nowhere near as good quality as American blades and made bloody cuts all over my face. Once or twice I found a kindly employee in an American embassy who bought packets of American-made blades for me. They also got me containers of dental floss, which was simply unavailable in many countries.

Toilets

Another source of discomfort for any traveler, but especially for low-enders, is toilets. It can be pretty miserable when you're wandering around a strange city desperately in need of a bathroom. There aren't always public toilets available, and even if you find one, it may be pretty dirty. And it may be hard to find a deserted alley to hide and relieve yourself.

I remember finding myself in such a situation in Paris. I had searched for a restroom for half an hour, asking various shopkeepers in my minimal, heavily-accented French if they could let me use their facility. Nobody was willing to accommodate me. Growing increasingly desperate, I finally found a filling station that I hoped might answer my needs, just as gas stations in the U.S. usually would. I approached the proprietor, but he seemed to take an instant dislike to me and refused even to hear my plea. When I started to take off my backpack, he shoved me so hard that I lost my balance and fell over. I had a fantasy about shoving him back – he wasn't any bigger than me – but I knew that would be stupid. I plotted revenge – maybe I would return at night and defecate on his doorstep or throw a rock through his window. Also stupid, and besides I didn't want to waste a whole day. For the next fifteen minutes I hated all Frenchmen, until I finally found a kindly shopkeeper who spoke some English and allowed me to use the restroom in his basement and partially restored my faith in his countrymen.

The further east you travel, the dirtier the toilets get. By the time you get to the Middle East they can be pretty filthy. Often in the Arab countries they don't have toilet seats, so you sit directly on the cold ceramic toilet bowl. At first this nonplussed me, but then I realized that it was easier to wipe off a ceramic toilet bowl than a wooden toilet seat, and I was just as glad to forgo the more comfortable seat. You learn to wash your hands carefully after using a toilet in that part of the world.

Some of the toilets in Middle-Eastern countries had bowls with handles on the sides, apparently to hold onto and pull your body downwards and thus achieve a bowel movement. This caused me to speculate that maybe too much pita or spicy food in your diet could make you constipated.

From Turkey to Japan oriental-style toilets were more common than western-style. These consist of a hole in the floor perhaps six inches in diameter, located in the center of a ceramic depression about two feet square, with a pair of slightly-elevated foot stands. You put your feet on the footrests, pull your pants down to your knees, and squat down with your bottom hopefully directly above the hole. It's supposed to be good for your body to have bowel movements in this squatted-down position. It's extremely awkward the first few times you use it, but you get used to it. And if I had to use a dirty toilet, I quickly decided I'd rather it be an oriental one than a western-style one.

Toilets in that part of the world frequently don't have toilet paper. Rather, there'll be a pile of newspapers and a waste can. You tear off a piece of newspaper to wipe your bottom and then discard it in the waste can, which gradually fills up with brown-smudged papers. Makes sense, because the newspapers would quickly plug up the toilet if you tried to flush them down. Seems repulsive, but you get used to it.

I learned early in my travels to carry some items that could serve as toilet paper: facial tissues, paper napkins, paper towels, bits of newspaper or sometimes just plain paper. Today I still carry these things when traveling: even middle-aged voyagers should know the benefits of self-provisioning.

You adapt to local customs in other ways too. Hitching across the desert in Sudan, whenever we stopped, I watched the Arab men walk a few yards from the truck and squat down. I soon realized they were urinating. Apparently the polite thing was to conceal your penis between your legs while you did it. Well, I squatted down too. When in Sudan, do as the Sudanese.

Dangers

The chances aren't great, but there is the possibility of personal danger, of being robbed or raped or beaten up or even murdered by some guy who picks you up. Statistically, more hitchhikers have been victims of crimes by the men who gave them rides than vice-versa. The number of murders and rapes of hitchhikers by their hosts has increased a great deal in the forty-plus years since I did my 'hiking. I've seen stories in the newspapers about serial killers who have murdered dozens of hitchhikers over the years. You can say, "I'll be careful who I accept rides from. I'll get out if the guy tries to take me to some remote and isolated spot." But you can't be sure to recognize you're in a dangerous situation until it's too late. Sometimes the guys who seem to be the nicest turn out to be the violent ones. One of my college classmates hitched from Amherst to Skidmore College in Saratoga Springs, New York, to visit his girlfriend. On the return trip he disappeared; no trace of him has ever been found. Sobering thought ... In retrospect, maybe I was just lucky that no driver ever attempted any violence against me.

A couple times I got rides with drivers who acted suspiciously, like they were considering robbing or molesting me. Once a guy pulled a pistol out of a shoulder holster and waved it around while steering with his other hand. I was scared even after he re-holstered it, although maybe he just wanted me to know he was armed. Another time two guys muttered together in the front seat like they were on their way to rob a gas station or something; I wondered if they might be planning to hold me as a hostage if they were apprehended. I got out of that car as quickly as possible.

The dangers are much greater for female hitchhikers, of course. Women may have made great strides toward equality in employment and status in most of the industrialized countries, but they're still more likely to be targets for rape and violence anywhere they travel. Fortunately neither of my daughters ever wanted to hitchhike, but I would certainly have discouraged them if they had.

Much more frequent is the danger of getting rides with unsafe drivers. Most of my hosts were careful, sensible drivers, but every so often I got in with some cowboy who wanted to drive 80 mph on a two-lane road or power-slide around corners on a gravel road. Occasionally I was picked up by a guy who'd been drinking, and a couple drivers seemed absolutely stoned on something-or-other. These situations create a dilemma: do you stay in the car and hope the driver doesn't have an accident, or do you ask him to let you out and take your chances on finding another ride?

Once when I was an undergraduate hitching south out of Chicago, I got into a bad situation on a narrow freeway with cars whizzing by at 60 mph and no place for drivers to pull over and stop. Then some guy zipped past, saw me, hit the brake and skidded to a stop fifty yards down the road. I picked up my suitcase and joyously ran to him, and off we went, tearing down the road at 70 or 75, way too fast for the conditions (the speed limit was 50). I cowered in the suicide seat, silently praying. Twenty minutes later a highway patrol car flagged us down. I waited in the car while my host went to talk to the officers. Pretty soon he came back and announced, "I gotta go pay me a fine." So I got out with my suitcase, not sure what to do next. My erstwhile host got in, turned the car around and started heading back. The officers ignored me, so I moseyed down the road a few yards and stuck out my thumb the next time a car came by. That was one of the few times I was glad to be stopped by a cop.

Another harrowing experience was in Thailand, hitching south from Chiang Mai toward Bangkok. A couple young guys in a late-model Chevrolet sedan picked me up. They spoke fairly good English and told me they were medical students. They were clearly from the wealthy elite – in those days nobody else in Thailand could have afforded a car like that – and had a kind of self-confidence bordering on arrogance. I cowered in the back seat as they tore down the gravel road at 50 or 60 mph, occasionally skidding from side to side. The guy in the passenger seat had a pistol that he periodically fired out the window. It made me ill-at-ease – I prayed he wouldn't decide to point the thing at me … for whatever nefarious purpose. We got stuck behind a truck going about 30, which I thought a much safer and more comfortable speed even though the truck stirred up dust into our faces. But my host-driver was impatient to pass and blasted away on the horn. The truck made so much noise that the driver apparently couldn't hear us, so he rattled on down the middle of the road. In a fit of rage the pistol-packing passenger reached out the window and fired the weapon into the air. Maybe the truck driver heard us at that point because he swung over onto the right-hand side of the road, finally allowing us to pass. I could have gone all the way to Bangkok with those guys, but I was just uncomfortable enough that I got out in the next town. Better safe than sorry.

Despite the occasional hazardous driver, I preferred getting rides in cars rather than trucks whenever possible. Trucks were slower and frequently less comfortable than cars, and of course it was quite uncomfortable when I had to sit crammed three or four into the seat or, worse yet, stand in the rear. But I will say that virtually every truck driver who gave me a ride was sensible and careful, and in some of the remote regions of Third-World countries they were the only option available. To this day I have a soft spot in my heart for truckers the world over.

Rip-offs

Most of the merchants from whom I purchased food, lodging and incidentals didn't try to overcharge me, but I was aware that some did. For one thing, prices aren't rigidly set in the bazaars and *souks* in many Third World countries, and locals as well as foreigners expect to bargain for their purchases; the difference is that the locals usually know what the approximate price should be and aren't as likely to be vastly overcharged. And some merchants – not all, but some – feel perfectly legitimate in charging more to strangers than to locals. Over time I developed a kind of combative attitude towards such merchants, especially in some Middle Eastern countries. I must have communicated this attitude to some merchants, who sometimes became antagonistic toward me. (This happens to upscale tourists too.)

A potentially greater source of trouble was the occasional petty thief or con artist. Young and/or low-budget travelers are probably less of a target because they usually have less money and they're more likely to fight back or flee if attacked. However, such travelers are more likely to encounter people at the bottom of the economic scale who might be happy to take advantage of any target of opportunity. It's a low-risk, high potential situation for the would-be scammer or mugger. I encountered a few would-be tricksters: a guy in Bujumbura, Burundi, tried to talk me into giving him money to repair his car so he could drive me for sightseeing, and another in Colombo, Ceylon (now Sri Lanka) tried to entice me to play some kind of card game. These were both pretty unsophisticated schemes, and easy to resist.

You develop a sixth sense when you're walking down the street and somebody falls in step with you: 'This guy wants to get something out of me.' Sometimes you're wrong: he turns out to be an innocent who just wants to be friendly or practice his English, but too often he's an aggressive beggar or an opportunist intent on seeing how much money he can rip off from you.

Foreigners are obvious targets for such grifters, especially if you look like you don't know your way around the locality. Even though you're a low-end traveler on a shoestring budget, they may think you're rich, and indeed you may be by their standards. If you're carrying a hundred dollars cash, that's the equivalent of a year's income for many people in the Third World. Stolen cameras and wrist watches can be converted into easy cash in the black markets in many cities: a guy offered to sell me an expensive Leica camera, obviously stolen, for 100 shillings (about $14) in the streets of Mombasa, Kenya. (I rejected him.) During the course of my travels I had two cameras, two wrist watches, about eighty dollars cash, and a few items of clothing stolen. These were taken by sneak thieves, not by any threats or violence to my person, but it still makes you feel both vulnerable and violated.

I experienced only two incidents where somebody tried to steal something from me bodily, both of which happened to be in Egypt. One was when I was walking on an isolated country road near Luxor: a guy fell in step with me and tried to stealthily lift the ballpoint pen that was sticking out of my pants pocket. When I realized what he was doing, I stopped and shouted, "No!" He stood there for a moment – I don't know if he was considering attacking me physically – but then he walked on.

The second was when I had gone to visit an out-of-the-way tomb off the usual tourist track. I was walking back to the town along a cement road on top of an embankment when a young boy fell in step with me. After a few words of broken English, he suddenly grabbed the ball-point pen from my shirt pocket. I turned on him as he scooted away. He stumbled on the pavement and fell face-first into the ditch alongside the embankment. I hesitated for a moment – didn't want him to drown in the ditch, but didn't feel comfortable hanging around and possibly facing some villagers' wrath. As soon as I saw the boy move, I hightailed it down the road.

Undeniably, if you end up in the back streets of a city like Cairo, Calcutta, Cape Town or Cali at night, there's always the chance that somebody would stick a knife in your ribs or hit you over the head in order to rob you. I've heard stories of travelers who were robbed at gun- or knife-point, but I never had any such experiences in my world travels. I never felt in any real physical danger: nobody ever tried to strong-arm me or hit me over the head. Maybe I was just lucky.

Ironically, the personal dangers were probably greater in parts of American cities than in most LDCs. The only time I was ever held up at knife-point was one evening some years later when my fiancée and I were taking an evening stroll on the lower east side of Manhattan. Four young African-American guys fell in step with us. One pulled a knife and said, "Don't shout, don't struggle, just stand there," so we stopped walking, and he put the knife back in his pocket. The other guys riffled through our pockets. One pulled my billfold out of my pockets, saw that I had only $7 in it, said "Shit," took the $7, and put the billfold back in my pocket. Unfortunately another guy dug deep into my front pocket and found the Rolex watch my parents had given me for graduation. He put it in his pocket, saying "That's mine." (The hell it is, I thought to myself, but what could I do?) Then the guys took off with a whoop. ... Ironically, they actually seemed like nice kids – not junkies or dropouts, not intending us any physical harm, but just some guys out on a lark.

People sometimes ask if I carried a knife or even a gun for self-protection. The answer is a loud and definite NO. If you pull a knife, that immediately escalates the situation – invites the other guy to pull *his* knife. What's more, even if I'd had a knife, I wouldn't have known how to use it. Far and away the better strategy is to avoid threatening situations in the first place, or if you do end up in a potentially dangerous situation, walk away rapidly or run if necessary. The experts say if confronted, maintain calm and try not to be threatening to the potential assailant. If you're stopped by somebody with a knife or gun or by a group of toughs, it's better to give up your money than to suffer bodily harm. And of course, in today's climate of fear of terrorism, you can get yourself into serious trouble with the authorities if you try to carry a knife or a gun onto a plane.

Photography
I carried a camera and took photos on almost all my hitchhiking trips. I considered the pictures to be part of the educational aspect of the trips. I figured they would help remind me of people, places and experiences and would also allow me to share my trip with family members and others after I returned home.

However, I soon learned that the photos didn't capture the most memorable parts of the trip. You can't take pictures of an interesting conversation or a memorable incident. It's hard to take decent pictures from a fast-moving car, and as a 'hiker you can't ask your host to stop for you to take snaps too often.

Even where I could take pictures, the lighting might be wrong or the image too fleeting to catch on film. So you end up with photos of buildings, beautiful scenery and random people, but these are not really the core of your memories. Furthermore, a lot of things don't look like much when you look back at the pictures later: it's hard to get a good, interesting shot of a mountain valley or a dense jungle or a picturesque river. You can get pictures of some of the people you meet along the way, people who might have had something interesting to say at the time, but you may have trouble remembering who was who, or who said what, when you look at the pictures some time later. And if you try to take pictures of local citizens in colorful costumes without their permission, you may offend people and even be attacked.

And it's one more thing to keep track of, to hassle with. I almost lost my camera twice on my trip to southern Africa. The first time was when I got a ride to a town in what was then called Northern Rhodesia (now Zambia). My host, a local resident, left me off on the far edge of town, saying that would be the best place to get my next ride. I thanked him, picked up my suitcase, got out of the car, and began waiting for another car to come along. There wasn't a lot of traffic, so I knew it might be a long wait.

A half-hour later my host reappeared, saw me still standing there and asked, "You missing something?"

"Umm, I'm not sure," I replied.

"How about this?" holding up the camera.

"Oh, my God, thank you!"

"Found it on my way to the grocers. Good thing you didn't get a ride yet!"

Another time was a rather similar incident, also in Northern Rhodesia. I again left the camera in somebody's car. This time I discovered it shortly after he drove away, but too late to retrieve it. It was near evening, so I found a place to stay. Next morning I walked to the edge of town and again stood and waited. After a while a police car stopped beside me, and the policeman asked, "Are you missing a camera?"

"Yes!" I exclaimed. Incredibly, my host, obviously a most honest and considerate soul, had discovered it and taken it to the local police station. He'd told them a hitchhiker had left it in his car, and the police had gone searching for me.

I eventually got tired of carrying the weight of the camera. That would be less of a problem with the small digital cameras available today, but then you've got problems of maintaining enough memory, recharging the battery, and so on. Another disadvantage of carrying a camera is that it identifies you as a tourist, thus making you a target for souvenir hawkers, beggars, grifters, petty thieves and anybody else who wants to get money from you. I finally gave up on the camera entirely and seldom carry one on my trips any more.

I do not intend by this disquisition to discourage you, dear reader, from carrying a camera and snapping away at whatever strikes your fancy. I am simply relating that the more I traveled, the less the camera came to mean to me.

———

People sometimes express envy for my having seen so much of the world and having had such a wide variety of experiences. They make comments like, "I wish I could have done more traveling when I was younger." They *think* they would have liked to have had some adventures like mine. But most people couldn't adjust to the uncertainties and discomforts I experienced. I'm tremendously glad to have done the things I did, but they wouldn't be right for most people.

Chapter 4. Student Summer in Europe (I): A Workcamp in Wales

Student Summer in Europe

My student summer in Europe (1961) was my first extended experience of limited-budget travel. Europe was less expensive than the U.S. in those days, but even so it wasn't cheap. However, you could stay in youth hostels for less than $1 a night, including a continental breakfast, and some hostels provided inexpensive evening meals or allowed you to buy food and prepare your own meal. You could get student rates for most concerts, plays and historical sites. You had to pay bus and train fares to get around in the various cities, but once you worked your way to the main roads leading out of the city, transportation between cities was free – that's what hitchhiking's all about, after all. So all-in-all you could have a pretty interesting summer on a limited student budget.

I went there on the Quaker Overseas Workcamp Program, which arranged for young Americans and others to spend two or three weeks in work camps in various countries. The camps generally revolved around some kind of community-service project, and they were enjoyable because they brought together young people from different countries for a common purpose. We had to get ourselves to the sites, but once there we got free room and board. The program directors encouraged us to hitchhike to and from the sites ("builds self-reliance," same thing the Amherst dean had said). We were to work on our projects for several hours each weekday, but the evenings and weekends were free for sightseeing and recreation, and we had two or three weeks of free time between camps. I thought it made a nice balance.

Our group of participants flew first to Paris for an orientation, which was held in a rundown camp on the outskirts of the city. While there I befriended an American girl named Sue, who became my sort-of-girlfriend during the three days of orientation. At the end of the orientation period she and I took the Metro into the center of Paris for some sightseeing, including the Île de la Cité in the middle of the Seine River and the Cathedral of Nôtre Dame. Unfortunately we missed the last train back to our camp, so we had to decide where to spend the night. We didn't want to stay in a hotel or take a taxi to the camp, either of which would have been prohibitive on our student budgets. Well, what the heck, it was a warm pleasant night and we were young, so we decided to climb the fence around Nôtre Dame and sleep on the ground. We found a secluded spot under a tree and slept pretty well. … Next morning we were awakened by some middle-aged American tourists staring at us and rhapsodizing, "Ah, Paris! City of young people and romance and love! Sleeping together in a churchyard!" We didn't tell them we were Americans too.

My first work camp was to be for two weeks in Wales, U.K. I hitched north out of Paris toward Calais, the cheapest place to cross the Channel to England. It took a full day to get there, followed by a few hours of fitful sleep on the overnight crossing, and another full day to hitch across southern England to Wales: two days elapsed time to save a few dollars on train fare.

There were about twenty of us in the work camp: three Americans, half a dozen Brits, and the rest from France, Sweden, and other European countries. We were supposed to build an extension on an old people's center, but we weren't very efficient in the construction: we were amateurs, and there were so many of us that we got in each other's way, but at least we were enthusiastic. I'm not sure how much our efforts benefited the old people, but to us it was a lark, a marvelous interlude.

After each day's work on the foundation we were covered with dirt. There was a tub, but hot water was in short supply, so we had to share bathwater. At the end of each working day there was a scramble to be the first in the tub, the only person to get completely clean bathwater. Everybody else had to start off in the previous user's water, then get his / her own water to finish the washing. Sounds gross, but we got used to it.

The director gave us a very limited budget, out of which we were supposed to take turns buying food and cooking meals. Since most of us didn't know much about cooking, the meals usually consisted of tasteless starchy stuff. We slept in sleeping bags on an attic floor. You don't mind these little tribulations when you're twenty-one and priding yourself on gaining Experience, and they helped me save up a little reserve in my budget.

We had several impromptu parties, dancing to records. I discovered the Swedish and French girls could follow my style of swing-dancing (we called it rock-n-roll in those days), but it didn't mesh well with what the English girls called "jiving." Still, I struck up a friendship with an English girl named Joy (the prettiest girl in the group, in my opinion). She was tall and slender and curvaceous in a small-breasted way. She had started studying theology at university "because I wanted to learn about God," but was disappointed since all the readings turned out to be disputations of trivial academic points. She was afraid to drop the subject, however, because her father was an Anglican priest. She seemed pretty uninhibited – the old saying is that preachers' kids are the wildest of all.

We had opportunities for a little sightseeing. The most memorable was a trip down a deep-pit coal mine. We rode an open-air elevator down into the bowels of the earth, where some miners were preparing a coal face for a dynamite blast; they waited until we were safely back on the surface before setting off the blast. It was the only time I've ever seen actual coal miners at work. (Because of fear of liability, I strongly doubt that any American mine would allow students or any other sightseers to go down into a working mine.)

When the camp was over, a half-dozen of us – three guys and three girls – took the train to London, where one of the girls invited us to stay in her apartment for a couple nights. The apartment was in a small three-story building in Kensington Park, one of the toney districts of the city. We had planned to sleep on her floor until an older woman banged on the door and complained about our noise and said she didn't want any "fun and games" in the building. (I learned later that "fun and games" was Brit-speak for sexual activity.) It was a warm night, so we three guys decided to pitch our sleeping bags in a small park across the street. The park was surrounded by a ten-foot fence. We went out about midnight, tossed the bags over the fence, clambered over ourselves, and fell asleep on the ground.

At six the next morning a bobby woke us and demanded to know what we were doing there: "Don't you know you're in violation of the law and could be fined 10 pounds each?!" That would have been a budget-buster, about $28 at the time, more than a week's living. We of course apologized profusely and explained why we were sleeping there, and he responded, "Well, get back to the apartment then!" So we banged on the front door and eventually roused the older woman, who let us in. ... The next night she changed her mind and said she wouldn't object if we guys slept on the apartment floor "as long as you behave yourselves."

My second camp was to be in an industrial complex in East Germany. I had three weeks to get from London to Berlin, which allowed time for some adventures along the way. I took the tube (subway) to the northeastern edge of London, on the motorway to the seaport of Norwich, and stuck out my thumb. A couple blokes in a lorry stopped. They didn't have room in the cab for me, but they invited me to ride on the rear flatbed and even set up a chair for me. I got quite a kick out of riding in solitary splendor on my open-air throne, but in retrospect I realize how dangerous it was to sit on an unanchored chair at 55 miles per hour – could have been killed if they'd made a sudden stop. Fortunately we didn't have any mishaps.

I took the overnight ferry to Hook-of-Holland and landed in Rotterdam the next morning. I wandered around the city for a while, but it had been badly destroyed during World War II and didn't have much of tourist interest. That evening in the youth hostel I met Michael, a British teacher / student about my age. He suggested that we hitch together for a few days. I wondered how compatible we would be and thought it might be harder for two guys together to get rides, but I agreed. He turned out to be quite interesting: he'd become a 'master' (schoolmaster, or teacher) in an English primary school at age 18 and was teaching while pursuing his university degree.

It took us most of the next day to hitch down through the Netherlands and Belgium to Aachen, Germany (French name Aix-la-Chapelle) – turned out it did take longer for two guys to get rides, but I was still glad to have his company. In Aachen we visited the famed Cathedral, one of the best examples of Romanesque architecture, although to my eyes it was modest in size and was dark, dreary and 'heavy.' However, it inspired Michael to confide that he might like to become a Catholic priest, except that he was raised as an Anglican. I gathered he was quite shy around women.

The following day we headed east toward the small town of Rosbach in the Rhineland, Germany, the town from which my grandfather had emigrated to the U.S. in 1890. My family still had some relatives there, including my father's first cousin, Emil, his wife, and their daughter Heidi, my second cousin, four or five years younger than me. They had hosted my family most graciously when we had visited there three years before. They weren't expecting me, let alone Michael, but were most hospitable when we showed up on their doorstep. Emil had his own business and was able to turn it over to his employees and show us around for a couple days.

Heidi was in secondary school and seemed intrigued at having a visit by a relative from America, a University Student, no less! She cuddled in my arm whenever we ended up in the back seat of her father's car. She was blond-haired and slender and could speak a bit of careful, school-girl English. Michael was attracted to her but reluctantly conceded the field to me, although he did exchange mailing addresses with her.

Michael and I split up after the Rosbach visit: he headed back to England, while I set out for Berlin and my second work camp.

I learned later that Michael went back to Rosbach a year later to visit Heidi. He had stayed with the family for several nights and had even mentioned the possibility of marriage, but she had gotten involved with another fellow by that time and had to discourage him.

Chapter 5. East Germany: Imprisoned by the Secret Police

The Quaker Overseas Workcamp directors had negotiated long and hard with the government of communist East Germany to get permission to send a half-dozen young people to a work camp in that country. This was 1961, the height of the Cold War, so called because of the highly confrontational face-off between the countries of the so-called 'free world' and those of the communist bloc. The free world included the U.S., most countries of Western Europe, Japan and various countries of Latin America, Africa and Asia. The communist bloc was led by the U.S.S.R. (Union of Soviet Socialist Republics, often called 'Russia' even then) and included East Germany, Poland, Czechoslovakia, and other countries of Eastern Europe, as well as mainland China and a few other countries scattered around the world. It wasn't a shooting war, but it certainly couldn't be called 'peace' either; each side actively competed to convert other countries to its economic and political system by diplomatic, economic, and propaganda means and even by threats of military action.

> Many countries of Asia, Africa and Latin America refused to adhere to either camp, preferring to remain non-aligned; they were sometimes called the Third World. More about them in later chapters.

Germany had been effectively divided into two countries at the end of World War II, with West Germany (officially called the Federal Republic of

Germany – *Bundesrepublik Deutschland,* or BRD) aligned with the free world and East Germany (officially called the German Democratic Republic – *Deutsche Demokratische Republik*, or DDR) as part of the communist bloc. Berlin, the former capital located in the middle of East Germany, was similarly divided into West and East Berlin. American, British and French troops were stationed in the western sectors, while Russian troops (frequently called 'Soviets') occupied East Germany and East Berlin.

The Quakers, also called the Religious Society of Friends, believed that sending even a small number of young people to the East German camp could be one small step toward reducing tensions between the two sides; this was consistent with their belief in the peaceful resolution of disputes. I was one of three Americans selected to go to the camp, doubtless because I spoke fairly good German. It was something of an honor to be selected.

We were instructed get ourselves to Berlin and to meet at the Quaker Overseas Work Camp office in West Berlin on Sunday, July 30. From there the Quaker representatives would escort us to the East Berlin office of the *Freie Deutsche Jugend* (FDJ) [Free German Youth], the official youth wing of the East German communist party, which was to be our host while at the East German work camp.

To go overland to Berlin, you had to take one of three transit autobahns that crossed over East Germany. I hitched to the West German border post at the 'middle' autobahn on July 27, arriving in late afternoon. There I approached a driver and asked if he could take me to West Berlin, to which he readily agreed. It took the East German border guards half an hour to process his application for a transit visa – he was a West German citizen – but an hour and a half for mine. They asked all sorts of questions that seemed irrelevant to me: Why do you want to travel to West Berlin? Do you have any connections with the American government? Do you have any relatives in West Berlin? Any contacts in East Berlin? Any relatives or contacts in the DDR? Are you carrying any goods for sale? Do you have enough money to support yourself? How much currency are you carrying? Any East German marks? and so on. They were obviously highly suspicious of Americans.

My host waited patiently for them to process me. When we were finally underway, I apologized and asked why he was willing to wait for me so long. He said he'd known it would take much longer for an American, but

"Es freut mich sehr einen Amerikanischen Freund zu helfen [I'm very glad to help an American friend]." The West Germans knew the American forces stationed in their country were their first line of defense against an invasion from the east.

I was nervous and excited to be traversing a communist country for the first time. The American newspapers were so full of stories about the horrors of life in communist countries – Cold War propaganda? – it had made me suspicious, almost paranoid, about what might happen to me. I half expected to see powerful searchlights and jack-booted soldiers with machine guns bearing down on our car.

But the transit journey was uneventful. We got to West Berlin about midnight. My host dropped me at a workers' hostel in the city center – lots of beds crowded together in a dank, smelly room. (I saw later that about a third of the occupants were students, and the two-thirds down-and-out laborers.) Cheap enough – 2 deutschmarks ('DM') (50 US cents) – I felt lucky to find such a place at that hour.

But it didn't seem so lucky when the cleaning women roused us at 6:00 the next morning and chased us out of the hostel. Bleary from insufficient sleep and weighed down by the heavy backpack, I wandered the streets for a couple hours. West Berlin was an impressive city with lots of new modern buildings and open green spaces. It had been rebuilt after the war partly as a propaganda showcase against the communist regime in East Berlin. One especially prominent symbol was a brightly-lighted Mercedes star-in-a-circle logo thirty-three feet in diameter revolving slowly on a tower some two-hundred feet up, where it would be clearly visible from the eastern sector.

Later I checked my backpack at a West Berlin subway station and headed toward the famed Brandenburg Gate (*Brandenburger Tor*), a major crossing point between West and East Berlin. En route I passed the Soviet War Memorial commemorating the 'heroic Soviet soldiers' who had entered Germany from the east as the war was winding down and had 'liberated' Berlin from the Nazis. I was surprised to see that it was guarded by Soviet soldiers even though it was located maybe a hundred yards inside West Berlin. I watched as an armored vehicle drove through the gate, dropped off some soldiers at the memorial and picked up others to take back into East Berlin – a routine changing of the guard except for the Cold War tensions. But the presence of those soldiers with fearsome-looking automatic weapons strapped to their backs discouraged me from approaching too close.

Erected in the 18th century, the Brandenburg Gate consisted of six huge stone columns holding up massive stone lintels, with lesser columns on each side; it supposedly symbolized peace but seemed to me like a fitting monument to German imperial power. After the war it became symbolic of the division of Europe into West v. East, free world v. communism.

Passing through the portals into East Berlin, I saw more Soviet guards with the ever-present assault rifles. They were stopping most cars for quick searches and routine processing of papers, but they ignored me and all the other people walking through the gate. It was common knowledge that many East Berliners simply walked through the gate to the West and didn't return. In order to stanch this outflow the DDR government had begun requiring East German citizens to obtain visas before they could enter East Berlin from the rest of East Germany. I presumed I wouldn't encounter any such problem when I returned to Berlin from my jaunt to East Germany.

The passageways through the gate led to the fabled Unter den Linden Street, which had been Berlin's most stylish street before World War II but was now dreary and depressing. Many of the surrounding buildings still hadn't been restored after the war, and those that had been restored or newly built were undistinguished grayish blocks of stone. Still, I found it interesting to wander around the nearby streets just to get an impression of what life looked like under communism. The contrast from the modern buildings and bright lights of West Berlin was dramatic.

I ate lunch in an outdoor restaurant in East Berlin, seating myself at an empty spot at a four-person table occupied by two other diners, according to the German custom. They were East Berliners, surprised to see an American joining their table, but most friendly and courteous. They seemed like ordinary people to me, hardly personifications of the Communist Menace.

My meal cost four DM. I paid with a five-DM West German bill, expecting to get one Westmark in change, but the waiter handed me four Ostmarks instead, a *sub rosa* acknowledgement of the black market. In theory an East German mark (Ostmark) was equal to a West German mark (Westmark), but the free- or black-market exchange rate was about 4 to 1. The waiter put my five-Westmark note in his pocket, took out five Eastmarks and put them in the cash register. I divined that you couldn't get change in Westmarks because the East Germans pocketed any such bills as soon as they saw them.

In the evening I crossed back into West Berlin and returned to the workers' hostel – and was duly roused at 6:00 the next morning. I wasn't eager to spend a third night in that hostel, so I decided to try and find a place to sleep in East Berlin. This time I carried my backpack to Friedrichstrasse Station, another of the crossing points between West and East.

I noticed a vending machine selling condoms in a men's room and – why not? – purchased one … just in case …

Having been alerted to the disjunction between Westmarks and Ostmarks, I changed some dollars into the latter currency in a bank, receiving about 16 to the dollar rather than the official rate of about 4, a perfectly legal transaction in the West, but illegal in the East. Somebody warned I'd have to smuggle the Ostmarks into East Germany, which made me more than a little fearful: my first foray into a black market.

I rode one stop on the (Soviet-run) *S-Bahn* [elevated train] over to the East Berlin checkpoint and tried not to appear nervous as I approached the East German guard post. I told the guards I'd been invited to participate in a work camp in the DDR *"als Gast der FDJ* [as a guest of the FDJ]." That seemed to carry some weight because they stamped my passport with no hassle and even gave me directions to the address where I was supposed to meet the next day. They never asked about the currency I was carrying.

The address turned out to be a shabby office in a dilapidated building, not the main headquarters of the FDJ. Fortunately it was open even on a Saturday. I had to talk my way in and then find somebody who knew about the arrangement with the Quaker program, but they ended up directing me to what they called the FDJ hotel and gave me a chit entitling me to stay there two nights for free.

The hotel was an old crumbling four-story building with no elevator, not fully restored from the war. It appeared to be a one-woman operation run by a plump middle-aged German housewife-type. She looked me over disapprovingly but then showed me into a room that was threadbare but spotlessly clean.

I decided this would be a good chance to catch up on my laundry and scrubbed up my dirty shirts, underwear and socks in the sink using my small packet of detergent. The clothes were still pretty gray when I draped them over the few pieces of furniture in the room, but at least I figured they were cleaner. Then I went out to see some more of East Berlin.

One thing that particularly struck me was the slogans painted on many walls: "*Wir bauen Kommunismus*! [We're building Communism!]", complete with pictures of smiling, heroic-looking young people. Propaganda everywhere.

But that contrasted with a trivial but revealing incident: I saw a Soviet soldier dressed in uniform and carrying the usual assault rifle. Several German boys fell in behind him and taunted, "Ya, ya, Russky!" as he walked along. He ignored them, obviously not daring to retaliate. So much for fraternal socialist solidarity, I thought.

When I returned to the hotel, I discovered that the proprietress had re-washed all my laundry, and the underpants and undershirts were now gleaming white. She refused my offer of payment. She may have been running a decrepit communist-youth hotel, but at heart she was still a fastidious *deutsche Hausfrau*.

That evening in the frayed hotel lobby I met a young Swedish girl nicknamed Sisi and learned that she too was going to the work camp the next day. Like most young Swedes, she was fluent in English. She said her father published Sweden's communist newspaper and wanted his daughter to attend the East German camp to see a socialist paradise firsthand. She was a curvaceous little thing of sixteen but had a rebellious, don't-mess-with-me attitude. I wondered if her father's communist beliefs had made her disaffected. She offered up that she'd been sleeping with her boyfriend since she was fourteen, which made me wonder if she might be interested in sleeping with me. But she went back to her room alone, leaving me to return to mine alone. In any case I'm sure the hotel proprietress would have highly disapproved and might even have thrown us out if we'd spent the night together.

Next morning I reported to the designated meeting place and encountered a group of 20 or 25 Young Communist Leaguers from British universities, a similar group from the French *Union des étudiants communistes (UEC)* [Union of Communist Students], eight or ten young English, Dutch and Americans from Quaker groups, and Sisi: all told, about 60 young people.

After some preliminary formalities, the FDJ officials loaded us onto three decrepit buses and drove us to the town of Hoyerswerda, about 100 miles south of Berlin. The group was about half boys and half girls, and the sorting-out process – who might pair up with whom – began as soon as the buses started up. We were all in high spirits. The British communists loudly sang a song about "Solidarity forever! … when the Red Revolution comes!", and the French kids responded with 'L'Internationale' in French. We from the Quaker groups, badly outnumbered and more skeptical about what might lie ahead, remained discreetly silent during these demonstrations of enthusiasm.

One of the first things I noticed in Hoyerswerda was more walls emblazoned with the ubiquitous *"Wir bauen Kommunismus!"* and similar slogans, plus more pictures of smiling young workers. Propaganda everywhere.

The work camp, on the outskirts of the town, contained 20 or 25 unpainted one-story wood-frame barracks, plain hastily-constructed buildings with very primitive facilities. Each barracks was divided into three rooms holding twenty cots with musty mattresses. The young male visitors were assigned to sleep in two of the rooms. We were each allocated a two-cubic-foot cubby-hole in a crude wooden shelf to put our personal items in, and we each claimed a few square feet of floor space for our suitcases / backpacks. We shared a bathroom (cold showers!) with German workers from an adjoining twelve-bed room. The girls had similar accommodations in an adjacent barracks. All-in-all, a very Spartan existence, but at least it was temporary for us, unlike for the German workmen. So this was the life one could expect under communism?

A couple of middle-aged English-speaking German supervisors introduced themselves as our hosts. I never learned their names. They said they were required to collect our passports and hold them till the end of the camp. I would have preferred to hold on to my passport, but I could see it might not be safe in the open barracks room, so I yielded it up, as did all the other young visitors.

They assigned our group to a couple tables in a large communal dining hall. The first evening we divided up linguistically, the French kids at one table and the English-speakers at the other, although we began to intermingle more as we got to know each other in the next few days. We got our food cafeteria-style, in a separate line from the regular German workers. The first several meals consisted of sausage, bread and a sizable pat of butter. The German workmen also got sausages and bread, but no butter, which, we learned later, was in short supply. (Don't ever let the visitors know there could be shortages of butter or anything else in the workers' paradise!)

Next day we were taken to our assigned 'work'. The camp had been established to build a huge lignite (brown-coal [*Braunkohl*]) processing facility. A six-foot-deep trench had been dug from one of the plants by a giant piece of earth-moving equipment. We never learned where the trench originated or ended – it was just *there* – from our perspective, one tiny section of an endless mini-canyon. We were given shovels and pickaxes and were assigned to smooth out the walls of the trench. We weren't quite sure *how* we were supposed to do this: should they taper from top-to-bottom or be exactly vertical? Should the floor slope upwards to the left or the right? We asked some workers, but they seemed to think it wouldn't make any difference.

Still, being young and naïve, we dug into our task with enthusiasm and were soon hefting shovelfuls of dirt out of our ditch. The exercise felt good at first, but it was hard physical work, and people began to flag after an hour or two. Sisi and some of the other girls gave up and climbed out of the ditch after less than an hour and spent the rest of the day lounging under a tree. A 'supervisor' showed up at noon, told us to take a rest, and distributed box lunches with more bread, butter and sausages. He pretended to inspect our work and was very praiseful of our efforts.

That evening our supervisors led us to a sort of clubroom in the town and invited us to partake of wine and cookies. A five-piece band played music for us to dance to. I asked several of the girls to dance including Françoise, a French university student who struck me as one of the more sensible participants from the communist-youth groups.

The supervisors invited us to participate in a talent show, and a few people sang popular songs from their respective countries. One French guy named Gilles sang a song, and then another, and then a third, all without accompaniment. The band became visibly impatient by the time he plunged into his third, and the bandleader waited with poised baton until the third number was finished and immediately led the band into a dance number, obviously intended to cut Gilles off from singing yet a fourth. We all dutifully clapped, and he looked very pleased with himself, but I thought he wasn't really very good. All in all, not the best party I'd ever been to, but a pleasant evening.

The following days were similar: digging in our ditch during the days, meals in the dining hall – at least the food became more varied after the first couple days, although still very plain and basic – often followed by wine and cookies and dancing in the clubroom.

Members of our group had different reactions to what they saw and heard. One British girl, a Young Communist League member, waxed enthusiastic about how much better relations between bosses and workers were under the communist system. "I saw some workers relaxing under a tree, and the boss came by and saw them, and they just smiled and greeted him. A British boss would've bawled them out," she enthused. Others commented about how the supervisors of our group didn't seem to care if we weren't working very hard. Sisi and some of the other girls were the most obvious slackers; they played around in our ditch for a few minutes each morning but then climbed out and spent the rest of the day lounging around, flirting with whatever boys chose to join them. Our supervisors ignored them. All well and good, I thought, but if people can get away with goofing off like that, no wonder productivity was so low under communism.

On the free evenings we took the opportunity to go to a nearby beer hall, where we had a chance to mix with the German workmen. The younger workers wanted to ask about life in the West. The more cognizant ones said they recognized they'd been fed propaganda about how awful life was in the West and how much better it was under the socialist system. One young guy leaned forward conspiratorially and confided to me, "*Ich bin kein Kommunist* [I'm no communist]." I'm sure many of his fellow workers felt the same but were reluctant to admit it publicly.

I used the Ostmarks I'd bought in West Berlin to pay for my beers. The coins were made of aluminum, resembling the play money I'd had as a child – didn't seem like 'real money' at all – and in fact the Americans joked about them as 'Monopoly money.'

One evening after a few beers I headed back toward the camp alone. Foggy in my brain, I got lost and ended up wandering across a huge switching yard, stumbling across eight or ten railroad tracks. A watchman confronted me and demanded to know what I was doing. I explained that I was attending the work camp, which he knew nothing about. He obviously suspected I was a spy or a saboteur or something, especially when he heard my American accent. I had a hard time persuading him not to haul me into the local police station, which might have been especially frightening since the U.S. had no diplomatic relations with the DDR. Pounding on the table and hollering "I'm an American citizen! You can't do this to me!" certainly wouldn't have done any good.

One evening we were invited to meet for a 'discussion' with a group of about twenty young German students from the FDJ. Our supervisors promised "a free exchange of ideas, a social opportunity to get to know each other." But the two groups didn't mix: the FDJ students sat on one side of the clubroom, and we visitors sat on the other. A master of ceremonies, a middle-aged German official, said we would discuss various topics in German with English translation. (Many of the French students spoke at least a little English.) He read off the first question, something like "How can people in the socialist countries and those in the West learn to live more peacefully together?" A young German raised his hand and read an answer from a piece of paper, obviously prepared in advance. A second question, and a second 'volunteer' read another prepared answer. All told, there were 15 or 20 questions and assigned answers. On one of the questions no 'volunteer' responded; another student explained that the assigned 'volunteer' was ill and couldn't come. The leader asked if there was another student who could answer, but nobody was willing to give an unrehearsed answer. It was painfully obvious that the whole thing was a propaganda show scripted in advance.

After the Q-and-A charade was over, the leader asked if any of the visitors would like to ask a question or make a statement, and none of us responded. The FDJ students left immediately – so much for our 'free exchange of ideas' and our 'social opportunity to get to know each other'.

One day I got a particle of dirt in my eye from all the debris flying around as we picked and shoveled. It was large enough to be quite painful, and I couldn't get it out by blinking. Dirk, a Dutch medical student, offered to see if he could help. He pulled my eyelid up with his fingers and exclaimed, "I can see it!" He dabbed at it with the corner of a handkerchief and fortunately got it out without hurting my eyeball. Didn't take a lot of medical knowledge, but I'm sure his year of med school gave him the knowledge and confidence to treat it for me. I doubt if a first-year American med student would have dared take the same risk.

Our clothes got pretty dirty in the ditch. One morning I washed out a wash-and-wear white shirt I'd been wearing and left it to soak in a basin in the men's room. When I returned in the evening it was gone, doubtless purloined by an East German workman. "Stupid!" I muttered to myself. The shortage of consumer goods under the communist system was notorious.

Sisi began showing some interest in Dirk. "She looks at me and licks her lips; she wants me to kiss her!" he exclaimed. Well, too bad, I mused – he gets her; I don't. Wonder if he's going to sleep with her ...?

A forty-ish German fellow named Horst showed up one day and insinuated himself into our group. We weren't sure why he was there, although we became suspicious when he started talking about opportunities to learn more about socialism. My curiosity finally got the better of me, so I asked about visiting Russia. He immediately offered to arrange a free trip to Moscow for me. I was actually tempted – spirit of adventure – even though Moscow sounded remote and forbidding in those Cold War days. But I figured the visit would just be more propaganda and indoctrination, and I knew my parents would be extremely distressed if they found out I'd gone, and I didn't want to be late for college, which was starting in less than a month. More than that, I was afraid if I accepted his offer, I might not be able to leave when I wanted. The American government would not have known I was there and so wouldn't have been able to extract me if the Soviets had detained me. So I never followed up on the invitation ... better safe than sorry ... young, adventurous, foolish, but not *that* foolish ... but it would have been a memorable experience.

A couple days later I saw Dirk talking with one of the French girls for fifteen minutes, and soon after that I saw Sisi actually try to bite him on the cheek. Little vixen. Short-lived romance.

I talked some more with Françoise. She and her sister Iliane had joined the UEC, which had sent their group to the work camp. Their father owned a factory back in France. She admitted that as an entrepreneur, he wasn't enthusiastic about his daughters' flirtation with the communist student organization, but he viewed them with an amused tolerance. He'd been glad for them to come to the work camp to dispel whatever illusions they might have had about life under communism. She and I ended up walking to a secluded area and necking a bit.

There was a very small *Evangelische* (Lutheran) church near the camp, a small unpainted wood-frame building with a half-dozen wooden pews and plain glass windows. On Sunday seven of us from the Quaker groups who spoke some German decided to attend, both to see what church was like under the officially-atheist communist regime and to offer our moral support. We didn't have dress-up clothes and indeed were rather bedraggled after our week in the ditch, but we dressed up as best we could and tramped into the church. We had misread the schedule, however, and walked in in the middle of the service. There weren't more than ten or twelve people in the congregation, all old and grey. The minister blanched when we walked in but relaxed visibly when we sat in the pews and turned respectfully toward him. He interrupted his sermon to welcome us, then continued with the service.

After the service the parishioners gathered around, and the minister explained that the government encouraged young people to disrupt church services in an attempt to stamp out religion; seeing our scruffy clothes, he had initially feared we intended to do the same. He tremendously appreciated our show of support once he saw that we weren't there to harass him.

After the first week our supervisors put us on buses, hauled us to a woodsy summer-camp-type place, and invited us to relax. It was a pleasant enough weekend: we swam, rowed boats around a lake, played impromptu games of volleyball, organized a couple foursomes for bridge, danced in the evenings, and conversed and flirted a lot. Dirk joined up with Iliane, Sisi took up with one of the French guys, and other couples similarly paired off. Françoise and I wandered to a secluded spot and lay on the grass together. I took her bra off and caressed her breasts, but when I reached for her lower private parts, she demurred, saying, "That's dangerous." OK, fair enough: I could enjoy her company without going all the way.

In the evenings the organizers provided more wine and cookies and dance music. Some middle-aged German workmen who were at the recreation area also came to the dances. Since there were almost no German women, the workmen swarmed around the female visitors, who were, after all, young and attractive. The guys from our group felt compelled to fend them off, partly because many of them were drunk and partly because the girls were 'our' women.

On Monday, back in the work camp, we settled into the familiar routine: meals, ditch, wine-and-cookie parties many evenings – the parties actually got boring after a while. More and more members of the group spent more and more time lounging under the trees rather than digging in the ditch, and some absented themselves completely. Sisi and her French boyfriend (who couldn't speak much English) took to hanging around the women's dorm during the days. Dirk stayed back one day and later reported, "I heard them having sex!"

On the second weekend the organizers again brought buses to take us to the same recreation area. The first weekend had been pleasant enough, but I thought another weekend there would be repetitive and boring and decided not to go. I told Françoise, but not the German supervisors, and simply hid out when they loaded up the buses.

So here I am alone. Don't want to just hang around the camp. So what to do, where to go, instead? I saw on a wall map that Hoyerswerda was only about twenty miles from the Polish border and thought I might as well hitch over that direction. Didn't expect to be gone very long – most likely return that evening – so I slung my jacket over my shoulder and headed for the road eastwards.

Hitching turned out to be surprisingly easy, different from what I'd expected in a communist country. Got a ride very quickly in a comfortable sedan to some small town on the Neisse River, which had been established as part of the German-Polish border shortly after World War II. Creating that border had been controversial because it forced Germany to give up a lot of land that had been German territory before the war. I stood on the German side of a bridge over the river and saw two Polish soldiers on the other side with the usual automatic rifles. I wondered if I dared walk across the bridge and see if I could enter Poland, another country then under Soviet domination. But I didn't see anybody else crossing the bridge and decided I'd better not try it. Once again, so much for fraternal socialist solidarity.

After a ham sandwich for lunch, I wondered, now where? Didn't want to go back to the work camp yet, so how about the town of Zittau, maybe fifty miles south, down near the corner where Germany, Poland and Czechoslovakia came together? Not that there was anything special to see there, but it made a convenient short-term destination. Could probably make it there and back to Hoyerswerda before nightfall.

A twenty-ish girl came along driving a small motor scooter. I stuck out my thumb, and, somewhat to my surprise, she stopped, and I settled myself on the rear. I had to hang on to her waist as we puttered along, which wasn't so disagreeable, after all.

A few miles later we had to stop at a roadblock. The police were looking for a guy who had stolen a car. They showed me the description the owner had given them: young man in his twenties, brown hair, 175 cm [70 inches] tall, speaks German with a foreign accent. Matched me, undeniably.

They waved the motor scooter on but detained me. They put me in a police car, drove into Zittau, and deposited me at the police station, which was an old wooden two-story building with badly-faded paint, wire mesh over the windows, and a caged area at one end of a long central hall. There were bulletin boards along the walls with various notices thumb-tacked up. In the hall were a couple tables and several rickety chairs. One window held a broken-down non-functioning air-conditioner. Police officers and others were milling up and down the hall.

They sat me at a table and asked to see my papers. I explained I was an American, was attending a work camp in Hoyerswerda *as a guest of the FDJ* – I emphasized that – and the bosses had taken my passport and were holding it till the end of the camp. The officers looked suspicious but didn't say anything. I worried at first whether they were going take me to a back room and rough me up, as American cops were sometimes accused of doing, but they were pleasant enough. They escorted me to a restroom when I requested but otherwise kept me sitting at the table and kept an eye on me.

It would have been interesting to watch the station activity if I weren't being held there involuntarily. I saw officers bring in two teen-aged boys accused of writing graffiti on walls and an old bum they'd picked up urinating in the street, although I never saw how those cases were resolved.

The time wore on: 4:00, 5:00, 6:00 p.m. I was getting uncomfortably hungry and was beginning to wonder when this episode would end. I asked how long they were going to hold me, but they only responded, *"Warte nur. Hab' Geduld* [Just wait. Be patient]."

Sometime after 6:00 they escorted a middle-aged woman into my area. She looked at me briefly and shook her head, obviously saying I wasn't the car thief. Much relieved, I asked again when they would release me, but they again replied to just wait.

Why hold me now, since I wasn't the car thief?

I said I was hungry, and one officer dug some coins out of his pocket and bought a sandwich for me at a concessionaire down the hall. Paid with his own money. Decent gesture, maybe a good omen, and I thanked him, although it wasn't enough to satisfy my hunger.

There I remained, just sitting and waiting .... seemed like ages ...

Maybe 9:00 or 10:00 p.m., three middle-aged men came in and walked over to me. They were dressed in heavy overcoats (in August??!) and looked bulky and forbidding – big bruisers. They led me out to a waiting car – it resembled a mid-sized American car from the late 1940's, with boxy fenders and a sloping rear frame. They told me to get in the back seat and closed the door behind me. The door handle had been removed, making it impossible to open the door from the inside. Two sat in the front seat, and the third sat beside me and kept his hand inside his overcoat – was he holding a gun?! One instructed (in German), "Stay in the car. Do not try to escape. Do not say anything. Do not resist. Do not make any sudden moves."

Oh, God!!

We drove off into the void, down the shadowy streets and into the countryside, rumbling along through the gloom. The men occasionally muttered together but otherwise said nothing.

I was scared but still felt strangely calm – nothing I could do but just wait and see what was going to happen. No choice but to trust them ....??!!

After a while I saw a highway sign: DRESDEN 60 [60 kilometers], then DRESDEN 40, then DRESDEN 25.

Some minutes after that we drove into the outskirts of a city and down the city streets until we came to a ten-foot-high masonry wall surrounding a six-story building. Despite the darkness I could see bars on many of the windows. We drove up to a metal gate, the driver honked twice, the gate swung open, we drove in, and the gate swung closed behind us with a metallic *clang!*

Oh, God!!!!??

Prison? years of confinement in a tiny cell? torture? 'third degree'? beat a confession out of me? force me to sign some document admitting to trumped-up charges? I'd read horror stories in American newspapers about exactly such things happening to Westerners arrested in communist countries.

They led me through a small side door into the building and before an officer sitting at a desk, who instructed me to take everything out of my pockets, take my jacket off, take my belt off (suicide prevention?), take my watch off, take my shoes off. He carefully wrote an inventory of each item. He confiscated my wallet and recorded the exact amount of dollars, Westmarks and Ostmarks I was carrying – are they going to charge me with currency smuggling? He asked me to sign the sheet, which I did – no choice.

A guard led me down the hall – without my belt I had to hold up my pants with one hand – into an elevator and up several flights. He unlocked a cell door and commanded, *"Drinnen*! [Inside!]"

The cell was about seven feet square, with bare unpainted walls and a single light bulb suspended from the ceiling maybe three feet above my head. There was a tiny window eight feet up, too high to see out of. About half the floor space was taken up by a wooden platform intended to serve as a bed. There was a toilet, a bare ceramic bowl with no seat or flush lever. The guard said I could use the toilet, but not to put any object into it or flush it; I should call him after using it, and he would inspect it and then flush it from outside the cell. He told me to wait and not go to sleep, then locked the door and left. The time must have been after midnight.

So here I am in a ***prison cell*** … in ***Communist East Germany*** … with ***no communication to the outside world,*** no way to notify my parents or the American government or the Swiss Embassy or anybody else who could help me get out …!!??

The cell was cold, and all I had on was a T-shirt and wash-n-wear cotton slacks and socks. I lay on the wooden platform and shivered. I contemplated the light bulb over my head and wondered if it concealed a microphone; I'd seen movies where the evil prison guards installed microphones in light bulbs in order to trick a prisoner into revealing some secret, something incriminating. (Don't let yourself be frightened by remembering too many movies …)

The helplessness of the situation ….

!!!!!!!!!!??????…..

But I will say I didn't panic, didn't start screaming or pounding my head against the wall, didn't break down sobbing or curl up in a ball. I accepted that there was nothing I could do but wait and see ... wasn't guilty of any crime ... was legally in their country ... hadn't violated the DDR's sovereignty or secrecy ... was only a student, not a spy or a saboteur ... didn't have anything to hide .... They might want to make some kind of example of me, but then again, why would they ...? I wouldn't be worth much as a propaganda tool. Maybe the FDJ connection would give me some kind of protection ...?

I tried to stay awake, but the cold and the hunger and the lateness of the hour ....

The guard awoke me an hour or two later, berated me for falling asleep, and led me to an office somewhere deep inside the prison. In the office a man wearing a green uniform with gold trim was seated behind a large desk. "*Sitze!*" he pointed to a stool maybe eight feet in front of the desk, so I sat down. Over his head was a light shielded from his eyes but shining into mine, the stereotypical setting of what cop movies showed as the 'third degree' – intense questioning intended to break down a prisoner into confessing.

TERRIFYING ...!!

But what could I do but cooperate ...?

He was all business – typical German bureaucrat? His first question: "*Weiß du wo du bist*? [Do you know where you are?]," using the familiar '*du*' rather than the more polite '*Sie*'.

"*Wir sind in Dresden. Sonst weiß ich nicht* [We're in Dresden. Other than that I don't know]".

"How do you know that?"

"I read the road signs as we drove here."

He didn't clarify where we were, and I was afraid to ask. Instead, he proceeded to question me for an hour, writing down each question and my answer in longhand on yellow legal-sized pieces of paper: What country are you from? Where is your passport? What other documents do you have with you? Any official or secret documents? Any microfilms? Why are you in the DDR? What are you doing here? Where have you been staying in DDR? Why were you traveling away from your group? Do you have any connection to the American government? Are you in the army / the diplomatic service / the CIA / any other government agency? Any connection to the government of the so-called *Bundesrepublik*? (Each of the two Germanys referred to the other as "the so-called ....") Do you have any luggage in DDR? where is it? any microfilms? (second time that question) and so on.

After he'd questioned me for an hour, I timidly ventured a question: *"Konnten Sie mir erzählen wo wir sind?* [Could you tell me where we are?]," trying to be as polite and obsequious as possible.

He replied, *"Diese ist eine Institution der Staatssicherheitspolizei* [This is an institution of the State Security Police]" (popularly called the *Stasi* or the *Geheimnispolizei* [secret police]).

EXCRUCIATING!!! Imprisoned by the secret police!!!

After that his manner began to soften a little. He called me to his desk, showed me the three pages of questions and answers [*Frage* and *Antworte*] he'd recorded, told me to read them through and say if anything was false, and then told me to sign each page at the bottom. I read them through – could decipher his handwriting and understand most everything he'd written – had to ask him the meaning of one or two words and phrases. It was a reasonable record of what I'd said, but I was still afraid to sign because I'd read stories about officials in the communist countries cutting up statements like these pages and splicing them into confessions. However, I conjectured that as a government official he had to make a record of his office's actions, and anyhow, I didn't have any real choice – had to trust him(!!?) – so I signed.

The guard led me back to my cell and again told me not to sleep. But this time I thought, to heck with it, I'm tired and hungry and cold, and what're you gonna do about it?, so I drifted off very quickly.

Sometime later he awoke me again, again berated me for falling asleep, and led me back to the green-and-gold-clad officer behind the large desk. This time the stool was much closer to his desk, and the light had been shaded away from my eyes. "You said you were in a work camp in Hoyerswerda," he said. "Where exactly is this camp?"

"I don't know. Somewhere near a beer hall and a dance hall with a band. Somewhere near a rail yard. They are building a *Braunkohl* plant."

He scribbled these down, asked a few more questions, and then said, "We'll have to check your story."

"Konnten Sie mir sagen, wieviel Uhr ist es?" [Could you tell me what time it is?]" I asked.

"Drei Uhr morgens [three a.m.]." .

"Dankeschön," as polite as I could.

"Go to your cell," he said. "Now you can sleep." The guard led me back; this time he brought me a blanket, which helped, but still wasn't enough against the cold. Despite the lighted bulb overhead I fell asleep immediately.

A different guard pounded on my cell door and woke me in the morning. He opened a slot in the door and passed in a tin plate with sausage and bread and a mug with 'coffee.' The food was predictably unpalatable and the coffee tasted like dishwater, but I was famished and glad to consume anything I got.

After 'breakfast' I sat in the cell wondering if I was doomed to spend the rest of my life sitting in a prison cell in a totalitarian dictatorship. I recalled a story about an Englishwoman who'd been similarly imprisoned; she had estimated how many steps back and forth in her cell would add up to a mile and had set out to 'walk' the distance from the French coast to Istanbul, Turkey. Maybe I should do the same ...?

In mid-morning a guard knocked on my door and said I could take a shower. He handed me a piece of soap and a towel, led me to a wide stairwell enclosed in a wire fence, called to another guard three floors down, locked me into the fenced enclosure, and told me to walk down, which I did. Another guard met me at the bottom, unlocked the cage, escorted me to a shower room, told me to stay within sight of a peephole in the door and to call him when I was done, and locked me into the room. ... Well, the room was clean, and there was hot water, so, what the heck, I took a nice long leisurely shower – nothin' else to do. The guard was visibly irritated by the time I was done, but (strange to say) I was feeling kind of defiant and refused to apologize to him. He locked me into the enclosed stairwell, called to the guard three flights up, and sent me back up.

Back in my cell again ... even more bored than before ...

Another knock on my door. This time it was some kind of official, judging from his uniform. He handed me two books (in German) and said, *"Hier, du kannst diese lesen* [Here, you can read these]."

I thought it curious that they would be giving me books until I saw the subjects. One was titled *Wer hat die beste Raketen?* [Who has the best rockets?] It had been published a year or two earlier, when the U.S.S.R. had placed a satellite ('Sputnik') in orbit around the earth and the Americans had had several well-publicized failures to do the same. It was only forty or fifty pages long and consisted mainly of diagrams and statistics comparing the Soviets' and the Americans' records up to that time – not very satisfying reading.

The other book (whose title I don't recall) was an obviously-fictitious tale of a man who had become a *Kommunist* in the early 1930's and had suffered all kinds of persecution by the Nazis for his beliefs. The protagonist had supposedly been imprisoned and denied food and water, forcing him at one point to drink his own urine. Heinrich Himmler, Chief of the Interior Ministry (one of the highest-ranking and most-notorious Nazis) had supposedly confronted him in the prison, but the protagonist, brave soul, had defied him and refused to foreswear being a *Kommunist*. The book ended triumphantly with the defeat of Nazi Germany and the founding of the DDR. It was utterly stupid, but it was easy reading and I could understand most of it, and reading it was better than staring into space.

Around noon the guard brought me another serving of bread, sausages and coffee. You're hungry enough, you'll eat anything.

By mid-afternoon I'd finished the *Kommunist*-prisoner book.

The situation was both frightening and boring. I wasn't ready to start my Calais-to-Istanbul walking journey just yet, so ... nothing to do but sit and stare at the walls, curse my bad luck / foolhardiness (take your pick), daydream about my life in the past, speculate about what the future might hold ...

In mid-afternoon I used the toilet, then called to the guard as instructed. I waited ten, fifteen, twenty minutes for the guard to come; meanwhile the toilet began to get smellier and smellier. When the guard finally came, he didn't even glance into the toilet before pulling the flush lever from outside the cell.

Besides the boredom and the nagging fear, one of the worst things about being in jail is the lack of control over your own life: you sleep when they tell you, eat when they tell you and what they give you, go when and where they say. Another downer was the isolation, the lack of contact with anybody but the guards and officials.

It was beginning to get to me: I wanted *out*!!

Evening meal: more bread, sausage and coffee.

Still had the blanket from last night. Fell asleep ... who knows what time? – the hours kind of melded into one another ...

Awoke before breakfast ... the guard brought yet more bread, sausage and coffee ... not looking forward to yet another boring day ... would they at least bring me something else to read? ... probably more stupid propaganda, but better than staring at the walls ...

No shower this morning.

No more books ...

Lunch was ... guess what ...? Am I gonna develop vitamin deficiencies?

Later that afternoon the guard led me back to the office where I'd been interrogated two nights before. The same green-and-gold officer was waiting. "We've checked your story," he said, "and it's true. We'll send you back to the Hoyerswerda camp. Don't leave the group again. But we had to be extra careful, *besonders in dieser Zeit* [especially at this time]."

What did he means by that last? What's so special about this time?

"Here are your possessions," he continued, pointing to a table with the things they'd confiscated. "Check that they're all here." He handed me the list I'd signed, and sure enough, everything was there, including every dollar, Westmark and Ostmark; the only thing missing was the condom I'd purchased in the men's room vending machine. (Were condoms also in short supply in the workers' paradise?!) "Please sign this paper that we've returned everything to you."

I signed.

He handed me another paper that said I had not been tortured, starved or mistreated and told me to sign it too.

I signed.

I will say that even though the prison was cold, grey, forbidding, dank and dreary, it was cleaner and better-maintained than the three or four American prisons I toured as a law student. Never saw any evidence of rats, cockroaches, bedbugs or other vermin.

The guard led me out to the street, where two young fellows in uniforms were waiting beside a car. "They'll take you to the camp," he said.

This time it was an older, rather banged-up car. They invited me to sit in the front seat, from which the door handle had not been removed. One guy drove, while the other sat in the back seat. They wanted to talk, to ask questions about America and West Germany. I was glad to respond. They said they were new recruits in the *Stasi*; they hadn't been eager to join, but it was the best job they could get. (I speculated that if they spent enough years in the organization, they'd get socialized into it and become just as doctrinaire and officious as the other officers and guards I'd met.)

We got back to Hoyerswerda in time for supper. My two escorts took me to the work camp office, where the supervisors greeted me with subdued anger: "You caused us a lot of trouble," one fumed. It seems the *Stasi* officials had contacted them in the middle of the night – rousted them out of bed – to verify my story. The supervisors had had to search through their records to confirm that I was in fact participating in the camp.

I joined a table of my camp-mates who were just back from their weekend at the recreation area. Except for Françoise, most of them weren't even aware I'd been gone. I was itching to regale them with tales of my imprisonment, but most of them just wanted to talk about who had paired up with whom – had we already become a gossip-mongering ingroup?

Françoise said the weekend had been pleasant enough, although just the same as the first one. She'd danced with several guys from the group but was glad to be back with me. She told me she lived in the city of Annecy in southeastern France, gave me her address and invited me to come visit her there.

Next week we were back in our ditch. Each day fewer and fewer group members actually got down into the ditch and hoisted dirt out; the rest hung around the dormitories, lounged under the trees or disappeared in twosomes.

The supervisors hadn't come to 'inspect' our work for more than a week, so several of us approached them and asked if it was satisfactory. One finally admitted it didn't make any difference: they were going to run a mechanized finisher through the ditch after we left anyhow.

That made official what some of us had suspected: the ditch-straightening was only make-work – keep us busy during the days, let us believe we were contributing to the building of socialism. Our participation in the work camp had been nothing but a propaganda exercise, and a rather amateurish one at that.

Alright, no harm: from my perspective it had still been an extremely interesting, enjoyable and educational experience (even including the 48 hours in prison, except for the fear factor). I wondered if it had disillusioned any of the British or French young communists. Françoise and Iliane admitted they were reconsidering their ideas.

The supervisors had parties for us on three more evenings, the same cookies and wine and five-piece band. They organized another talent show, and Gilles sang his same three songs again. The parties had become completely routine and same-old, same-old, although I did enjoy dancing and occasionally necking with Françoise.

The following Saturday they drove us back to the FDJ office in East Berlin. I stayed one more night in the FDJ hotel and discovered Sisi was staying there too. Maybe tonight she'd be interested ...? But no, she was preparing to go back to her boyfriend in Sweden (little vixen!) and her father and his communist newspaper. I never learned what she thought about the whole work camp experience.

Next day I went back to the Friedrichstrasse Station, showed the East German border guards my passport and DDR visa, and crossed back into West Berlin without incident. As instructed, I went to the Quaker office in West Berlin, where I met the other American and British participants from the Hoyerswerda camp. The Quaker representative exclaimed, "We're so relieved to see you back safe-and-sound! We had no word about your situation until yesterday."

"What happened?! Why so worried?" I asked.

"You know the East Germans put up that barbed-wire 'fence' along the border between East and West Berlin last week. They're preventing East Germans from crossing over to West Berlin."

"Hunh!?" I responded, open-mouthed. "We didn't know anything about that; they didn't tell us. ... Well, one official said something about *'besonders in dieser Zeit,'* but I didn't know what he was referring to." I thought it better not to mention it was a prison official and I'd been in the secret police prison when the fence was erected.

"Yes, they've got tanks and anti-tank obstacles at some points, and now they're not letting West Berliners into the East. They blocked most of the elevated and subway lines between the two parts of the city. We were worried whether we'd be able to get you back out. We're responsible for you, you know."

The original barbed-wire barrier was put up on the night of August 12-13, 1961. Over the next weeks the barbed wire was gradually replaced by a concrete wall extending more than thirty miles between the East and West portions of the city. It became known as the Berlin Wall and remained in place until the end of the Cold War in 1989.

"Well, they didn't give us any problems at the work camp," I replied. "They tried to be good hosts."

"Anyhow, welcome back to the free world!"

CHAPTER 6.
STUDENT SUMMER IN EUROPE (III):
SOME MISSED OPPORTUNITIES

Despite my experience with the *Stasi*, I was intrigued at the possibility of visiting another country in the communist bloc. I wrote my parents a postcard saying I was considering the idea of hitchhiking into Czechoslovakia, which in those days had a reputation as one of the strictest, most Stalinist of the communist countries. I also said I expected to return home for a week or so before the start of fall semester at college.

Then I set out to get a visa. The Czech embassy had extremely limited hours: open 3:00-4:00 p.m. Tuesdays and 9:00-10:00 a.m. Thursdays – two hours a week. It was located in a residential area of East Berlin, quite far from the city center. I took a bus that poked along and finally got me to the embassy at 3:45 on Tuesday. Despite my pleas, however, the guards said I was too late and refused me entry. Naïve on my part, I realized too late. Once again, so much for fraternal solidarity of the Communist bloc, I thought bitterly, and so much for my plan to visit Czechoslovakia.

> (I wonder, in retrospect, if I could have hitched to the Czech border and gotten a visa there …?)

As an alternative, I saw a poster advertising the *Leipziger Messe*, the famed Leipzig Trade Fair that had been held almost continuously since the

Middle Ages. Oughta be interesting, I thought, to see what it looked like under the DDR: would it be just another propaganda display? So I decided to take my chances on another encounter with the *Stasi* and go see it.

Leipzig was accessible either by local roads or at a turnoff from the transit Autobahn that ran southwesterly out of Berlin. At the West Berlin exit point the guards said I could walk over to the East Berlin border post, some ten yards distant. I wondered what kind of reception I would get from the soldiers there, especially in view of the tensions following erection of the barbed-wire Wall, but I bravely, resolutely, marched across the no-man's-land.

The East German guards watched me coming, striding into the lion's mouth, as it were. But they proved to be surprisingly helpful despite the usual automatic weapons strapped to their backs. They invited me to wait at their station until they could find me a ride to Leipzig.

After a while one motioned me over and invited me into a waiting car. The driver glared at me as I got in and demanded, *"Hast du Pistole mit?* [You got a gun on you?]"

"Nein, ich bin Amerikaner [No, I'm an American]." He relaxed visibly when he heard my accent. I asked why he had agreed to give me a ride, and he replied, "THEY (pointing to the Soviet soldiers) told me to take you along. I couldn't refuse."

Nice to have help from guys with really persuasive powers.

We took local roads to Leipzig. I had a pleasant conversation with my reluctant host, who turned out to be a West German businessman going to the fair in the hope of generating business for his company.

The fair was moderately interesting. A surprising number of Western businessmen were there, both to sell their products and to look for possible purchases from the communist countries. However, there were very few consumer products on display; most of the exhibits were photos of industrial products rather than actual pieces of equipment, rather sterile and boring to me. The soviet bloc was obviously more interested in developing industrial facilities than in producing for consumers.

I took the opportunity to visit the famed Leipzig University, founded over 600 years ago. Goethe, Wagner, Nietzsche, and numerous Nobel Prize winners had studied there. The East Germans had renamed it Karl Marx University. It seemed only slightly less bleak and doctrinaire than East

Berlin. The buildings were dingy and crumbling, badly in need of refurbishing. There were still pockmarks on the buildings and piles of rubble from World War II bombings. The main administration building had a prominent office for the FDJ but almost no other evidence of student clubs or activities. A bulletin board showed a list of classes, including many hours of political economy – the study of (i.e., indoctrination in) Marxist economic theory. Being a university student under those conditions must have been rather confining and depressing.

Next day I left the fair and got ride to an overpass over the transit Autobahn. Making my way down to the highway, I saw immediately that this was another bad situation. Transiting cars weren't supposed to stop on the freeway, so who would ever risk picking up an unknown hitchhiker, possibly an escaped political prisoner or a refugee from the *Stasi*? And predictably, the first hundred drivers wouldn't even glance at me as they whizzed by.

But Fortune smiled surprisingly soon: a West German man and his family transiting back home swerved off the road beside me. The wife moved into the back seat with the two kids while the husband invited me into the front. I was embarrassed at this act of hospitality until I saw his motivation: he was a Baptist lay preacher who wanted to bring me to the Light. "*Sind Sie Christian?* [Are you (a) Christian?]" he asked.

"*Nicht genau. I suche doch* [Not exactly. I'm still searching]," I replied, my standard reply to preachers. He spent the next couple hours extolling the virtue of being Saved. I listened politely and replied when I had to. I found his exhortations repetitive and 'heavy', but I didn't want to offend him and risk losing this (Heaven-sent??!) ride.

We crossed back into West Germany without incident. My host dropped me in the city of Bayreuth, where I spent the night in the hostel. I saw on a map that we weren't too far from Salzburg, Austria, which was known for its music festivals and student life, and decided to go see if I could find a party.

Next morning I headed back to the highway. Almost the first car that came along was my Baptist lay preacher and his family. The preacher seemed overjoyed to see me, explaining that God must have sent him to me this second day to ensure my salvation. I endured another hour of his exhortations, glad to have the ride but not unhappy when they had to turn off the Salzburg road.

I arrived in Salzburg in early afternoon. In those days there was a youth hostel on the edge of town, accessible by a 45-minute bus ride and a fifteen-minute walk. I got to the hostel in mid-afternoon and discovered that it didn't open until 5:00 p.m. It didn't make sense to go back into the city, so nothing I could do but hang around until the hostel opened. After a while a few other student travelers began arriving, and we carried on a desultory conversation until we were finally allowed to enter. After claiming a bed in the boys' dorm room, I went back to the mess hall where a meal of sausage and potatoes was to be served at 6:00 p.m. I tried to find a group to join, but everybody clung to their own small circles of friends, and I never really got into a satisfactory conversation.

The hostel doors were locked at 10:00 p.m., and bedtime (curfew) was at 10:30. Next morning the staff awoke us around 7:30. After the typical hostel breakfast of bread, jam and coffee, they said we all had to leave by 9:00: all-in-all, a rather regimented existence.

I decided to spend another day in Salzburg, which was famous for its concerts and traditional architecture, so I left my backpack on my bed and took the bus into town. Dutifully visited the cathedral, the abbey and the Old City, which were interesting enough, although I would have preferred to have had company. I checked the schedule at the famous festival hall and discovered there was a concert that evening. It began at 7:00 and finished before 9:00, which I figured would allow just enough time to catch the bus and get back before the hostel closed.

During the intermission I got into a conversation with a Swedish girl, comparing notes about our respective colleges/universities and our summer travels. She was alone and was staying at a tourist home in the Old City. I had a feeling we might have been compatible and desperately wished I could have stayed and talked with her after the concert ended. She indicated, however, that she was sharing her room with three other girls and couldn't invite me in (even if she'd wanted to, which wasn't clear). So I had to dash for the bus back to the hostel: another of the summer's missed opportunities.

Several other student travelers, fellow hostellers who'd attended the same concert, also got on the bus. It poked slowly along the road back toward the hostel, arriving at the nearest bus stop just at 10:00. The other hostellers and I ran to the hostel, but the door was already locked. We banged on the door and shouted until the proprietor opened it a crack. "You're late," he frowned. "I shouldn't let you in." We protested that we'd attended the concert and the bus had run late, and he finally, grudgingly, let us in.

Now where to go? Two nights in that hostel were enough.

Well, I had a couple weeks until college began again, so I decided I might as well accept Françoise's invitation to visit her home in Annecy, even though I had never actually told her I would come. I had no idea where Annecy was until I studied a map of France and discovered it was in the French Alps, a little south of Geneva, Switzerland, within view of the famed Mont Blanc.

Hitching in that part of Europe turned out to be quite slow and unsatisfactory. The area was rife with tourists whose cars were loaded down with family members and luggage – no room for riders even if they'd been willing to pick me up. The roads through the mountains were slow and tortuous. I had to wait a long time between rides, and then they were only for short distances. If somebody dropped me in a city, I sometimes had trouble getting information about routes to the outskirts and ended up carrying my backpack for long stretches.

I only made it to Innsbruck, Austria, the first night, less than 100 miles. The hostel there was more centrally located but was jammed with kids in their early teens who ran around noisily disrupting any attempts at conversation.

Youth hostels, at least in Europe, have gotten much fancier (and much more expensive) since my student-traveling days. Now they advertise on the Internet, touting their proximity to night spots, ski areas and other recreation possibilities. Many have 24-hour concierges with no lock-outs or curfews. Many offer single and double rooms, rather than the large twenty- and thirty-person dormitories I remember. They now offer more sumptuous meals and bars to relax in in the evenings. They've become much more like standard hotels. On one hand, they're less Spartan and more attractive, but on the other hand they seem to have gotten away from the original idea of providing safe and inexpensive havens for young travelers.

Next day I got lucky and got a ride with a guy going all the way to Switzerland. But the road led through the tiny principality of Liechtenstein, and I decided to stop and see a bit of the country. I soon regretted giving up my nice ride, however, when I saw how crowded the capital city of Vaduz was with tourists and the concomitant souvenir (i.e., junk) shops. The mountains were impressive, and the National Museum might have been interesting, but there really wasn't much reason to stay in the town, so after an hour I went on.

It took me another two days to make my way across Switzerland, a total distance of maybe two hundred miles. In retrospect I might have done better to pay for a bus or train to some interesting town rather than spending hours standing by roads watching cars whiz by.

I do recall a couple of memorable rides, though. One was with a youngish German woman, probably early 30s, who picked me up on a mountain road. She spoke excellent English, and we had a pleasant conversation. After half an hour we reached a mountain pass, and she pulled off the road and parked on a gravelly spot and asked, "Would you like to have a picnic?"

"Well, yeah, sure, but I don't have much food with me."

"Oh, I have plenty of food. Please be my guest."

"Well, thanks."

She opened the trunk and produced a picnic basket. We climbed a little ways up a mountain path, and then she spread out a small blanket on a grassy spot and took out slices of ham and cheese, bread, fruit and a bottle of wine. "Have whatever you like. Make yourself a sandwich," she said.

It was a beautiful sunny day, and the mountain air felt crisp and clear. We ate and continued conversing, a very pleasant interlude, but a question kept running through my mind: 'What's going on here? Is there something beneath the surface I haven't cottoned onto yet? Did she have some ulterior motive?' (Sex ...?!)

After the meal she gathered up the uneaten food and put it back in the basket. "Wasn't that pleasant!" she exclaimed.

"Yes, wonderful! Thanks for treating me."

"It's so nice to share your meal with somebody," she said. She carried the basket back to the car and put it into the trunk. "Shall we be off?"

We drove another half hour, and then she pulled over to the side and said, "I'm turning off here. I wish you luck in finding your next ride."

"Well, thanks very much for the ride and for sharing your picnic lunch with me ... um ... it was very enjoyable."

"You're most welcome. I enjoyed it too," she replied, and off she went.

Another ride that sticks in my memory was outside of Interlaken when a guy drove past in a new convertible sports car with the top down. He slammed on his brakes when he saw me and, when I ran up him, said, "Sorry. I was daydreaming. Where ya heading?"

From his accent I knew he was a fellow American. "Heading for Annecy in France," I replied.

"I can take you a little ways toward there. I'm heading to Milan, if you want to go with me. See a bit of Italy."

"Thanks for the offer. Let me think about it," as I climbed in, thinking it would be a treat to cruise along with the wind in my face and a thrill in my heart.

Soon turned out to be more of a thrill than I'd bargained on. My host roared into each Alpine curve, touching the brakes just in time to avoid hurtling off the road, then jamming on the accelerator and careening around the curve. He seemed to be a pretty skillful driver, but my heart still skipped a beat every time he entered a curve, and I broke out in a cold sweat. "Trying out my new Porsche, wanna see what she can do," he said.

"Wow!" I gasped, "some car, alright!" cowering in the suicide seat and staring transfixed as the speedometer soared to 120 km/hr and dropped back to 40 (75 mph to 25), trembling in fear that he might miscalculate on some curve, or skid on a gravelly spot, or meet a large truck on a blind curve, or some other disaster.

After maybe 45 minutes of this terror we reached a turn-off toward Annecy, and I told my host, "I think I really ought to get out here. I got some people expecting me in Annecy," which wasn't exactly true, but sounded good.

My host hit the brakes and skidded to a stop. "Enjoyed having you with me for the little while. Hope you enjoyed the ride."

"It was ... *breath-taking*!" Truer words were never spoken.

I made it to Annecy late that evening, too late to go to Françoise's house. I was lucky and found a cheap *pension* (guest house) for the night.

Next morning I left my backpack at the pension and made my way to the address Françoise had given me, which fortunately wasn't too far from the center of town. It turned out to be a rather pretentious house in a neighborhood of large elegant homes, suitable for the owner of a sizable manufacturing company.

With some trepidation I knocked on the door. A woman answered, and when I tried to explain who I was in my two dozen words of French, she interrupted, "*Attende*! [Wait]" and went next door and brought back a girl of about thirteen. The girl, whose name was Madeleine, was about five feet tall and just beginning to develop into adolescence. She had studied several years of English and spoke it with careful schoolgirl diction. With her as translator, I explained how I'd met Françoise and how she'd invited me to come for a visit. The woman, who turned out to be Françoise's mother, said her daughter hadn't informed her parents that I was coming – no surprise, since I hadn't written – and had gone to Italy to refresh her Italian in preparation for an exam. The mother was very gracious, however, and invited me to come for dinner that evening.

Madeleine, seeing a chance to practice her English, offered to guide me around the town, which turned out to be quite picturesque, if overly touristy: zillions of souvenir shops, pretentiously quaint little cafes, crowds of people speaking German or English. Surrounded by mountains, it fronted on the Lac d'Annecy, with thirteenth-century stone bridges over a smallish river winding through the center of town. The Old City section was crowned by a historic chateau and had narrow winding streets, some cobblestoned, lined with magnificent old multi-hued townhouses. Madeleine eagerly led me down charming back streets, pointing out monuments and historic buildings and attempting to tell me their stories. It was quite an effort for her to formulate her thoughts into English sentences, however, and she grew visibly tired as lunchtime approached. Eventually I proposed that we get something to eat, and we stopped in a small bakery shop on the river bank and got some crusty French *baguettes* and cheese and grapes and a couple éclairs and shared them on a riverside park bench.

In the late afternoon Madeleine led me back to Françoise's house. As I prepared to go in, she took my fingers in her hands and gave a little squeeze, sort of halfway between childlike and budding-young-womanhood, the first time she'd touched me all day. Then she disappeared into her own house.

That evening at dinner I met Françoise's father, who was fairly fluent in English. He talked about the difficulties of running a business under a government that interfered in every little decision under its doctrine of *dirigisme*. Françoise's younger sister Iliane was also present; she remembered me from the Hoyerswerde work camp. She spoke fairly good English and helped translate between her mother and me. The mother seemed quite fascinated that her daughter had met an American young man in Germany who had traveled all the way to Annecy to visit their home. Wished I could have communicated with her better ... have to take French next year at college.

We talked until late in the evening. Too bad I'd missed seeing Françoise – another missed opportunity – but the dinner with her family and the guided tour with Madeleine had made Annecy special.

Next morning before leaving the pension I wrote a letter home. I bought stamps from a local shop (French shops often sell postage stamps) but put the wrong postage on it, and it went by sea mail rather than airmail.

> I learned later that my parents became increasingly anxious after receiving my postcard about hitchhiking through Czechoslovakia and then receiving no further word from me for almost a month: had their son been detained in that Communist bastion? sent to a labor camp? *executed?!* They were much relieved when my letter from Annecy finally arrived in early September. ... I decided never to tell them about my 48 hours in the East German prison.

I worked my way back across France toward Ostend, Belgium. In those days France either had no speed limits or didn't enforce them – I was never sure which – and I got rides with a couple of speed maniacs who tore down the curvy two-lane roads at 120 to 150 km/hr (75 to 94 mph). Always the dilemma: do you give up a ride going where you want to go for the sake of safety, or do you stay with it and grit your teeth and pray silently for your life? Made me appreciate the relative sanity of most American drivers.

I met a couple of English girls in the Ostend youth hostel who were going around inviting everybody to come stay in their flat in London's East End. I accepted the invitation along with a couple other guys and, after crossing the Channel next day, made my way to the flat. Once there I discovered it was quite full, and the two girls who had invited us were nowhere to be seen. We learned later that the inviters had been feuding with their apartment-mates and were harassing them by throwing out invitations to all-and-sundry. However, the permanent residents were quite gracious and managed to find spare beds and couches for everybody to sleep on. It was kind of a menagerie with seven or eight of us crowded in together in a three-room apartment, but it was also lively and a lot of fun. The student life: seven or eight guys and girls crowded in together in three small rooms.

After supper my last evening one of the British guys invited me to play poker. He won couple hands, putting him up maybe £1 ($2.80), prompting him to brag, "Not bad for a bloke who failed the eleven-plus." [The eleven-plus was an exam that effectively divided English schoolchildren into the university-bound vs. everybody else.] He knew I was a college student, and I speculated that he had a mild inferiority complex for having finished school at fifteen. Half an hour later I won a fairly large pot, leaving him owing me about £2. "I don't have the money with me," he said. "I'll have to go get it,"

"Sure, go ahead," I said, knowing perfectly well that he knew that I knew he wouldn't return until after I'd flown out the next day.

I ended up flying from Heathrow Airport to New York three days before classes started. Back in New York I called a classmate who lived in the city, who very cordially invited me to spend a night in his parents' home and ride back to college with him the next day. The visit to my parents would have to wait until Christmas.

I added up my remaining funds and calculated that the entire summer including airfare had cost me less than $500 (mind you, in 1961 dollars). Traveling so cheaply, I had doubtless missed some opportunities, but I'd also had some experiences that few high-end travelers would ever have and had met more people from more different walks of life than most tourists ever would. And I'd learned a lot more about my own likes and dislikes, capabilities and weaknesses, potentialities and limitations. I wouldn't have had it any other way.

And it whetted my appetite for more adventure travel.

CHAPTER 7.
THREE DOLLARS A DAY

My trips in Africa (chapters 8 – 16) were my first extended experience in less-developed countries (LDCs). I budgeted myself to $3 a day – $100 a month – to cover food, lodging, transportation and incidental costs. This was in the mid-1960s, when $1 was a significant amount of money in many developing countries. American dollars were the most widely-accepted currency in the world and were eagerly sought after in every LDC I visited.

Even today dollars are the nearest thing to a world currency, although their position is gradually fading. There's been a lot of inflation since the 1960's, and the dollar has lost more than 90 percent of its purchasing power. So $3 a day then might translate into $25 or $30 in the early 21st century, when this was written. The stories below are based on 1960s prices.

My informal limit was $1 for a meal and $1 for a night's lodging. Sometimes I had to exceed these limits, but sometimes my meals and nights' lodgings were free, so on average I found it just about possible to stay within the budget. You couldn't begin to live on that amount of money in the U.S. even in those days, but it was possible in the cheaper parts of the world if you were willing to live at the local level. And living at the local level actually gave you a better feel for the country's people and culture than staying in first-class hotels.

Trying to live on that amount of money for long periods, you develop the habit of stretching every penny and, frankly, of looking for free lodging and meals whenever possible. This doesn't mean you become a bum or a leach, but it does mean you accept legitimate meal invitations and try to find free sleeping places. During the course of my travels I slept on beaches, couches, temple floors, wooden tables, luggage racks, cement floors in abandoned buildings, and God knows where else. I also traveled by the cheapest means possible when I couldn't hitch rides, including half-price fourth-class train fares in India and hitching rides on planes in Thailand and Vietnam.

In later years I've stayed in my share of high-rise first-class hotels and eaten my share of elaborate meals in expensive restaurants, usually on business, but I don't particularly care for them. Hotel staff, of course, are trained to smile and call you by name, and they're certainly agreeable, but I still find big hotels cold and sterile. My heart is still with the small local places. I don't mind if it's not the fanciest décor or the clerks and waiters don't speak English – to me they're warmer and friendlier than first-class places.

Meals

One problem of any do-it-yourself travel is finding meals at times you want to eat at prices you want to pay. This is especially difficult if you're on a tight budget and/or constantly moving on. There's a temptation to skimp on meals, partly as a way to cut costs and partly because of the difficulty of finding suitable places. You end up grabbing a few bites of local food or something sweet to kill the hunger pangs, but this isn't an adequate amount of food and often isn't nutritious. So you tend to lose energy, to tire more easily. I also gradually lost weight on my longer trips: went down from 160 lb. to 145 lb. on my eighteen-month jaunt around the Middle East and Asia [Book II]. (I was too thin; I gained it back the first couple months after I returned home.)

I didn't worry about cleanliness in the U.S. and Europe, but I did when I started traveling in Africa and Asia. I was well aware that the standards of hygiene were lower in those lands. But I wanted to eat the same food in the same places as ordinary local people: aside from being much cheaper, I figured it would be more interesting and 'genuine' than the internationally-oriented fare in fancy restaurants and hotels.

So I ate a lot of meals in food stalls and mud-brick restaurants. I decided I would eat anything that was thoroughly cooked, and I worked out ways to find out what was available and how it looked. Sometimes I learned the names of a few foods in the local language, sometimes I would walk around the dining area and examine what other patrons were eating, and sometimes I would drag a waiter to the kitchen and peer into the various pots and point to the things that looked most appetizing. These approaches also solved the problem of not having a common language with the food servers.

I tried to be very careful about beverages, although they tended to be more problematic than finding food. I preferred to drink water, but I settled for soft drinks or tea when I couldn't be sure the water was safe. I avoided ice almost everywhere, so the soft drinks were warm, and I got tired of them. I also got overcaffeinated from tea a few times.

I got diarrhea several times; the worst cases happened to be in Egypt, India and Vietnam. Usually it wasn't too severe, but it really knocked me out a couple times. I remember searching frantically for a toilet more than once. (A Peace Corps volunteer in Pakistan commented on the need to develop a strong sphincter muscle to guard against 'accidents'. He described one such accident he couldn't avoid: *sploosh* straight into his underpants.) I carried Kaopectate and swigged it down whenever my stools got too soft. Still, considering where and what I was eating, it was remarkable that I didn't get ill more frequently. Maybe I developed resistance to some of the bugs.

Prices

One problem every traveler faces when first arriving in a new country is to learn about local prices. Translating them into your home currency may not give an accurate idea of what the local prices should be. Prices for many items aren't fixed or at least aren't displayed in many LDCs. Locals will usually know how much things should cost, but tourists from wealthier countries often won't know. Tourists are seen as wealthy, and indeed they often are wealthy compared to denizens of less-developed countries. Even a low-end traveler may be carrying a few hundred dollars, more than a year's cash wages for the poorest people in developing countries. In some societies it's considered quite legitimate to charge wealthy persons more for a good or service than a poor person would pay. It's also culturally acceptable to overcharge strangers. All this makes even a low-end hitchhiker a target for price-gouging.

As a foreigner you're almost automatically a target for sharpies, especially in Third World countries, and sometimes in industrialized countries too. Taxi drivers the world over are notorious for taking advantage of newly-arrived travelers who don't yet know the lowest-cost route or the true fare from one place to another; this can be a particular problem if the taxis don't have meters. Souvenir sellers – street peddlers, bazaar merchants and many small shopkeepers – are notorious for overcharging foreign travelers. Some restaurant proprietors aren't above jacking up prices for people they assume they'll never see again.

You can try to avoid disputes by negotiating the price in advance, but if you do you immediately identify yourself as a newcomer and a potential target, and the taxi driver or vendor may simply set the price too high. For example, many of the taxis in Izmir, Turkey, used to be horse-drawn carriages that weren't metered. I negotiated a price of five Turkish lira before taking a short trip in one of these conveyances, only to learn later that the standard fare was one lira. Another time I negotiated a fare of 8 pesos for a taxi ride in Mexico City. The driver ran the meter, which said 4 pesos when we reached my destination. When I handed him 4 pesos, he insisted on holding me to my bargain.

One trick is to spread out a map and (pretend to) follow along as the driver takes you to your destination; that *may* encourage him to take the most economical route.

In Third World countries you have to bargain for many purchases. (You bargain for certain things in Europe and the U.S. too – cars, houses, stuff in flea markets – but you bargain for many more things in developing countries.) You have to recognize when you're in a bargaining situation. Sometimes I got it wrong: paid the asking price for something and later learned that I should have bargained it down. And occasionally I tried to bargain for some purchase and realized that the seller had offered his legitimate price at the beginning. Bargaining is viewed as a kind of game, a social event, in large parts of the Middle East and Asia. You do best if you take it in a spirit of fun – smile and keep a civil tone even as you haggle. The process takes time, of course – if you're in a hurry to make your purchase, or if you want the item too badly, you're likely to overpay.

You have to accept that you're at a disadvantage – the vendor has a much better idea of the real price than you do. As a generalization, the initial prices for tourist items sold by street vendors or bazaar merchants are likely to be ridiculously high – two or three or even four times the item's customary market price. So you may bargain him down from 80 pesos to 60 and think you've gotten a good deal, whereas the rock-bottom price might have been 20 or 30.

Weak currencies and black markets

Some countries' currencies are weak, that is, the currency (pesos, lira, rupees, shillings, etc.) may be losing value rapidly. This normally occurs when the country's inflation rate is high or when people don't have confidence in the strength of its economy. When a country's currency is weak, you may lose value if you exchange too many dollars. A related problem is that you may not be able to change your leftover currency back into dollars when you're leaving the country.

Other problems arise when the government sets the official exchange rate too high; the currency is then called overvalued. For example, when I first arrived in India the government had set the official exchange rate at $1 = 5.5 rupees (i.e., 1 rupee = 18¢) when the true market rate was probably around $1 = 8 rupees (or 1 rupee = 12½¢). Thus if you changed dollars into rupees at the official rate, you were only getting about two-thirds as many rupees as you really should have. This would make travel in India rather expensive if you changed at the official rate.

When the currency is overvalued this way, a black market (also called an informal, unofficial or parallel market) is likely to emerge. Economists say that if the official exchange rate is overvalued, the black market tends to undervalue the currency. In my example from India, the official rate was 1 rupee = 18¢, the true market rate was probably about 1 rupee = 12½¢, and the black market rate was 1 rupee = 10¢. Thus $1 would get you about 10 rupees on the black market, so you could get more local purchasing power than the dollar was really worth. That made it cheap to travel in India.

Governments often try to suppress informal/parallel markets, that is, to make them illegal and try to prevent people from changing money on them. (They're called black markets in countries where governments are trying to suppress them, but they're called free markets in countries that don't try to control the currency. Most of the prosperous industrialized countries fit in the latter category.) The enforcement may be very strict or may be quite loose. In the former case you may be risking confiscation or a fine or even a jail sentence if you're caught buying local currency on the black market. In the latter case it's sometimes called a grey market because even though it's technically illegal, the government tolerates it.

Foreign tourists often encounter the black market when people approach them in the streets near major hotels and tourist sites and whisper, "Change money? Change money?" Another frequent place is small shops selling tourist souvenirs. You have to be cautious if you decide to change on the black market: aside from any danger from the police, street sellers and shopkeepers are quite willing to take advantage of a newly-arrived traveler who doesn't know what the black-market rate is and offer him/her a rate way below the going market rate. When I first arrived in India, for example, street traders approached me and offered to sell me rupees at 6 or 8 to the dollar (as noted above, the free- or black-market rate was about 10 to the dollar at that time). Hence this is another piece of information you want to gather before entering a new country or immediately upon arrival. You can often learn the rate from other travelers who have recently been in the country or sometimes even from banks, newspapers or currency-trading offices in other countries.

You have to be cautious when changing money on the black market. I've heard stories about shady characters who promise great exchange rates and then, when unwary tourists put dollars into their hands, scamper off into the back streets. This never happened to me, maybe because I was young and could have given chase, or maybe I was just lucky to find honest black-marketers (if that's not an oxymoron ... honor among thieves?).

I did get 'taken' a few years later on a tourist trip with my wife in Cartagena, Colombia. A guy approached us in the Plaza Bolivar, the central square of the Old City. He said, "I need dollars," and offered me

1100 pesos per dollar when the grey-market (semi-official) rate was about 1000. I offered to exchange $300. He looked around warily and, not seeing any police, counted out thirty-three 10,000-peso notes, which he then rolled up and put into his pants pocket. So I gave him three hundred-dollar bills, which he also put into his pants pocket. He then fumbled around in his pocket for a while, which should have made me suspicious. I could have made a fuss and said I wanted to cancel the deal and get my dollars back, but I didn't. After 15 or 20 seconds, he produced a wad of pesos from his pocket and handed them to me. I could see the 10,000-peso notes. I should have insisted on counting them, but I didn't, and he disappeared. Later I realized that there were only a couple 10,000-peso notes on the outside of the wad, and the rest were all 1000-peso notes. I lost about $250 – my own damn fault – to one of the oldest and simplest scams known. My old World-Traveler instincts had failed to alert me. Well, live and learn.

You may try to buy the currency on the free market before you enter the country. However, most countries with black markets try to prevent you from importing their currency, so you'd have to hide it somewhere and smuggle it in. Since most such countries require you to declare how much currency you're bringing in, you'd have to underreport how much you have. You could probably get away with this, but if they discover that you're carrying a significant amount of their currency, they might seize it and maybe fine or even jail you.

Many countries in Asia and Latin America have started to grow economically, to prosper, and their governments have devised more sensible and effective economic policies than they followed in the 1960s. Consequently many fewer of those countries have currency black markets today than when I was student-traveling. On the other hand, many African countries' currencies were stabilized by their European colonial 'mother countries' in the '60s, but they're weaker today. So these are the countries where you're more likely to find black markets in the early 21st century.

Currency management

If you're on a really extended trip like my eighteen-month hitchhiking odyssey, you probably don't want to start off with enough cash to pay for the whole trip. You can carry travelers checks, but you'd need several thousand dollars' worth, a lot of money to tie up, and they're kind of expensive – commissions of 1½ percent or more – and you may have to pay another percent or two to cash them in. They're not completely risk-free: if they're lost or stolen, it can be quite a hassle to redeem them. And they're not accepted everywhere. In particular, most black marketers will take only cash.

You might have somebody send you cash through the mail, but this runs the risk of being stolen: postal employees in some countries are notoriously theft-prone. My parents did mail me some $10 bills during the two months I spent in Cairo, but they weren't willing to risk larger sums to the honesty of the Egyptian postal service.

> Years later I mailed a five-hundred-dollar bill to my wife in China; she never received it, doubtless stolen by some postal clerk.

So you may have to arrange some way to periodically get additional funds from home. These days you can probably do it with a debit card if you have funds in the bank, but such cards didn't exist in my days of adventure traveling, so I had to write a check to a foreign bank and wait about three weeks while they sent it for collection. This was especially troublesome at times when I wanted to keep moving on.

A related problem for any traveler, luxury or low-budget, is to ensure that you have enough local currency for your spending needs. You don't want to exchange too many dollars – for one thing, you'll probably have to pay a substantial commission every time you change money. On the other hand, you don't want to run out of local currency when you need it and don't want to have to keep returning to the bank or money changer to get more of it. So you want to gauge how much local currency you're going to need as accurately as possible.

If you fly into a country, some airports have good facilities for changing money and may give you a good rate; others, however, may give you a very poor rate and/or charge high commissions, and some don't even have facilities for changing money. If you're traveling overland, you may find banks, shops or money changers when you arrive at the border, but at other crossings there may be no way to change money, and you can get pretty desperate for local currency.

You want to keep the various currencies separate: put your local currency in one place and your dollars in another, or better yet, spread each of them around to several places. You don't want to attract attention by flashing a large sum of money around, so you put a modest amount of local currency in your billfold – say $50 worth, or even less if the country's really poverty-stricken or thief-ridden. The rest you spread around: some in your pants pocket, some in your purse, backpack, shoulder bag or money belt. That way if somebody picks your pocket or steals your backpack, at least you won't lose *all* your money.

In Third World countries it's highly desirable to carry an adequate supply of small bills and coins of the local currency. In the first place, it's difficult to get change for larger bills in some countries. And if you get into an argument with a taxi driver or vendor who you think is trying to overcharge you, it's very helpful to be able to hand him or her the exact amount you want to pay rather than giving a larger bill and trying to get change. One disadvantage is that small bills may be torn and dirty, but it's still better to have them when you need them. On the other hand, if you want to change local currency back into dollars when you're leaving some country, a bank or hotel may be reluctant to accept a large pile of small bills. So you have to plan your needs carefully: small bills until you're ready to leave the country, and then large bills to redeem at the money-changer.

You're likely to be carrying a larger amount of your home currency or dollars than of local currency, depending on how long you're planning to stay in the given country and how long you're planning to travel to other countries. Just as with local currency, you want to spread the dollars around: some in a pants pocket, briefcase and/or handbag, maybe some in a money belt, and some wrapped up in a shirt in your suitcase or backpack. And make a list of the various places you've stashed it away.

On an extended trip some years later I thought I was running out of money and had to cut back on my expenditures, and then when I got home and unpacked, I discovered two stashes in my luggage totaling several hundred dollars that I'd lost track of.

Just as with local currency, you have a similar problem balancing large and small dollar bills: large bills to change at banks vs. smaller bills if you need to change or spend small amounts.

———

Money management is less of a problem today than when I was student-traveling because credit and debit cards are more widely accepted now. However, they aren't accepted everywhere, especially not by the local restaurants and cheap lodging-places frequented by low-end travelers (and I've never heard of a black marketer who would take cards). Furthermore, you have to arrange to make payments every month, which can be difficult on an extended trip. And sometimes you may get screwed on the exchange rate or commissions, depending on the terms of your particular credit-card issuer. So you still have to pay attention to planning your finances.

One disadvantage of spending so many years as a very-low-budget traveler is that I find it hard to change from that mentality even as a mature adult. Even traveling with a wife and children in middle-age, I found myself constantly searching for budget-priced accommodations and low-cost meals. Fortunately my wife was game to accompany me to local eating and lodging places, and my daughters have taken up the budget-traveler spirit.

CHAPTER 8.
AFRICA: VENTURING
INTO THE WILD

African Travels

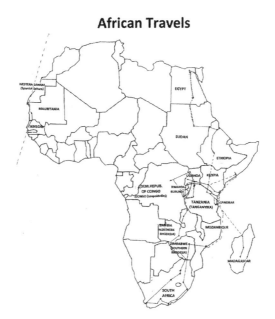

Four weeks after graduating from college I was on a plane with about eighty other young Americans bound for Kampala, Uganda, where we were scheduled for nine months of teacher training, to be followed by a two-year teaching stint in Uganda, Kenya or Tanganyika (later Tanzania). We were participants in a foreign-aid program called Teachers for East Africa (TEA), run by the U.S. Agency for International Development (USAID). The training was to be at a college called Makerere University College, which was then an overseas affiliate of the University of London.

Uganda was still a British colony when we arrived in July 1962. The college campus was on the outskirts of Kampala, two or three miles from the center of town. It was possible to walk into town, although I usually stuck out my thumb after I got to the main road and frequently got rides.

After I'd been there three or four weeks, I'd gotten used to being one of the few white faces in a sea of Africans and decided it was quite safe, so I determined to venture out a bit. My first foray out of Kampala was to Jinja, a small town about fifty miles away on a paved road. It was near the source of the Nile River, where it flowed out of Lake Victoria. I had to walk a couple miles through Kampala to get to the Jinja road, but once I'd gotten to the outskirts of the city, I only had to wait a few minutes until an Englishman came along and gave me a ride.

Jinja itself was anticlimactic, a dreary little town, except that I got a ride to a brewery at the edge of town and managed to talk the Belgian brewmaster into giving me a tour of the brewery. No free beer, though.

I soon discovered that a white skin was a tremendous asset when hitchhiking in Africa. You might have to wait a long time – several hours – for a vehicle heading your direction to come along, but when one came, it almost invariably stopped.

Having proved that hitchhiking was possible, I decided that my next foray would be to the town of Fort Portal, toward the western edge of Uganda, near the Rwenzori Mountains (also spelled Ruwenzori and sometimes called the Mountains of the Moon), fabled for having snow caps so near the equator. I stuck a couple items of clothing and some toiletries in a suitcase and headed to the outskirts of the city.

That journey turned out to be more challenging than Jinja, about 200 miles over rough dirt roads. Heading out of Kampala I got a ride in a shared taxi – had to pay something like five shillings (70 US cents in those days).

It was a slow journey, especially since the taxi driver made several stops to go greet friends. He got out of the car each time, slapped the friend on the back, and conversed in the local language (Kiganda) for several minutes. I got impatient at our slow progress.

Once a peasant farmer held up a chicken – the local marketing strategy? – as we drove past, and the driver slammed on the breaks and went over to negotiate the purchase of the chicken. He told the farmer to hold it for him till he came back a couple days later. A very informal kind of commerce!

Later I got a ride in a truck that went grinding along at 12 or 15 mph over the rough roads. At an especially rough spot I saw an eight-foot wooden pole sticking out of a hole in the ground with a crude wooden sign with the hand-painted words 'POLE POLE.' Why in the world would somebody want to put a sign announcing a *pole* that way?? Then the driver explained that 'pole,' pronounced POH-lay, meant 'slow' in Swahili, and 'pole pole' meant 'very slow'.

It took me the whole day to get to Fort Portal, by which time I was tired, hungry and covered with dust. I figured I could find another young single TEA participant teaching in the local secondary school to put me up for the night but ended up in the home of a middle-aged American couple who were amused at their unexpected drop-in. They offered me a bath, a welcome relaxant after the hard day, but were dismayed at how long it took me to wash off all the grime. Still, they offered me a comfortable bed and were very gracious hosts.

The next day I got a ride a few miles into the Rwenzoris, although not far enough to see any snow-capped peaks. I was a bit nervous about being out in the jungle at the base of the mountains because of a low-level rebellion going on: the so-called Rwenzururu movement in which a couple of small local tribes were trying to assert their independence from Uganda. There were rumors of gangs of men charging around with machetes and intimidating people. Fortunately I never saw any such gangs.

I did, however, encounter an obnoxious little fellow dressed in a loin-cloth and not much else who approached me hollering, "Me pygmy! Me pygmy! Take photo! Take photo! Five shillings!" Well, I knew the 'going rate' for taking photos of local citizens was one shilling, and I wasn't going to be another typically-overcharged tourist. More important, I didn't think he was a real pygmy, so I ignored him.

I didn't have any information about the Rwenzoris – didn't know what, if anything, to see – and I didn't see any traffic on the road into the mountains, so I gave up on the idea of visiting there and instead decided to head down to Queen Elizabeth National Park, which was famous for its variety of large animals.

> Uganda made the region into Ruwenzori National Park in 1991. It is famous for its spectacular valleys and its biodiversity. It is conjoined to Virunga National Park in the Democratic Republic of Congo.

It was a short enough distance to QE (as the Brits sometimes called it), and I got a ride fairly quickly. Shortly before we got to the park we saw a crowd of people standing by the road and stopped to see what was happening. Turned out some man had shot an elephant that had wandered outside of the park boundaries, intending to 'harvest' its tusks for the ivory trade (even though they weren't especially large tusks). He murdered the magnificent animal for its ivory.

> The survival of elephants was threatened in many African (and other) countries as a result of their wholesale slaughter starting in the 1960's and up to the present. Several attempts were made to 'regulate' the ivory trade, until it was supposedly banned by an international convention in 1989, but widespread poaching continued into the 21st century.

Murdered Elephant
Outside Queen Elizabeth National Park, Uganda

The main road ran right through a section of the park. My host offered to take me further, but I declined, saying I wanted to stop and see at least a bit of the park. "Well then, I'll drop you at the Kazinga Channel, where you can look down into the river and maybe see some hippos," he responded.

The Kazinga Channel flows between Lake George and Lac Eduard, two of Africa's so-called great lakes. From the channel bridge I was indeed able to see a few hippos lolling in the water and even some elephants in the distance. However, without a car I couldn't travel further into the park and hence couldn't see any of the buffalo, warthogs, chimpanzees and other animals that were also major attractions of the park. Herein the disadvantage of hitchhiking.

Later that afternoon I stuck out my thumb again. Luck was with me, and I got a succession of rides back to Kampala (on a different, better road than the one I'd come out on) and got back to Makerere by midnight.

In reflection, it'd been a fairly successful jaunt. I'd covered more than four hundred miles in two days, pretty good for hitching in Africa, although I hadn't really seen as much of the interesting sights as I would have liked … as I should have. But a brief exposure was better than none. And it whetted my appetite for more.

CHAPTER 9.
MOMBASA TO ZANZIBAR
ON A DHOW

.

East Africa Trips

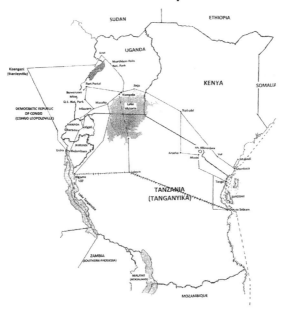

We got a two-week break from our teacher-training program in late
September. By this time some other guys on the program had also tried

hitchhiking, and several of us decided to head for Mombasa, a seaport on the Kenya coast. We agreed we'd have better chances to get rides if we went singly or in pairs, so I agreed to go by myself and link up in Mombasa.

In those days the three British East African protectorates – Uganda, Kenya and Tanganyika (later Tanzania) – were linked in a common market, and you didn't need a visa to travel from one to another. And indeed, many countries in Africa were just emerging from colonial overlordship by European countries, and either you didn't need visas to enter them, or you could get them (almost always for free) at the borders. Still, I decided to take my passport on the Mombasa trip and later was glad I had it.

> I believe conditions have changed radically since then: now you often have to get your visa in advance or pay a bribe to get one at the border.

The road from Kampala to Nairobi, the capital of Kenya, was paved the whole way and was fairly well-traveled, and I made the entire distance, about 300 miles, in one day. I had learned in advance about a nice YMCA in Nairobi. It cost 10 shillings ($1.40) a night, affordable enough for most Europeans but beyond the means of most Africans. It bothered me a little that almost all the guests at the Y were white, but it didn't really make any difference.

I ran into several other guys from the program at the Y. We spent a wild night drinking in a local pub, where we met some British soldiers. Late in the evening several of the TEA guys and the Brits decided they wanted to go to a whorehouse. That wasn't my cup of tea, so I retired for the evening. … Next morning the guys were full of stories about taking taxis to some dive on the outskirts of the city and about all the African women they encountered there. They made jokes about what strains of syphilis or gonorrhea they might have picked up. Not my cup of tea, as I said.

Next morning I hitched out to Nairobi National Park, a game park thirty minutes out of the city, where I found a ride around the park with a British couple who had an extra seat in their Land Rover. We saw some drowsy lions and some slow-moving elephants – I think the animals in that park got bored with tourists.

In the afternoon I took off for the coast. This road was gravel, and very dusty, and occasionally blocked by herds of cattle.

Cattle in main Nairobi-Mombasa road

I got a ride to what the map showed as the town of Voi; there may have been a town somewhere, but all I could see was a crossroads. When the driver dropped me off, I saw two other guys on the TEA program. "Good ol' Bill! Got us a ride!" they exulted, but were then disappointed when they saw that I was getting out of the car and was going to be looking for a ride too.

The place was completely deserted except for us – no people or cars in sight – and we were getting cold and hungry and also more and more apprehensive as the dusk gathered. We shivered in dread at the prospect of spending the night on the open plains of African big-game country. The road ran right through the middle of the Tsavo Game Preserve, which in those days had a problem of overpopulation of elephants. We had visions of a herd of elephants trampling through or maybe a leopard or a pride of lions deciding we would make an easy snack. We armed ourselves with the biggest sticks we could find, just in case ...

Then, fortunately, about 8:00 p.m. a vehicle came along, a truck hauling a load of oranges to Mombasa. The African driver stopped and motioned for us to climb up the back, on top of the oranges. Suddenly the trip was fun again, an adventure, as we peeled our eyes through the darkness, hoping to catch a glimpse of animals and meanwhile enjoying a welcome snack of oranges.

We got to Mombasa about 9:30 and inquired if there was a clean, cheap hotel. Somebody directed us to the Rainbow Hotel, a two-story wooden frame building with a restaurant and bar on the main floor. Many years before it had been a watering place for British colonials, but it was long past its glory. However, the rooms were clean and in our price range, making it a welcome oasis. And fortunately we managed to talk the restaurant staff into providing us a simple meal, even though it was long past their usual closing time.

Later that evening we visited the bar, which turned out to be full of white men and African women. The women were obviously available for sex, for which I was told the going price was 20 shillings ($2.80), and it was convenient to take them to a room right there in the hotel. This could be called prostitution, but it had a different spirit, a different 'feel,' from prostitution in American cities. It was much more acceptable to have a variety of sex partners in African culture than in American culture. Young people generally became sexually active shortly after reaching puberty, and by 'sleeping around' each person would find the partner he or she liked best and could settle down with. If a girl bore a child, she was more desirable as a wife because it proved she was fertile. The women in places like the Rainbow were somewhat analogous to the *courtesans* who hung around European capitals during the Middle Ages. They mostly came from the countryside and had little or no education, and the hotel offered the best chance most of them would ever have at a glamorous night life. Most of them spoke a kind of knockabout English they'd learned from the men, and it was possible to converse with them even if you didn't choose to have sex. … Well, I was intrigued by the situation but didn't feel comfortable about paying for sex, whatever the justifications, so I chose just to converse. I didn't get to bed until after midnight that night.

Next morning I was awakened at 6:00 a.m. by a hotel worker banging on my door to offer me a cup of tea. This was in the old British colonial tradition of having one's servant bring 'morning tea,' but I wanted to sleep in. Later that morning I instructed the hotel desk not to wake me or bring me morning tea again.

Mombasa had a little to offer in the way of sightseeing – a 400-year-old Portuguese fort, palm-fringed tropical streets, an open-air market, the seaport – enough to occupy me for a day.

During my wanderings I met Monique, a Frenchwoman about my age, and ended up asking her for a date. I picked her up that evening at her hotel, which was several cuts above the Rainbow, way beyond my student budget. But then how to entertain her? I didn't know my way around the city, didn't have a car, didn't have a lot of money to spare, didn't know where to go or what to do. I ended up lamely suggesting that we walk down the road to another bar for a drink. We carried on a desultory conversation for an hour and a half, during which time she ordered some expensive hors d'oeuvres and a couple drinks, stretching my budget. She was curvaceous and pretty, if a bit haughty. I could understand how a woman could become conceited when she's one of the few white women attended by lots of lonely, horny white men. I never figured out how she'd landed in an end-of-the-earth place like Mombasa, or what she was doing there. Eventually she said it was time for her to get back to her place. She seemed to expect me to call a taxi, but by then I wasn't eager to spend any more money on her. We ended up walking back in silence.

Back at the Rainbow I ran into two of the TEA guys. I told about my less-than-successful date, and they told about the African women they'd hired for the evening. "I got more for my 20 shillings than you did for yours," one of them said.

Well, a lesson learned: it's not easy to have a date in an unfamiliar city with somebody you don't know very well. Next time, think twice.

Next morning I discovered that several more of my TEA colleagues were also staying at the Rainbow, including a married couple who'd driven to Mombasa in their Volkswagen. Somebody had learned about a motorized dhow that was scheduled to sail to Zanzibar next day, and several of us decided to take it. The married couple considered the idea but decided it might not be wise for the wife to be the only woman on board. So the husband amused himself and us by pretending to read headlines from a newspaper: 'French Couple Murdered on Dhow;' '13,000 Dhows Sunk during

Last Monsoon Season;' and so on. We were amused but not discouraged from making the trip.

The original dhows were small sailing ships that Arab traders would sail down the east African coast on the monsoon winds. They would engage in trading (and slaving) and then would sail back up to the Arab countries when the winds shifted a few months later. The more modern dhows still traveled under sail when possible, but they had auxiliary inboard gasoline motors.

I was much reassured the next day when I saw that the passenger trade on dhows was well regulated. We paid our fares and registered with the British port master, who recorded our names and passport numbers and the ship we were sailing on in an official register.

Our dhow, the M.V. *Mwafak*, was maybe 30 or 35 feet long, made of wood, with a main deck and a hold below the deck that was used for carrying cargo. It had a raised prow and a raised deck in the rear (the 'poop deck'?) and a mast and booms for rigging a sail. A canvas cover had been rigged over the rear deck, giving us some protection from the sun. There were no cabins or beds; we'd been warned that we would have to sleep in the open air on the wooden deck. We'd also been told to bring our own food since the crew wasn't prepared to feed a bunch of outsiders. The 'toilet' consisted of a round hole on a board stuck out over the side of the ship, obviously affording no privacy. If they only had to urinate, the crew members just did it over the side, so it was probably just as well the married woman had decided not to join us.

M.V. Mwafak

Raising the Sail on M V _Mwafak_

We counted about a dozen crew members. They were loading some kind of logs while we watched. The loading winch consisted of three fifteen-foot poles roped together at the top and spread apart at the bottom to form a triangular base. A rope was rigged to a pulley at the top, thus allowing cargo to be hoisted in the air and swung over the deck to be lowered into the hold. The entire system worked on human muscle-power: three men alternately pulled on the rope to lift the logs and eased it down to lower them, while other men pushed them into place once they were in the hold. Dhow seamen had to have strong bodies.

We took off in mid-morning, our ship using the engine to sail out of the harbor. It was fascinating to see all the other dhows and ships in the harbor and then to watch the shore fade away until it gradually disappeared over the horizon. Once on the open ocean the crew turned off the engine and proceeded purely under sail. We had a sunny clear sky, a gorgeous day for an ocean voyage. The ship rocked gently on the mild ocean swells.

Toward evening a couple crew members, presumably cooks, started roasting some kind of meat over a small charcoal grill. It smelled delicious, much better than the bread, processed meat and fruit we'd brought for ourselves. We envied their enticing repast as we masticated our cold dry sandwiches.

Still later a wind came up, and the ocean swells turned into fairly large waves, causing our ship to roll sickeningly from side to side. The motion didn't seem to bother the crew (not surprising), but several of us passengers had to vomit over the sides. Still, I spread out some cloths for a bed and got a fairly good night's sleep.

Next morning we landed in Zanzibar, an exotic island if I ever saw one. The smell of cloves and cinnamon wafted through the air – Zanzibar is a major producer of both. The town of Zanzibar consisted of narrow, winding streets and quaint stone houses. Known as 'Stone Town,' it was the headquarters of the East African slave trade until the British more-or-less stamped out slaving during the nineteenth century. Plantations with neat rows of pineapple plants filled most of the interior of the island, which was only about twenty miles across. It was still a British protectorate when we were there and was nominally governed by a sultan who had a palace in the town and a summer palace on the coast a few miles outside of town; sightseers could ride by and look at the outside of the two complexes. It hadn't yet been 'discovered' by tourists and consequently retained much of its traditional character. The beaches were lined with gently-swaying palms and were deserted. There were no first-class hotels, only some quaint guest houses.

I understand Zanzibar has since become a popular tourist destination and is now well-supplied with luxury hotels and crowded with tourists, mostly Europeans. It's brought development and lots of dollars, but it's destroyed a lot of the island's charm.

Somebody steered us to one of the guest houses, a very casual place with an open-air common room and no locks on the doors. It was run by an older woman whom everybody called "Mama." She was quite a character, known for her story-telling, and we were invited to listen in as three or four women gathered around to hear one of her stories. She told about a nearby house that was supposedly haunted by the ghost of an English sea captain who'd been murdered by a pirate. I listened for a while and enjoyed her colorful language and expressive mugging, but then lost interest and drifted on.

Next day three of us rented face masks and snorkels from Mama. She charged us three shillings (42¢) each, "a special rate for my guests." We'd been told there was good snorkeling in the bay, although the reefs were a goodly distance out. We were all good swimmers, young and vigorous, and we figured we could swim out without too much difficulty.

The water was clear and blue and the sun was bright, a gorgeous day. After applying suntan lotion we swam half an hour out into the bay, taking it slow and easy, breast-stroking all the way and using our masks to increase flotation, until we reached the approximate location that had been described to us. There we had to search for a while, taking turns diving down, until we finally located the coral reefs. And they were spectacular: extensive and colorful, varying from a few inches to six or eight feet below the surface. They were populated by myriads of larger and smaller vividly-colored fish, waving their fins slowly in the undulating waters. We had to hold our breath and dive down to see the deeper structures, which was a bit tiring. We could put our feet down on the shallower structures, although they were sharp-edged and some of the corals gave our feet sharp, painful stings, so we couldn't really rest. We were well aware that each of us had his life literally in his own hands: keep paddling or drown.

After maybe an hour we decided to head back, another half-hour of swimming. All told, we were constantly in the water for about two hours. It had been a spectacular trip, well worth the effort, although quite tiring and in retrospect rather risky. And we'd gotten some sunburn: the suntan lotion wasn't as effective as the products available today, and it got washed off by the salt water, so our skin got decidedly pink. Fortunately it wasn't too painful, and it faded after a couple days.

After a couple days we were ready to head back to the mainland. Somebody inquired at the shipping office and learned that a German freighter was scheduled to sail to the city of Tanga, on the Tanganyika coast, the next day. The shipping agent at first refused to sell us tickets, saying the ship didn't have accommodations for us and the captain didn't want to take responsibility for our comfort and safety. So several of us went down to the dock and walked up the gangway onto the ship and asked to see the captain. He was a bit nonplussed to be confronted by a group of American and British students. He didn't speak much English, but fortunately I remembered enough of my German, so I became the spokesman for our group. We told him we'd sailed to Zanzibar on a dhow and only wanted one night's passage on his ship and were willing to sleep on deck, and he relented and contacted the agent to sell us tickets.

Once again we had to take our own food, no big problem. We scrounged up some bread and fruit and tins of meat in a tiny shop in Stone Town. We were becoming experts at self-provisioning.

On board the ship the captain invited us to his quarters for beer and conversation. We eagerly scarfed down the pretzels and peanuts he proffered. Once again I was the interpreter. He showed us a souvenir he'd bought from a street peddler, a hideous garish straw elephant about eighteen inches tall. He'd paid the first asking price, 100 shillings ($14), so we gently tried to explain that you have to bargain with the peddlers, especially in the port cities. I'll bet he could have gotten the ugly thing for 25 shillings if he'd haggled long enough.

Sleeping on the freighter's metal deck proved to be much more uncomfortable than the dhow's wooden deck. I was fortunate to find a pile of canvases and actually got a few hours' sleep, but next morning some of my fellow venturers said they hadn't gotten any sleep at all. But at least the freighter didn't roll as badly at night as the dhow had done.

We split up after we hit Tanga. It was fairly late in the afternoon, so I made my way to Tanga Girls School, hoping to find somebody on our TEA program who could put me up for a night. And I was lucky: a couple young British women teachers offered me supper and invited me to use their couch – we young expatriate teachers had a strong mutual-aid ethic.

And I think the two British women were happy to see a new face since there weren't many other Europeans or Americans and they liked being able to relax with someone from a more familiar culture.

Next morning one of the teachers gave me a ride to the edge of town. I was dreading the seven hundred miles stretching between me and Kampala, the majority over dusty gravel roads, not much to look forward to. But I was again lucky and got a ride straight through to Arusha, in north central Tanganyika. We arrived in early afternoon. My host, an Englishman who lived outside of Arusha, apologized that he couldn't put me up for the night but offered to drop me wherever I'd like in the town. So I asked if he could take me to Arusha Boys School, on the hope I'd meet somebody there.

At the Boys School I approached the first teacher I saw, who turned out to be an American who coached the softball team. I told him I was looking for a place to stay. He replied, "My wife and I will be glad to put you up if you'll agree to umpire the softball game my team is playing against the Agha Khan School this afternoon." (Secondary schools were divided by race in those days. The pupils at Arusha Boys were black African, while those at Agha Khan were Asian, that is, of Indian and Pakistani descent. So it seemed to be important to have a neutral umpire.)

"I'm willing to do it, happy to do it," I replied, "but I haven't played the game since high school and don't know all the rules in detail."

"Don't worry about it," he replied. "You'll remember enough. This isn't the big leagues. Just make it a good show: holler convincingly and wave your arms when you make a call, that's all."

Umpiring the game turned out to be rather fun. I hollered "Ball!" and "Strike!" and "Safe!" and "You're out!" with gusto, gesticulating vigorously, and the kids seemed to think I knew what I was doing.

Arusha is on a high savannah, approximately 4600 feet above sea level and about thirty miles from Mt. Kilimanjaro, which rises out of the plains to 19,455 feet. Once I glanced up from my umpiring and saw the mountain in all its magnificence, glowing in the late-afternoon sun. The teachers and pupils were blasé about it – not surprising since they saw it every day – but it was dramatic to me. Exercising my umpire's privilege, I called a break in the game and ran for my camera and took a couple spectacular photos of it.

Mount Kilimanjaro above Softball Game

Next day I got a ride a short ways out of Arusha on the road north toward Nairobi, until my host dropped me where he turned off on some side road. As I was standing by the road a man dressed in the traditional reddish-brown blankets of the Masai tribe came walking along. I was a bit nervous – the Masai have a reputation as ferocious warriors – until he stopped and smiled. I tried, "Hello," and then "Jambo" (Swahili for hello), but I don't think he understood either greeting. So I pointed at my camera, and he willingly stood for me to take his picture.

Masai Man on Arusha-Nairobi Road

My next ride took me all the way to Nairobi. The most eventful thing about that ride was when we saw a cheetah in the middle distance running very fast, presumably chasing a gazelle. I've read that cheetahs can run faster than sixty miles an hour for short distances. They're much more elusive than lions, who loll about in the game parks and seem to have no fear when vehicles drive up close to them. That was the only time I ever saw a cheetah in the wild, but it was a spectacular sighting.

I barely stopped in Nairobi, just long enough to buy a quick meal, and then headed on out to the road to Kampala. Again I was lucky and got several rides, the last of which took me all the way to Kampala by 10:00 p.m. or so. Four hundred fifty miles in one day: pretty good time for hitching in Africa!

Chapter 10. Uganda: Celebrating Independence: A Pretend Journalist (I)

After about a hundred years of colonial domination and 'protectorates' over most of Africa, the various European powers suddenly decided to get out of the colonialism business in the late 1950s and early '60s. Uganda was one of the smaller British colonies and one of the later ones to be granted independence. Their turn came in October 1962, at which time I'd been in the country about four months.

Before independence Uganda, like many former British colonies, had a sort of three-tier socio-economic structure. At the apex were the British who occupied most of the top positions in the colonial government and the largest business enterprises. Second were the Asians, who held many of the middle-level government positions and who controlled most of the country's smaller stores and other businesses. They were resented by the majority black Africans and were fearful about their future when the British left.

The vast majority of the population were black Africans. They were divided into numerous ethic groups (they used to call them 'tribes'), each of which had its own traditional ruler (tribal chief or 'king'). The British had entered into treaties with the four largest tribes around 1900. The largest group in Uganda was the Baganda, for whom the country was named. Its king was called the Kabaka. One such Kabaka, Mutesa II, had attended Cambridge University in the 1930s, where he was known as 'King Freddy.'

At the time of independence the British government honored its treaties by creating a kind of federalism with the Kabaka and three other traditional rulers retaining considerable powers in their respective 'kingdoms.' Thus independent Uganda was unique, having four kingdoms within one small-ish country.

The former African colonies vied with each other to put on the most ostentatious show celebrating their newly-won status in the world of nations. The Ugandan government-to-be arranged to have ten Rolls-Royces flown in to chauffeur visiting dignitaries around. They spent some £10,000 (about $28,000 at the time) for fireworks to light up the Big Night plus thousands of pounds for flowers and paper bunting to display around the city. (Some observers questioned whether all this money would have been better spent on programs to alleviate some of the country's poverty, but the Ugandans wanted to have their moment of glory.)

Other parts of the celebration were more home-grown. The government commissioned local artists to paint the newly-designed national flag on hundreds of 12" x 15" boards, which were also put up all around the city. And they wanted a pageant, which was to be staged in the largest available auditorium, in a local cinema. They recruited some British and American housewives to help organize the pageant, probably because the housewives had had experience arranging similar pageants for Sunday schools and grade schools back home. The program predictably included speeches by local dignitaries, shows by local musicians and dance groups, and flag-waving demonstrations by dozens of Ugandan schoolchildren dressed up in red, yellow and black, the new national colors. A group of African students from Makerere wrote a short play presenting their rather self-glorifying version of Uganda's history. The housewives also recruited four married couples on the TEA program to put on a fifteen-minute square-dance demonstration. Nobody bothered to explain what a square dance with a bunch of white Americans had to do with the independence of an African country, but it made a lively addition to the show with the participants dressed up in colorful cowboy costumes.

Various foreign governments designated Official Somebodies to be their representatives at the ceremonies. Queen Elizabeth II of England had designated a member of the royal family to serve as her representative as each African colony became independent. By the time Uganda's turn came, the more famous royals had all had their turn (or served their duty, as the case may be), so the queen selected the Duke and Duchess of Kent as her representatives to Uganda's festivities. They were an attractive young couple, but relatively inexperienced at Officially Representing.

Other foreign governments also sent representatives to attend the ceremonies. President John F. Kennedy of the USA chose Massachusetts Senator Benjamin Smith as his emissary. Smith had been Kennedy's roommate at Harvard, and Kennedy had arranged to have him appointed to the Senate seat that he (Kennedy) had vacated when he was elected President in 1960. Smith was a loyal supporter of Kennedy and a gentle, easy-going man, but a poor speaker; some observers considered him rather unimpressive to be the Official Representative of the United States Government.

I hit on the idea that it might be useful for those of us on the TEA program to host a reception for the senator. I tried to talk up the idea among my fellow TEAers, but initially they weren't very responsive. Fortunately we managed to enlist the help of Mrs. Beckwith, the wife of a visiting American history professor who had had experience arranging this kind of thing and lent a certain *gravitas* to the enterprise. Once she was on board, the idea took off.

Even a simple reception like ours took quite a bit of doing. We arranged for the use of the reception hall at Makerere, ordered the food and drinks, planned some simple decorations, and so on. We sent invitations to various dignitaries – the Ugandan Minister of Education, the Headmaster and higher administration of Makerere, higher-ranking African civil servants, a few of the local British government officials and businessmen, and so on. Most of them R.S.V.P.'d within a reasonable time, although the Minister of Education failed to respond.

Other participants in the TEA program didn't seem especially excited about the impending independence ceremonies, but I thought it was an opportunity to witness a bit of history being made and decided to go see what I could see of it.

Like most every African country approaching independence, the Ugandan government-to-be had set up a press office to assist foreign journalists and advertise its newly-won status. I thought it might be neat and might gain me access to some privileged places if I could get a press pass, for which I would have to be accredited, so I made my way to the press office.

When I arrived, half-a-dozen men and women were milling around while a harried-looking young Ugandan shuffled through a pile of papers trying to find the letters of accreditation from their various news agencies. As he found each letter, he dug through another pile and handed the person a badge saying PRESS and the name of the paper or magazine. I waited until he'd processed everybody else, then approached him and asked, "Could I get a press pass? I want to write this up for my hometown newspaper and some others."

"Yes, surely. Is your letter of accreditation in here?" he asked, gesturing to the pile of papers.

"No, it's not. I'm a freelancer."

"Press pass?"

"I haven't gotten one yet."

"What paper are you writing for?"

"*The Ames Daily Tribune* and *The Southern Illinoisian*, my two home towns."

"Wait!" he commanded as a couple more newsmen approached him. He extracted their credentialing letters from the pile of papers and handed each a PRESS badge, then turned to me again. "Who are you working for?"

"*The Ames Daily Tribune* and *The Southern Illinoisian*."

"Haven't heard of them."

"They're small-town papers, both dailies. They'll be interested in a story about a home-town boy attending Uganda's independence. Human-interest stuff. You could reach an audience who wouldn't otherwise pay much attention to you."

"Unnnh .... Wait!" He turned to assist another reporter, then back to me after a minute. "You want a press pass ...?"

"Yes, please."

"We don't have your letter of accreditation ... What paper are you with? ... Well, just a minute. The reporter from *Trud* [the Russian labor newspaper] hasn't arrived, prob'ly won't show up. I can give you his badge." He handed me a badge saying

```
{ _____ }
{             }
{    PRESS    }
{             }
{    TRUD     }
{ _____ }
{             }
```

"Thanks!" I exclaimed as I eagerly stuck it in my pocket. I was amused at the idea of masquerading under the press pass of a major propaganda organ from the leader of the Communist Bloc.

Thus armed, I took my little 35-mm camera and went out and joined several others crowded into a car with a sign PRESS in the window. I didn't know where it was going, but I figured it must be someplace significant.

Turned out my 'fellow newsmen' were Americans, and we were going to the airport to see Senator Smith's arrival. When we got there we saw a sizable crowd of Asians, the women dressed in colorful saris and the men in suits. Somebody explained that they were members of a Muslim sect called Ismailis and were awaiting the arrival of their spiritual leader, the Aga Khan. Soon a DC-3, a two-engine propeller-driven plane widely produced during and after World War II, landed and taxied up to the terminal. (Those were the days before jet aircraft became common.) A youngish man dressed in a business suit came out, and the whole crowd of Ismailis started clapping, ululating and ringing bells. He acknowledged the crowd with smiles and nods and seemed quite comfortable in his role as their leader. He spoke a few words into a microphone and then was driven away in a car. I thought he was quite impressive.

Shortly thereafter a DC-6, a huge (for that time) four-propeller plane landed and taxied up to the terminal, and Senator Smith emerged. He almost stumbled as he walked down the steps. Somebody thrust a microphone at him, and he mumbled something about "Glad to be here ... um ... Kenya's ... um, Uganda's independence ...." To me he paled in comparison to the Aga Khan despite having arrived in twice as big a plane.

Milton Obote, Prime-Minister-to-Be of independent Uganda, was waiting on the tarmac to greet him. They spoke a few words, then were led off to a car waiting to whisk them into the city.

Various ceremonial events took place that afternoon: a parade through the city, a regatta of traditional African rowing boats on Lake Victoria, a flyover of RAF jet fighters, the dedication of a new children's hospital, and so on. I attended the official opening out in front of the Parliament building crowded onto a small platform with a dozen other newsmen. We were shaded from the hot sun but still sweltering in the 95° heat. We stood for a couple hours, and my legs started aching. Newsgathering isn't as glamorous as it's sometimes made out to be.

The official ceremony marking the transfer of power was held that evening at Nakasero, the national stadium. My press pass got me into the center section of the bleachers, with the most comfortable seats. Interestingly, the crowd around me were almost all white; Africans were relegated to the less-comfortable bleachers on the periphery. A camera crew trained spotlights on us, and someone instructed us to look to the left and wave, and we all did; I suppose that makes good news footage.

The loudspeakers blared forth an announcement in Kiganda, the language of the Baganda people. An Englishman seated beside me said the authorities were concerned about how the uneducated populace might react at the idea of being 'independent.' The announcement was telling them to go home peacefully at the end of the ceremonies and not to expect to find anything different in their lives tomorrow. They were to stay sober and work hard to start building their new nation.

A battalion of maybe two hundred African soldiers marched onto the field, and then the Duke and Duchess of Kent were chauffeured in in an open Mercedes phaeton. The duchess was escorted to a chair in a royal box, while the duke was led onto the field to review an honor guard. He strode down the line of soldiers and stopped a couple times to fiddle with something on some men's uniforms. It struck me as unusual, maybe even disrespectful, but maybe you're supposed to do that when you're reviewing an honor guard.

Shortly before midnight the battalion commander called out orders: "Fourth Battalion of the King's African Rifles, presennnnnnt arms!" The men raised their rifles and then snapped them smartly on the ground, almost as a single *crack*! The stadium lights were dimmed, and the Union Jack (English flag) was lowered in darkness. Then the lights were turned back on, and spotlights were trained on the flagpole as the Uganda flag was proudly raised. The commander ordered: "First Battalion of the Uganda Rifles, presennnnnnt arms!" The men raised their rifles again, fired a volley into the air, and again snapped them sharply down. The ceremony concluded with a twenty-minute fireworks display, quite comparable to ones I'd seen at Fourth-of-July celebrations in American towns.

After the ceremony was over at about half past midnight, I wanted to head to the Parliament Building, where Milton Obote was scheduled to hold his first press conference as the newly-installed Prime Minister of the newly-independent country. However, I couldn't find any press cars to take me there, so I started walking through the unfamiliar dark streets. I was rather nervous since I was the only white face in the rather large crowd and didn't know whether any Africans might decide they could harass me or even rob me since they were now 'independent.' A car came along – a chauffeur-driven Mercedes – so I stuck out my thumb. The car stopped, and an African gentleman in a suit and tie in the rear seat rolled down the window and asked where I was going. "To the Parliament Building," I replied.

"I'm a Member of Parliament. You are welcome to ride with me," he responded, and opened the door. An African man in shabby clothes happened to be standing right next to me. He moved to get in too, and the M.P. shrugged his shoulders and let him in. "I can't give you a ride and refuse him," he said, rather apologetically. The shabby-clothed man puffed out his chest and leaned back in the seat, obviously intent on enjoying what may have been the only ride he ever had in a Mercedes, or maybe even any car.

At the Parliament Building I flashed my *Trud* pass and went into the press room and sat near the front. P.M. Obote appeared shortly after. After some introductory remarks, he made several announcements obviously intended to be portentous. He said Uganda would accept aid from everybody. This was mildly significant in the context of the Cold War at the time, when the so-called Free World competed with the Communist Bloc for influence in the newly-emerging countries of the so-called Third World. Obote also declared that his government would recognize and exchange ambassadors with the Republic of China (Taiwan) rather than the Peoples Republic of China. This was a minor victory for the 'free world' and especially for the American government, which adamantly refused to recognize the government of so-called Red China thirteen years after the Communists had seized power.

I stood up and took several photos of Obote while he was making these pronouncements. In my naïveté I must have betrayed some sense of excitement because the other newsmen in the room shuffled restlessly and tried to intimidate me into silence with their stares. They looked rather bored with the whole show – I wondered how many similar ceremonies in other African countries they had attended.

The next afternoon the Kabaka held a reception on the grounds of his royal palace in an area of Kampala with a heavily Baganda population. It was attended by numerous Ugandan and foreign dignitaries, thereby clearly reaffirming his position as *primus inter pares* among the four regional kings. I got a ride there in a press car and circulated among the assembled guests. A young white American woman, fresh out of college, was confiding to anybody who would listen that she had met the Kabaka (who was about forty) and become his mistress.

Hearing a stir in another part of the grounds, I went over in time to see the man known as Jomo Kenyatta progress through the crowd like a ship through a stormy sea, parting the waters on either side. He had assumed this name: Jomo is translated as 'burning spear' and Kenyatta as 'the light of Kenya.' He'd been arrested, tried and imprisoned as a leader of the radical Kenyan anti-colonial society known as the Mau Mau, which had murdered over a thousand pro-British Africans and a few white settlers during the 1950's. [Historians later cast doubt on his alleged involvement with the Mau Mau.] He had been released from custody and admitted to the Kenyan Legislative Council in 1961, and by 1962 he was generally regarded as most likely to become the first Prime Minister / President of independent Kenya. I stepped in front of him and snapped his picture as he walked past. He accepted my intrusion as the natural obeisance due to a Man of Destiny.

> Kenya became independent in 1964.

Another man of only slightly less Destiny was Tom Mboya, also a Kenyan politician-in-waiting. A trade unionist, he had received financial support from the AFL-CIO, the American umbrella labor organization, and had been on the cover of TIME magazine in 1960. He was widely considered a likely successor to the aging Kenyatta. I went over and put my arm around his shoulders, thrust my camera into the hands of a nearby Englishman, and said, "Please take a picture of us."

Tom Mboya (Kenyan politician) and the author at
Uganda independence

Mboya was assassinated in 1969 at age 38. There were rumors it was because he was a member of the Luo tribe (rather than the more dominant Kikuyu) or because Kenyatta wanted to eliminate a potential rival, but none of these have been substantiated.

The following afternoon I went down to watch the Independence Pageant. It went off smoothly enough and was reasonably interesting. I thought the square dancers conveyed more enthusiasm than almost anybody else. I was struck, however, by how few people came to see the pageant; the theater was less than half full.

The Independence Ball was scheduled for that evening. Kampala didn't have any ballrooms large enough to hold all the expected guests, so the official ball was scattered among several locations, but the premier site was in the Grand Hotel, Kampala's largest. (It had been the Imperial Hotel up to a month before independence, but the owners decided the name was no longer politically appropriate, so they took down the old sign and put up a new one. But the tableware still said Imperial Hotel.)

I didn't have the requisite official invitation, and I doubted that my press pass would get me in, but I thought I might as well try to crash the ball anyhow. It was supposed to be formal – tuxedos suggested – but I didn't own a tux, so I put on my blue summer-weight suit and a tie and set out across the campus. Walking down the road toward the exit gate, I heard a vehicle approaching and I stuck out my thumb. The vehicle stopped, and lo-and-behold, it was one of the rented Rolls-Royces! The African driver gestured toward the back seat, and I sprang eagerly in. He explained that he had just delivered the ambassador of the Republic of China to the university to visit an old friend and was free for a couple hours. He asked where I'd like to go, and I said the Grand Hotel.

When we arrived at the main entrance of the hotel, I offered the driver five shillings (70 cents, a decent tip at the time). He said he couldn't accept it because the drivers had been specifically forbidden to use the vehicle for personal purposes or to accept gratuities. Then he got out and opened the door for me. As I got out, I saw a phalanx of uniformed guards and hotel employees at the top of the steps, and it suddenly dawned on me they were watching me arrive in a chauffeured Rolls-Royce!! So I thanked the driver profusely and strode confidently up the steps, nodding and smiling to people on every side ... and they bowed and scraped and deferred obsequiously to me! No one would think of checking for the invitation of Important Guest arriving in a Chauffeured Rolls-Royce!

I proceeded grandly through the elaborately-decorated entranceway into the grand ballroom, which was decorated with the black, yellow and red stripes of the newly-commissioned Ugandan flag, complete with images of the crested crane, Uganda's newly-chosen national bird. But beneath the surface the room was still rather dingy and cramped, conveying a sense of faded glory and decay, somehow symbolic of a white-man's-outpost in a dying empire. The room wasn't air-conditioned and was uncomfortably hot and humid.

The attendees were a mixed crowd, some white and some black, with a few Asians thrown in. I noticed immediately that almost none of the men were wearing tuxes; most were in business suits, and some in shirtsleeves, so I fit right in with my blue suit. Most of the women were in evening formals or saris, however, and many were quite stunning. Senator Smith and his wife and party were there. P.M. Obote appeared briefly, made a short speech, and left, doubtless to make the rounds of other venues. I talked briefly with several of the guests. Many of the whites were 'old colonials,' British civil servants who had spent years in the colonies and who had been running the government on behalf of Her Majesty. They seemed comfortable enough intermingling with their darker-skinned colleagues, although they were obviously aware of the imminent change of roles.

The ball was actually something of a disappointment, however. It had none of the glitter of Events in Washington or London. A six-piece band was playing enthusiastically, if not always well. Eventually a few couples started dancing languidly, but it was too uncomfortable to put much effort into it. Most of the guests were in groups at their own tables, so I was basically an outsider. I asked a couple women who seemed to be unaccompanied to dance, but they excused themselves after one or two numbers, leaving me to wander disconsolately around the room. I decided to leave after a couple hours.

The day after the ball Senator Smith called a press conference. I showed up with my Trud badge, although only a handful of real reporters came, and anybody who wanted to could have walked in. Smith made some very brief remarks about how honored he was to be in Uganda and then threw the session open to questions. The other newsmen asked one or two desultory questions, and then there was silence, so I piped up, "Is there any truth to the rumor that you may be appointed ambassador to Uganda?" (Mrs. Beckwith had speculated that Kennedy had sent Smith to Uganda to consider this possibility; she thought it would be a convenient way to pension him off since he clearly wasn't going to run for re-election.) Smith reacted with a startled expression and stammered awkwardly, causing me to think that Mrs. Beckwith may have been right. [In any case, someone else was ultimately elected.]

Our TEA reception was scheduled for two days after the official ceremonies. The Minister of Education still hadn't responded to our invitation, so Mrs. Beckwith decided I should go downtown to the ministry and personally urge him to come. I took a taxi (unusual for a hitchhiker, but I wasn't paying for it) to the ministry and walked in the front door and followed the arrows to the Minister's office. I felt quite self-conscious about taking such a direct approach, but I knocked on his door and went in and introduced myself. He was busily writing something but stopped to listen to me. I reminded him of the invitation and said we hoped he would be able to attend that afternoon. He said, "I'm very busy and don't have time to prepare a speech."

"You don't have to give a speech if you don't want," I replied.

"Oh, but yes, for somebody in my position, I'd be expected to make a few remarks. And I don't want to come across as unprepared. It's part of the job."

"Well, it'd be a chance for you to meet Senator Smith. He's President Kennedy's personal representative. Might be useful to get to know him. And it would be a way to show your support and appreciation for the TEA program. You know about our program, I'm sure ..."

"Yes, of course. But I'm very busy. This is a very busy time – we're just getting started here. ... But I'm sorry to disappoint you."

So I went back to Makerere and reported my lack of success to Mrs. Beckwith and the others.

The reception was scheduled for 6:00 p.m. Senator Smith and his party arrived half an hour late, but then he was all smiles and very gracious as he began to circulate among the guests.

Shortly thereafter the Minister of Education showed up, much to our surprise. Since I'd met him only a few hours before, I took it on myself to greet him and introduce him to the senator and the assembled guests. He proceeded to make a fifteen-minute speech – mostly pleasantries and inanities – something we hadn't expected. It fouled up our schedule a bit, but no great problem.

Mrs. Beckwith had arranged that we would have a reception line to introduce each TEA participant to the senator. She had decreed that since I'd been the one to initiate the whole idea of the reception, I would be the one to make the introductions, although I think she was a bit nervous about how well I would do at the head of the line. I too was nervous about being thrust into the limelight, but once the line started, I was pleased to find that I was quite comfortable in the role. I tend to freeze up in front of a camera, but I found it easy to smile and make small talk with each TEAer before introducing him/her to the senator.

After the reception line the senator and his party departed as quickly as possible. He confided to me that they had planned to visit Murchison Falls National Park that day but had postponed their trip so that they could attend the reception. I think he viewed the reception as more of a duty than an honor.

Chapter 11.
Rwanda and
Burundi ... with a Girl

Our studies for the teaching diploma at Makerere College weren't too challenging, so I decided to take a long weekend and hitch down to Rwanda and Burundi. These two small countries had obtained their independence from Belgium only a few months earlier (July 1, 1962) and were still feeling their way as sovereign nations. They were located off the southwest corner of Uganda. From a map I estimated the distance from Kampala down through Rwanda to Bujumbura, the capital of Burundi, to be about 360 miles, which I guessed I could cover in a couple days. Two days down, two days back, with one-day stopovers in Kigali (Rwanda's capital) and Bujumbura – should be able to do it by missing only a couple days of rather boring classes.

I happened to mention my plans to an English girl I'll call Phoenecia, a British participant about my age in the teaching program. I'd heard other program participants talking about her, saying she "had her problems" and that she had been sort of dating an African student who lived in my dorm and who had broken off contact with her after a few weeks. These things should have made me cautious, but the idea of having a female traveling companion intrigued me, so I casually asked if she'd like to go along. To my surprise, she said yes.

We set off on a Thursday morning. Makerere College was on the north side of Kampala, so we had to make our way through the city to the road heading southwest out of town. Kampala in those days had a central core of elegant houses mostly occupied by Europeans, surrounded by a sea of low-rise adobe dwellings occupied by Africans. We tried hitching along the major roads through the city but still had to walk a couple miles carrying our luggage. Fortunately Phoenecia had a backpack – it was too heavy, but at least she didn't have to strain her arm carrying it. Still, she was already looking weary by the time we got to the southwest outskirts of the city and could begin hitching in earnest.

We got rides down through Uganda fairly quickly and arrived at the Rwanda border in early afternoon. The Uganda border post was a forlorn shack out in the middle of nowhere, and the two uniformed officials seemed glad to see us to break the monotony of their jobs – evidently only few vehicles a day passed through there. By sheer luck an oil tanker truck was checking through the border just as we arrived, and the driver agreed to take us along. The border official said we might have had to wait a day or two for a ride if we hadn't chanced upon the tanker.

The tanker turned out to be contracted to the United Nations to carry fuel to one of its outposts in Rwanda. The driver was Italian. He said their mission in that part of Africa was supposed to be confidential – something about fighting a rebellion in the former Belgian Congo, the next country west of us – so we shouldn't tell anyone we had seen him and he'd allowed us to ride along. He had an African assistant whose job was to run errands and guard the vehicle at night. The assistant normally rode along in the passenger seat, but the driver assured us he wouldn't mind riding on top of the truck. I privately thought that would be pretty uncomfortable, but I also knew that Africans were accustomed to yielding place to whites and to being assigned to the dirtiest, most uncomfortable jobs. And sure enough, this fellow accepted uncomplainingly and rode along for hours perched precariously on the top of the fuel tank.

So Phoenecia and I crowded into the seat beside the driver, and off we went, over a rough dirt road barely one lane wide. The driver spoke a little English, and we attempted some conversation, but we couldn't communicate very much, so we mostly rode in silence, lost in our own thoughts. The truck rumbled along at 20 kilometers an hour – 12 mph – kicking up a trail of dust and jerking and shaking as we hit rough spots in the road. The road ran along the western border of Rwanda's Akagera National Park, which was supposed to have lots of game animals. I kept glancing over at the park, hoping to see a lion or a giraffe or something, but mostly it was just a vast empty savannah. Once or twice the driver pointed to the left, and off in the distance we could see the tiny figures of a few grazing animals, maybe wildebeest or zebra, but usually it was just empty. That's one thing about hitching in Africa: you're likely to spend many hours riding along staring at nothing.

Phoenecia didn't say anything for a long time, but I could see she was getting more and more uncomfortable. Eventually she asked us to stop, and she got out and threw up on the ground. I asked if there was anything I could do for her, and she put on a martyr-like expression and said no, she'd be alright. And in truth, what could I have done? Once we'd gotten into this situation, there was nothing to do but carry on.

Later we saw a vehicle heading toward us, stirring up its own trail of dust. As it got closer, I saw it was another oil tanker. When we met it, both vehicles stopped in the middle of the road, and the drivers got out and greeted each other with enthusiastic hugs. The other driver was a fellow Italian, also contracted to the U.N., taking his empty tanker back for another load. I asked Phoenecia if she wanted to go back with that truck, but she said no. After a few minutes we drove on. That was the only vehicle we passed for our first five or six hours in Rwanda.

We got to Kigali some time after dark. The driver parked the truck on a city street and left to stay with some friends. The African assistant spread out some blankets on the ground and evidently planned to bed down for the night under the truck. Phoenecia and I set out to find lodging.

Kigali turned out to be one of the most unimpressive national capitals I've ever visited. [Mogadishu, Somalia; was another one, and Vientiane, Laos; and Kathmandu, Nepal, would also make my list. I understand that Kigali has blossomed into a significant city in recent years, as is also true of Vientiane and Kathmandu.] It had one paved road about six blocks long, lined with a few stores, all closed at that hour. The street seemed deserted. Where to eat? Where to sleep? I could have figured out something for myself, but I felt responsible for getting Phoenecia into this mess and was desperate to find some accommodation for her. I prayed that we wouldn't encounter any strong-arm muggers.

Fortunately we finally spotted somebody who directed us to the only hotel in town. It was closed up, but we banged on the door and eventually roused the night clerk. (I wondered if we were the only guests in the hotel that night.) I don't know if Phoenecia was reluctant at first, but she agreed to share a room with me after the clerk said it had two separate beds. We explained in halting French that we were tired and hungry. The restaurant was long-since closed, but the clerk took pity on us and led us to the kitchen and let us rummage around in the refrigerator, where we found some cold leftover meat and potatoes. The meat was tough and the potatoes greasy, but we were grateful to get anything at all at that hour.

Our room was plain and small and not as clean as we would have liked, but it was (presumably) a safe place to sleep. I'd stayed in worse places, but I wasn't sure how Phoenecia felt about it. Anyhow, we collapsed onto our respective beds as soon as we entered. No suggestion of sex: by that time I'd realized I wouldn't be interested in this woman even if she were interested in me. I was definitely regretting bringing her along.

Next morning I ran into an American man on the main street. "You're not from here, are you?" he asked. When I said I was just a tourist, he said he was the American Ambassador to Rwanda. There were only four Americans in the whole embassy, including a junior officer, a secretary and a radio operator. There was such a small community of expatriates and educated Rwandans in Kigali that they were looking for new blood, new arrivals to provide some stimulation. He invited Phoenecia and me to lunch, which we accepted with pleasure. We swapped stories about our respective experiences in Africa. Not a high place on the prestige list for career foreign service officers.

In the afternoon Phoenecia and I headed for Astrida [now renamed Butare], in the southern part of the country. This was a much more populated area, and we had no trouble finding rides or hotel rooms or meals. Phoenecia, however, was getting unhappier by the hour, and by the time we got to Bujumbura (the capital of Burundi) the next day, she decided she was sick. She went to the British embassy (which, incidentally, also served as their embassy for Rwanda) and met an official who took pity on her. As an embassy official, he could buy plane tickets with Burundian francs; ordinary travelers had to pay in hard currency because the black-market price for the franc was about half the official exchange rate. He bought a plane ticket to Kampala, which he then sold to her for half price, in effect letting her buy it at the black-market rate. She flew out that same afternoon. I was glad to be relieved of the responsibility for her. A lesson learned: don't take a girl along when you're hitching in remote areas, or choose very carefully if you do take one.

Bujumbura was a larger and more cosmopolitan city than either Kigali or Astrida, although still small potatoes by international standards. Some people called it a 'sophisticated city' with style shows and fancy stores; I suppose it was by African standards of the time. Considering that it had been a French-speaking Belgian colony three months earlier, a surprising number of people, Africans as well as Europeans, spoke English.

I hung around for a day or so and did a little sightseeing: the market-place (which resembled open-air markets in every other tropical country I've visited), a small museum, a cathedral, a mosque. Nothing you'd go out of your way to see, but as long as I was there, interesting enough to occupy my time.

As I was wandering around, an African fellow about my age fell in step with me. By that time I had traveled in enough exotic places to have developed a sixth sense: this guy wants something from me. "You America?" he asked.

"Yeah. How'd you guess?"

"America dress different. You not look European."

"Oh? Where'd you learn English? You speak it very well."

"By talk to tourists. I'm friendly person, talk to many tourists."

"Oh?" Suspicion rising.

"You want I show you city?"

"Oh, thanks, no. I don't want a guide. I prefer to go on my own." I'd had my fill of people approaching me and trying to sell their services as guides. But you don't want to be outright rude to them.

"I give you ride my car and show you all interesting places."

"Oh, thanks, no." Please, just go away. Leave me alone.

"I have real nice car. I'll show you all sights."

"What kind of car is it?"

"It's a, um, Tchev-Ro-Lette."

"Shev-ro-lay" [Chevrolet], I corrected his pronunciation. Like hell this guy has a Chevy, or any other car. "How can you afford that? It's a very big car." This was back in the era when even Chevys had eight-cylinder motors.

"Yes. In garage, for repair. You loan me money, pay mechanic, and I pay you back and give you ride."

So that's his game. "No, I can't do that. Too much money."

"Then you loan me money, buy gas. Only I need, money for gas, and I give you ride, show you city."

This was beginning to get irritating. "Thanks, no. I just want to go sightseeing on my own, want to be alone."

"Please, I am street boy. Give me some money."

"NO!" I refrained from adding, Go away! Beat it!

"At least buy me some beer?!" This last in a tone that was half-plaintive, half-demanding.

Was this an implied threat? Well, it was bright daylight, and there were other people around. Didn't seem likely that he'd try anything.

Time to stop being polite. "NO!! Just go away. Leave me alone!"

He turned and dejectedly shuffled away. Have to find another mark. His line was too implausible anyway.

Next morning I headed north, back toward Rwanda and Uganda. By evening I reached the Gihindamuyaga Benedictine monastery in Gitarama, Rwanda, a tiny hamlet out in the middle of nowhere. The monastery was a large, imposing, two-story structure made of earthen bricks, surrounded by farmlands, like something straight out of the Early Middle Ages, a fortress against a hostile outside world. It appeared to be several decades old, probably dating back to German colonial times (pre-Belgian, pre-World War I), and built for defensive purposes, with only one small door along one wall.

I knew the monastic tradition was to provide respite to weary travelers, no questions asked, so I banged repeatedly at the door. Eventually a Belgian monk opened it and immediately let me in. I asked for lodging, and he asked to see my passport; evidently they did this as a means of screening their guests. Then he led me down a dark hallway to a small drab room with a crucifix on one wall, a bare bulb suspended from the ceiling by a cord, a rickety wooden night table and equally rickety chair, and a metal-frame bed with a tattered mattress and no sheets. Suitable cell for a Dark-Ages monk to sit and transcribe Biblical passages, I thought. "You can sleep here," he said. "I'll show you to the shower, and then I'll come to get you for the evening meal."

In the shower room he showed me how to turn on an electrical device on the shower head to heat the water, and then left. The shower gave forth a weak stream of lukewarm water, but it was welcome after the day's dusty travel. When I was done, I reached up to turn the heater off and got a nasty shock ... εεε !!! ... Well, what do you expect?: 220 volts, and I was standing barefoot on a wet concrete floor. Lucky I wasn't electrocuted ... I mean, *seriously* ...

There were six or eight monks and lay brothers at the table for the evening meal. The food was very simple: a biscuit, some beans and potatoes, a tiny piece of gristly meat. I figured as a guest I should make some conversation, so I ventured a couple questions about their work. They answered briefly but didn't volunteer any further comments, so I decided I'd better be quiet too, and we ate the meal mostly in silence.

After the meal the Belgian monk escorted me back to my cell. "Lights out at 10:00," he said. I glanced at the light bulb above me, fearful of trying to turn it off after my earlier shock. I settled down to read one of the paperback books I always carried, when I heard faint noises of conversation down the hallway and realized that the regulars were having a social hour after the meal, maybe even with a little wine. Well, I guess they didn't invite strangers to their little gathering. Too bad ...

The light bulb went off at 10:00 p.m. I have the impression they turned off their generator at that time.

At 6:00 the next morning the Belgian monk fetched me for breakfast, a couple of hard rolls with some jam and coffee. After the meal he asked if I could pay a little for the night's lodging. I gave him five shillings – about 70 U.S. cents – and he seemed satisfied.

It was an interesting experience, but certainly not a lifestyle I would choose. You'd really have to be dedicated to the religious life to live in those conditions.

I was worried about making my way back along the empty road north of Kigali, but I got a ride from a kindly older American Protestant missionary couple who took a different road, through a more populated region some miles west of the one we'd come down on. They spoke so gently and considerately to each other that I almost wondered if they were putting on a show for my benefit. They'd obviously been there many years and knew every side road, every dirt track in the region. We drove for several hours, and the population thinned out and the road became rougher as we got farther north. We occasionally caught glimpses of plains animals in the distance, wildebeest and zebra.

Eventually they stopped and let me out, saying they had to turn off here. There wasn't another car in sight, but they reassured me, "You'll get a ride here." They headed away on a dirt track so faint I could hardly pick it out, leaving me standing alone, feeling very isolated. Where there are wildebeest, there are lions, I thought; I hoped none of them would come along and decide I would make an easy meal. There were no trees or sticks anywhere in sight. Not that I would have been able to defend myself against a hungry lioness anyhow.

And then it started to rain. Here I was in the middle of nowhere, no shelter, getting hungry and thirsty, hadn't seen a car for an hour, fearful and tired, no apparent way out of this, and a cold rain besides. I had a plastic raincoat in my suitcase but no other protection. I opened it and tried to hold it over myself like a tent, but it didn't provide enough shelter, and my arms quickly got tired. I didn't want to get down on my hands and knees in the dirt, so I hunkered down and spread the raincoat over me, but my knees quickly got tired. Nothing I could do but squat there and suffer. Thank God Phoenecia wasn't with me then!

Fortunately the rain stopped after half an hour. And shortly after that a truck finally came by and gave me a ride to the Uganda border, which turned out to be only ten miles away.

On the Uganda side I was lucky and got several rides in the direction of Kampala. I reached the paved road in Mbarara, still a hundred miles from the capital, after nightfall, and again was extremely lucky and got a car going all the way to the city. We reached Kampala about midnight, and then I still had to make my way through the city to Makerere on the north side. I was cold and tired and hungry and miserable, so when a taxi came by I hailed it and told him to take me to the college.

To heck with the cost. Sometimes you have to break the hitchhikers' code of honor.

CHAPTER 12.
UGANDA: MURCHISON FALLS:
MAROONED ON A HIPPO ISLAND

My friend Doug Smith and I decided to cut a couple classes and take a long weekend to go visit Murchison Falls National Park (sometimes called Kabarega National Park) in the center of Uganda. The Nile River (the branch called the White Nile) originates in Lake Victoria on the southern border of Uganda. It flows north and westward for about 200 miles to where the entire river plunges through a gorge only 23 feet wide: 11,000 cubic feet of water per second dropping 141 feet, a spectacular sight. The park is also known for a high concentration of wildlife including hippos, crocodiles and numerous plains animals.

We loaded up our backpacks and headed for the road north. It was a short enough trip, less than two hundred miles over mostly paved roads. We had no trouble getting rides and made it to the park headquarters – in a crumbling one-room hovel – by mid-afternoon. We inquired about taking a cruise to see the falls up close and were told that the cruises were arranged at the Paraa Lodge, the park's only tourist facility at that time. The cruise would last about two hours and would cost over $10 a person, a lot of money to an impecunious student. Then somebody told us that a film crew happened to be there on an assignment to get shots of wildlife. They had chartered one of the boats and might be able to take us along as they filmed the next day. We met one of the photographers, who said they planned to take sack lunches and stay out for most of the day. They could take us along if we promised not to interfere with their work. We promised, of course.

We spent the rest of the afternoon wandering around the lodge area. We could walk to the river, but it was too far downstream to see the falls. We did see some hippos lolling in the river shallows and a few grazing animals off in the distance.

Somebody at the lodge told us there was a youth hostel nearby, so after supper we started walking down the gravel road. It happened to be a dark, moonless night, and we could barely see the road ahead of us. We heard grunting and snuffling sounds all around us, but it was too dark to see who or what was making them. We'd gone a few yards down the road when a Landrover came along. We stuck out our thumbs, and the driver stopped for us. When he turned on the headlights, we saw a mama hippo and her baby crossing the road not thirty feet ahead. Thank heaven we hadn't walked close enough to alarm her! – mama hippos are ferocious in defending their calves. Despite their size and blimp-like appearance, hippos can run twice as fast as most humans, and their jaws are strong enough to bite a ten-foot crocodile in two. If we'd walked much closer, this one might have attacked us and severely injured or killed us. Fortunately she ignored the Landrover.

The driver dropped us at the 'youth hostel,' which turned out to be a dilapidated oval-shaped adobe structure with a tin roof held up by mud-brick pillars. It was open-air, with large 'windows' all around, except they had no glass; we were sheltered from rain but not from wind. It was on a mud platform about three feet higher than the surrounding swampy ground, with a couple dozen decrepit metal cots but absolutely no other facilities. Well, it would do for our needs. We each selected one of the less-dilapidated cots and spread out our sleeping bags.

Sometime in the middle of the night I awoke and had to urinate. No problem: I could simply step outside the structure and pee off the raised platform. By that time the moon had risen, and I could hear lots of grunting and shnuffling and see lots of huge dark shapes moving around: mama hippos and their babies! They come up from the river to feed on land at night. They ignored me as long as I stayed on the platform, but I suspected they might have attacked if I'd ventured to walk among them. We were marooned on an island in a sea of hippos!

In the morning they were all gone, leaving no trace except for eight-inch piles of smelly dung.

Doug and I scraped together some breakfast from the food in our packs and then walked back to the lodge, where we met the film crew, two men and a woman. We watched as they loaded piles of equipment onto their boat: movie and still cameras, tripods to hold the cameras, reels of 32-mm movie film, rolls of film for the still cameras, telephoto and wide-angle lenses, light meters, specialized lenses for cloudy or bright lighting, carry-on bags full of who-knows-what equipment.

We tried making a little conversation; they answered politely but were intent on their work. We learned they didn't have a common language: the 'chief,' an Englishman, spoke English and German, the second man spoke German and French, and the Frenchwoman spoke French and English, so any two could communicate together but not with the third. But they'd been working together for a while and didn't seem to be hampered by their linguistic incompatibilities.

The boat trip was fantastic: the captain drove us a ways up the river under power and then turned off the motor, so that we floated silently back down. This allowed us to drift closer to the animals on the river-banks without alarming them. Even so, we seldom passed close enough to get good shots without telephoto lenses. The two men shot movie film while the Frenchwoman used a still camera with a huge foot-long telephoto lens. It was fascinating to watch them work. They were obviously making films and still shots for a particular purpose: every so often the Englishman would say, "We can use that in such-and-such sequence," or, "This would be suitable for the so-and-so scene."

Filming the crocodiles was the neatest, I thought. They would be sunning themselves on the river banks but then would dash for the water when our boat drifted too close. The result was like a choreographed action shot, each one sprinting in sequence as our boat passed by.

The hippos mostly just floated in the water, although I did see a couple of males engaged in a kind of combat: first they opened their mouths wide and slashed at each other, and then they turned around and sprayed dung at one another; they did this by thrashing their tails back and forth while defecating.

We saw some elephants in the distance moving in their slow grandmotherly way, lifting bunches of grass into their mouths with their trunks. The other grazing animals were interesting enough, although they didn't move around very much and were too far away to see very well.

I took a few shots of crocodiles and hippos with my 35-mm still camera. I had a small telephoto lens, but I still doubted whether most of the shots would be close enough to really see the animals. So mostly I just looked at the animals and watched the film crew.

We made two or three runs up and down our stretch of river but never got close enough for a really good view of the falls themselves. The chief eventually recognized our disappointment and told the boat captain to make a run as close as possible to the falls. The early-afternoon sun happened to be at a good angle and lit up the water droplets like crystal, and the three photographers eagerly trained their cameras on it: a shower of sparkling pixie dust!

Around 1:00 p.m. the chief proposed that we take some time to eat. A boat crewman fetched some containers from an ice box and laid out a fairly elaborate spread for the photographers; it had been prepared at the lodge. Doug and I got sandwiches and fruit from our packs and sat at the side and started to eat them. The chief saw us and invited us to join them, saying they had more food than they needed – how much better-tasting than our pathetic sandwiches! ... Even when relaxing, the three photographers didn't have a whole lot to say – is that a characteristic of professional photographers? – but we still appreciated their hospitality.

Late in the afternoon Doug and I returned to the lodge. We treated ourselves to dinner even though it was beyond our meager budgets and then headed back to the youth hostel before night fell – no hippopotamus encounters on the road, thank heaven! Our second night marooned on the 'island' passed uneventfully.

Next day we hitched back to Kampala, full of stories to tell our stay-at-home TEA compatriots.

CHAPTER 13.
SOUTHERN AFRICA:
WHITES AND BLACKS

We finished our finals in the teacher-training program in early December
and had six weeks' break over the Christmas season, enough time to make

a really extended trip. I sounded out several guys about trying for South Africa, but no one was quite that adventurous, so, once again, I decided I'd rather go alone than not go.

Africa was just emerging from decades of European colonization, and most countries / territories still had stable economies and non-repressive governments. It was easy to cross borders and safe enough to travel through most areas – even down the spine of Africa – so I didn't think I'd be taking any undue risks.

I learned there was a passenger-and-cargo steamer that traveled up and down Lake Tanganyika every two weeks. It was scheduled to sail south from the town of Kigoma on the Tanganyika shore three days after my last final. The map showed a road leading southwest from Kampala, some 500 miles to Kigoma. That meant I would have two days to cover 500-plus miles of dirt roads through some pretty isolated country. Was it possible? … Well, you certainly won't make it if you don't even try.

> The Republic of Tanganyika combined with Zanzibar and changed its name to Tanzania in 1964, but the body of water is still called Lake Tanganyika.

So I put $150 in travelers checks and $50 cash into my luggage and packed my suitcase in advance and carried it into the examination hall. As soon as I finished the exam I headed out for the road. I made it to Masaka that evening, only fifty miles, but at least a start. There weren't many youth hostels in Africa: in most places you had the choice of what passed for first-class hotels or little ten-room run-down inns, usually owned by Asians. I was initially cautious about the latter places but eventually decided they were adequate for my needs. I stayed in one such place in Masaka: seven shillings, about $1, just within my budget.

After that the trip became slow going. The road was rutted and unpaved and without much traffic. Red dust was everywhere; it billowed out behind every moving vehicle. Most of the rides I got were for short distances, with long waits in between. Just across the border in Tanganyika the road ran alongside Lake Victoria for a ways. I had hoped it might be a scenic trip, but it wasn't; I seldom got glimpses of the lake beyond the scrub brush and low hills. I only made a couple hundred miles that day, still leaving me about 250 miles from Kigoma.

Next morning I got a ride to some small dusty town where I found a comfortable spot under a shady tree to wait for the next ride. A wild-eyed frizzy-grey-haired old African fellow carrying a walking stick came along and stopped and stared at me. Maybe he decided I was an Evil Being because he started waving his fingers at me and muttering an incantation in the local language. I could have been frightened, but I decided he was no danger and just stared back at him. This must have frustrated him because he began poking at me with his walking stick. That made me more uncomfortable – might he turn violent, attack me personally? I tried to parry his thrusts with my hands. He was getting a little more aggressive when a British woman, apparently a local housewife, came along and chased him away. "He's harmless; he's crazy," she said. But I was still relieved to have him gone.

After a while a middle-aged Englishman named Hugh picked me up and drove me down the road to another small town. He wanted to talk. He'd been in Her Majesty's Colonial Service before Tanganyika had gained independence one year before and had stayed on in the employ of the Tanganyikan Government. He was one of many British colonial officers who'd stayed on since there were nowhere near enough educated Africans to take over the running of the government offices. The British government was still paying the bulk of his salary.

We arrived in his small town shortly before noon. He drove off the 'main road' (which was little more than a dirt track) and up a hill to his house. He introduced me to his wife Velma, who immediately invited me to stay for lunch. They had one child about seven years old. They were worried that he had no English playmates, although he did play with some of the African children. They wanted to raise him "at our level, not theirs," reflecting the old British colonial attitude of cultural superiority.

After lunch they both urged me to stay with them for some days: "You can go out with Hugh as he visits the villages; it's quite interesting," Velma said. I gathered they felt quite isolated and were hungry for English-speaking company. I demurred, saying I really did want to try to catch the Lake Tanganyika ship the next day. They then suggested that I wait in their home while they notified somebody-or-other in the center of town to keep watch for any cars heading toward Kigoma that might have room for me. I thanked them profusely for their hospitality and their kind offer but still insisted that my chances would be better if I waited by the road myself. Hugh finally, reluctantly, drove me back to the main road and said, "Do feel free to come back to our home if you don't get a ride."

No cars came along for the next hour. I was still about a hundred miles from Kigoma and was getting worried about missing the boat. I had wild ideas about trying to walk those hundred miles, but I knew that would be ridiculous even if I didn't have the suitcase to carry.

Then an Asian family in a nice comfortable Mercedes came along. Three adults and two kids were already snuggly fitted into the car, but they stopped for me. (I was sure they wouldn't have stopped if I'd depended on Hugh's contact person to get me a ride.) They squeezed me into the back seat alongside the grandmother and one child. I had to hold my suitcase in my lap, but it was a welcome burden, not all that heavy, and I was thankful to have the ride.

We rode along with the windows open despite the swirling dust. The whole family were fluent in English (as were most of the Asians in East Africa). They ran a store in some small town; they told how they'd jacked up their prices after a couple of African ruffians walked into their store one evening and robbed them at gunpoint. I was sympathetic, although I also knew that the Africans resented the Asian merchants precisely because of those high prices – a vicious circle.

It was just turning dusk as we approached the outskirts of Kigoma. We rounded a bend and there, suddenly, sitting in the middle of the road, was a leopard. He was a magnificent beast, his large spotted head higher than the Mercedes' fender. The driver screamed at us to roll up the windows as he slowed and swerved to miss the animal. What a shame! I would have loved to stop and look at him for a couple minutes, but we accelerated past him, and the driver wouldn't let us roll the windows back down until we'd gone another mile. ... As it happened, that was the only leopard I saw during my three years in East Africa.

Spent the evening in some cheap rundown hotel in Kigoma. Turned out my ship didn't sail until the next afternoon, so I had time in the morning to visit the town of Ujiji, a few miles outside of Kigoma, famous as the place where the explorer Henry Stanley supposedly met the missionary David Livingston ("Dr. Livingston, I presume?") in 1871.

The site of the storied meeting proved to be nothing but a grassy plain with a tiny stone monument, not a very impressive display for an incident that has become ingrained in British-American history.

While I was at the monument, a man approached me, introduced himself as a Baptist minister, and asked, "Would you like to come to our home for lunch?"

From his accent and manner he was obviously American. I was leery of missionaries, especially Protestants (even though I'd been a Congregationalist in my youth) who all too often made me uncomfortable by their efforts to Save me. So I replied, "Thanks, but I have to catch the ship from Kigoma this afternoon."

"I'll ask my wife to prepare lunch quickly, and then I can drive you to the port."

I didn't see any way to refuse him politely, and the meal and the company might be welcome, so I accepted.

Their house looked as if it had been transplanted directly from some American town: white wood frame with blue shutters, utility room with washer and dryer, air conditioning, dishwasher, and 1950's-style furniture. It seemed a little incongruous out here in the wilds of Africa, but maybe it gave the missionary family a needed touch of home.

At lunch the preacher and his wife and two school-age daughters took an interest in my teaching program and my travels, making a very pleasant meal.

After lunch the preacher obviously decided it was time to make his pitch. The rest of the family retired to other rooms while he sat with me at the dining table and asked, "Are you a Christian, Bill?"

I knew his definition of 'Christian' meant being 'born again' and accepting Jesus Christ as my personal savior. I had ceased attending church a few years before and no longer had much of any faith, but I didn't want to offend him, so I replied, "I'm still searching." That gave him the opportunity to expound upon the importance of accepting Christ into one's life and of the Southern Baptist faith. I listened politely and bowed my head when he prayed over me, but was relieved when he announced, "Now I'll drive you to the ship."

The ship, the MV *Liemba*, was the inspiration for the German gunboat in C.S. Forrester's novel, *The African Queen*, and the later film of the same name. By the time I saw it, however, it was a dirty, rusty old thing, having been built by the Germans in 1913, scuttled during World War I, and salvaged in 1924.

M V *Liemba* at dock on Lake Tanganyika

The *Liemba* was later refurbished and its steam engines replaced with twin diesels; it looks quite spiffy now and still regularly sails up and down Lake Tanganyika carrying cargo and intrepid passengers.

I had bought the cheapest fare, where you had to sit up on hard wooden benches in a lounge all night, the equivalent of deck class. Once on board, I approached the captain and asked if there was an unoccupied cabin or at least a bed I could use. He frowned but finally said there was a spare bed in a three-person room that I could sleep in. Being a *muzungu* (of European descent) was an advantage even in post-colonial Africa.

The voyage was quite interesting. We stopped at a half-dozen small coastal towns as we made our way southwards. Most of the towns didn't have docks, so we anchored offshore and hauled passengers and cargo to and from shore in small boats (lighters). Loading and offloading the cargos was extremely labor-intensive, requiring men with strong backs and shoulders. They chanted in order to coordinate their efforts in lifting the heavy cartons onto and off the lighters.

**Men loading grain sacks onto M V *Liemba*,
small village, Lake Tanganyika**

I was allowed to go ashore whenever there was room in the landing boats. The villages were unremarkable, similar to ones I'd seen in other places, but our arrival was a big event to the villagers. Crowds of people gathered to watch us come ashore; they stared at me like I was from outer space. In one village a 'witch doctor'(?) in a white round-faced wooden mask came out and did a little dance and flicked his fly-switch at me while murmuring an incantation. I didn't know if he was blessing me or putting a pox on me.

We reached what was then called Northern Rhodesia, at the southern tip of Lake Tanganyika, after three days. It was still a British protectorate; the British government had encouraged its citizens to emigrate to the African colonies after World War II, and Northern Rhodesia had about 75,000 white settlers and a few thousand Asians out of an estimated total population of perhaps 3,000,000 in 1962. The settlers had put down roots and become farmers, businessmen and professionals. They reminded me of the pioneering spirit of colonial times in America, when people had zeal for hard work, thrift, mutual trust and helping one another.

> Northern Rhodesia became the independent country of Zambia in 1964.

I probably chose the wrong road to head south from Lake Tanganyika. An Englishman gave me a ride to the town of Mansa, some distance off the more heavily-traveled Great North Road (which was supposed to run from Cape to Cairo, but only goes from Cape Town to northern Kenya). It was a pleasant little town – could have passed for a pleasant little town in the American Midwest, with well-kept wood-frame houses, grassy lawns, picket fences and friendly people. Its population was largely African, but there were British families and a few of the ubiquitous Asian shopkeepers. I found my night's lodging in a five-room inn run by an Asian.

From Mansa the map showed a road that crossed over a little strip of the Congo and then back into Northern Rhodesia, to a region called the copper belt. Seemed like a logical route, so after a modest breakfast I carried my suitcase to the edge of town about 9:00 a.m., found a spot under a tree with a little hillock to sit on ... and waited ... and waited ... and waited ...

I alternated between sitting and standing in order to keep from getting too stiff and sore. Only one or two cars an hour drove by, all local traffic. Some drivers passed by several times and began waving to me; a couple even stopped briefly to converse. At first I stood up whenever a car came by, but after a while I didn't bother.

In order to feel that my time wasn't being completely wasted, I started to read a paperback. I even remember the book: *The Moon and Sixpence*, by Somerset Maugham, a fictionalized account about the artist Paul Gauguin, who left a bourgeois life in Paris and sailed off to Tahiti to paint. It struck a chord with me because I fancied that I was doing something vaguely similar. I was concerned that I might get so absorbed in the book that I'd forget to raise my thumb if a car passed by. But I discovered that my ears were well-attuned to automotive sounds – they perked up whenever I heard a car, even a block away.

Noon – no rides. I found a package of cookies in my suitcase and made lunch on those -- not very satisfying.

1:00 p.m.;

2:00 p.m.;

3:00 p.m.;

… no rides …

A middle-aged Englishwoman came out from a house across the street and brought me a cup of tea and some biscuits. "I've watched you waiting there and thought you might appreciate a spot of refreshment," she said.

I was flabbergasted! – I doubt if any American housewives would take such pity on a scruffy hitchhiker like me. "Thank you so much," I stammered.

"Just put the cup and saucer back on my porch when you've finished," she responded.

4:00 p.m.;

5:00 p.m.:

… no rides …

6:00 p.m.: no rides. How can you bear to wait beside the road for *nine hours* and not get a ride??! What sustains you, I suppose, is the hope that your ride will miraculously appear in the next minute. Never give up hope …

Dusk was approaching, and I was becoming resigned to returning to the five-room inn and to my frustrating vigil the next day. Then, *mirabile dictu*, a flatbed truck came by. The Asian driver stopped and said, "We are heading for the copper belt. We are having no room in the cab, but you are welcome to ride on the back if you'd be liking."

"Wonderful!" I exclaimed, and scrambled eagerly up.

At first I stood on the hard iron floor as we rattled along; later I sat more-or-less cross-legged, even though it was pretty uncomfortable; and still later, as I got weary, I lay down and fell asleep. I was in a kind of groove in the center of the flatbed and figured I needn't worry about falling off: foolish, perhaps?

When I awoke, it was morning and we were back in Northern Rhodesia, and there was another guy on the flatbed beside me. In spite of the discomfort and noise and dust of my bed, I'd slept through the night, including picking up the second hitchhiker and passing through whatever border formalities there might have been entering and leaving the Congo.

The driver dropped me in some town. Getting back to civilization, I hoped the next ride wouldn't be so long in coming. It happened to be Sunday morning, and no restaurants were open. I found a hole-in-the-wall shop that sold packages of cookies and other small snacks and bought a few bites of things, staving off the hunger pangs.

The distance wasn't great, but traffic was light, and it took me the whole day to get to the town of Ndola, another quasi-British outpost. My ride happened to drop me at the entrance to a country club frequented by stereotypical British 'old colonials,' blustery types with handlebar mustaches and the confidence of innate superiority. I walked hesitatingly into the club, conscious of my dusty, bedraggled appearance, and asked if they would serve me even though I wasn't a member. The dining room was less than half full, and they were only too glad to do so.

The waiter, a tall African clad in a spotless white evening coat and red turban, brought me the menu, embossed on cream-colored velour paper and looked like something out of a fancy-gourmet cookbook:

THE NDOLA CLUB

MENU

APPETIZERS
Crab cake
Shrimp cocktail
Hot artichoke spinach dip

SOUPS
Potato and roasted leek soup with crab meat
Minestrone
Cream of spinach

SALADS
Mixed green
Garden fresh
Heirloom tomato and watercress

ENTREES
Filet mignon
Roast prime rib
Mixed grill
Pork chops Milanese

SEAFOOD
Grilled fresh Zambezi River bass with garlic lemon sauce
Shrimp primavera
Broiled tilapia with caper sauce
Yellow-fin tuna with salsa and arugula

STAPLES
Potatoes – *au gratin*, whipped, baked or French fried
Truffled macaroni and cheese
Fettuccini Alfredo

VEGETABLES
Broccoli florets with sweet homegrown basil
Eggplant sautéed with crushed garlic
Corn niblets with drawn butter sauce
Garden fresh green beans with sliced almonds

DESSERTS
Cherry torte
Brandy trifle
Ruby plum tart
Ice cream – vanilla, chocolate, or fresh mint - with topping of
choice

ASSORTED CHEESES

SEASONAL FRUITS

COFFEE, TEA OR MILK

Prix fixe £1

My eye fell immediately to the price, which was equivalent to $2.80, virtually a whole day's budget. "Can I just order … let's see … the mixed grill, and pay you just for that?"

"I'm sorry, sir, but the club policy requires that you pay the established price and select from the entire menu," the waiter replied in an impeccable BBC accent.

Well, I hadn't eaten much of anything (and hadn't spent much money) for 36 hours and was agonizingly hungry, and this looked like the only feasible alternative. So I decided to splurge. "Well, OK," I replied. "How many items can I have?"

"You may select from the entire menu," he repeated.

So I started at the top: Hot artichoke spinach dip, followed by Potato and roasted leek soup with crab meat, followed by Garden fresh salad, followed by Filet mignon, followed by Pork chops Milanese, followed by Grilled fresh Zambezi River bass with garlic lemon sauce, followed by Truffled macaroni and cheese, followed by Broccoli florets with sweet homegrown basil, followed by Cherry tort, followed by Brandy trifle, plus a couple glasses of milk. The waiter brought me each item on a fresh plate and placed it in front of me with an elegant flourish, but he began to look distressed when I got to the pork chops and looked positively agitated by the time I got to the Brandy trifle – obviously I was eating more than they budgeted for each diner. I cleaned up my plate each time, ate every bite, wasn't wasting any food, wasn't secreting it in my suitcase or anything. But when I requested the Ruby plum tart, he said, "No." That's all, just "No." No explanation, just "No." Not angrily or abruptly or disgustedly, just "No."

Well, I figured I'd gotten my £1's worth by that time, so I was willing to forgo the tart ... and the cheese ... and the seasonal fruit ... Still, it was one of the most memorable meals I've ever eaten.

Much reinvigorated, I left a 15% tip (10% was standard in Africa in those days, and 15% was positively squandering by my standards) and headed out to find a place to sleep.

Next day I headed on south to Lusaka, which was the capital city but had little of sightseeing interest. By the time I got through the city and on the road toward the famed Victoria Falls, it was after dark, and I was worried about getting picked up, especially since there was so little traffic: where'm I gonna sleep if I don't get a ride? ... Well, keep hoping ... I carried my suitcase to a spot with a long sight line and changed into a white shirt, trying to make myself as visible as possible in the gloom.

A few African pedestrians walked by, greeting me politely, almost deferentially. A couple trucks drove past but turned off the road a ways down. No other traffic ...

Then after an hour Fortune smiled: a youngish Englishman in a nice comfortable sedan stopped: "Saw you standing by the road, mate. Wouldn't want to leave a white man out here alone at night."

"Well, uh, thanks for giving me a ride," I replied, somewhat startled. I hadn't *felt* in any danger – discomfort, perhaps, but no *danger* ...?

The road was no longer a dirt track but was partially paved, with two strips of asphalt separated by a strip of vegetation. The effect was to create a sort of wide one-lane road, which was OK as long as we were the only car on the road, but rather unnerving the few times another car came toward us. My host played a game of chicken with every approaching car: eased somewhat to the side but kept barreling down the road, forcing the approaching car to pull over off the asphalt. Made me uncomfortable ... the perils of hitching ... but I figured I'd better keep the ride I had ... but I was glad when he dropped me in some small town.

Next morning I got rides to Victoria Falls, on the Zambezi River between Northern and Southern Rhodesia (now Zimbabwe). The falls were impressive, more than a mile wide, more than twice as high and twice as wide as Niagara Falls, claimed to be the largest sheet of falling water in the world during the rainy season. However, the water plummets off the edge of a cliff into a transverse gorge, and you can't stand far enough away to see the breadth of the water-drop from the ground. So I first stood on the Northern Rhodesian side and looked into one end of the chasm. It happened to be the end of the dry season, and the total volume of water going over the falls was much less impressive than during the rainy season; it looked like a series of rivers rather than one solid curtain of water. But the advantage was that you could see deep into the chasm, whereas during the height of the rainy season you can't much of anything because of the huge cloud of mist kicked up by the falling water.

Below the falls the Zambezi flows through a narrow gorge spanned by the Victoria Falls Bridge. The bridge is close enough that crossers are sprayed with mist. I carried my suitcase onto it and stopped to take a photo; if I had nobody to share the experience with, at least I could show the picture to my family later.

After viewing the falls from the Southern Rhodesian side, I looked for a place for lunch. I walked into a fancy tourist lodge overlooking the falls, but it was way too expensive. I was preparing to leave when an old fellow spoke to me: "You American?"

"Yes, heading for South Africa."

"The food's pretty good here. I've been here a week."

"I'm sure it is good, but it's out of my price range."

"It's not too bad. Most of the entrees are under two pounds."

"That's a lot to me. I'm budgeted to a pound a day for three meals and lodging."

He looked startled: "All your meals and lodging for a pound!?"

"It's possible to do it. Most of my meals cost five shillings or less." [There were 20 shillings in a pound.] "I'm a student."

"Well, um, I could, um, I'd be willing, um, to, um, invite you to be my guest ... if you'd like."

"Well, that's very kind of you. You don't have to do that."

"Please, be my guest."

So I accepted his offer and listened to his story. He was 70, widowed with grown children. He had come to the Rhodesias to spend Christmas and had just finished writing 75 Christmas cards to friends and family back in the U.S. Apparently he wanted to impress them by sending his Christmas cards from Victoria Falls. It struck me as rather expensive – the postage alone would have made half a month's budget for me. He spent most of the meal talking about those 75 cards. When I ventured to mention my trip, he didn't seem interested – probably couldn't relate to hitchhiking – so I dutifully listened to his meanderings. At the end of the meal I thanked him but could hardly wait to escape. If being rich made you that desperate and lonely, I was just as glad to be a budget-traveling student.

It took me a couple days to hitch through Southern Rhodesia. It was a beautiful country with peaceful, prosperous-looking farms, most of which were owned and managed by European settlers. Most of my rides were with Europeans, but some African truck drivers and an occasional Asian picked me up for short distances. The white drivers all sang the praises of the wonderful country of South Africa. Those were the days of *apartheid*, the (white) South African government's policy of 'separate development,' which in practice meant controlling and holding down the blacks, who made up the large majority of the population. Most white Rhodesians seemed to support the policy wholeheartedly, and they also tended to be scornful of the Asians. I kept silent but privately remembered the hospitality given to me by numerous African and Asian drivers.

In 2000 Zimbabwe's president, Robert Mugabe, allowed thousands of purported 'war veterans' to seize the lands previously tilled by white farmers. Murder, rape, robbery and other violent acts were committed against the whites. Zimbabwe's agricultural production plummeted, turning the country from one of Africa's richest into one of its poorest.

I reached the Limpopo River, which serves as the border with South Africa, late on the third morning. My ride took me across the bridge to the South African border post, where I encountered the immigration officer, an officious Afrikaner – a *boer* of Dutch descent, whose people were traditionally suspicious of English-speaking settlers. He seemed to be instantly suspicious that I was an *agent provocateur* or something, and demanded, "Why are you coming to South Africa?"

"Just a tourist, that's all."

"What're you planning to do in South Africa?"

"Just go sightseeing, that's all."

"Where'd you come from?"

"I'm an American, living in Uganda right now."

"What're you doing in Uganda?"

"I'm training to be a teacher at the university college there."

"You're a student?"

"Yes, a student teacher."

"Are you a student or a teacher?"

I was afraid to say I was a student because he might think I was coming to agitate the blacks against the *apartheid* policy. On the other hand, I was afraid to claim I was a teacher since that wasn't yet true. So I repeated, "A student teacher."

"ARE YOU A STUDENT OR A TEACHER?"

"Student, I guess."

"Oh, yeah, how'd you get down here?"

I had to answer. Couldn't claim I'd come by bus or anything because he'd know it was a lie. "I hitchhiked."

"*Hitchhiked*!?"

"Yes, sir."

"Oh, yeah, do you have any money? You can't come to South Africa and become an indigent, a free-loader."

"Yes, here, look," digging my $150 travelers checks out of my suitcase.

He glanced at them. "This isn't good enough. You have to show me you have money."

"Look, these are travelers checks. I can exchange them for cash at any bank or money changer."

"I want to see your *money*."

"Here, I've got twenty-two U.S. dollars," showing him the cash in my billfold and my pants pocket.

"That's not enough. You have to show me you have enough money. We don't want bums here."

"I'm not a bum. I'm a student preparing to enter a respected career, and I have enough money to support myself while I'm visiting your country."

"You haven't shown it to me."

"What am I supposed to do, go to a bank and convert these travelers checks into dollars cash?"

"Change them into rand" (Souh African currency).

"American dollars are accepted everywhere."

"RAND!"

Resignedly, "Can you tell me where's the nearest bank?"

"You can't do it in South Africa. I won't let you into the country until I see your money."

"You mean I have to go all the way back to Rhodesia and change these into South African money?"

"That's right."

So I reluctantly headed back to the main road and stuck out my thumb ... had to wait half an hour for a ride back to Rhodesia, then search for a bank.

In the bank I told the teller, "I'd like to change these into rand."

"Sorry, can't do that directly. Have to change your dollars into Rhodesian currency, then change those into rand."

"Does that mean I'll have to pay two commissions?"

"Sorry, but yes."

Well, I didn't have any choice ... ended up with a half-inch stack of rand worth about $144, down about 4% from the original $150.

I hitched back to South Africa and showed them to the immigration office. "Alright, I'll give you a visa for one entry to South Africa," he said.

Only one entry? You S.O.B. ... not that I expected to need more than one entry, but I still considered it mean-spirited. Maybe he was one of those petty officials who like to use their petty power to give people a hard time just because they can. Or maybe he just didn't like hitchhikers. Or me.

After he stamped the visa in my passport, I said, "I'm more likely to become indigent now, to need public assistance if somebody happens to steal this money. Travelers checks I could at least have gotten reimbursed."

"Oh ... well ... well, you can deposit the money in this office and pick it up on your way back out. Be safe that way."

F--- your bloody country. Damned if I'm gonna trust my money to the likes of you. But I bit my tongue, stuffed the wad of cash into my pants pocket, and turned and stalked out.

My feelings were soon mollified. The pioneering spirit that I noted among white settlers in eastern and southern Africa also extended to women, making them more willing to pick up (white) hitchhikers than women in North America or Europe would have been. One of the most memorable was Ursula, who picked me up shortly after I'd crossed into South Africa. She was heading toward Pretoria, some 300 miles away, a long ride over rough two-lane roads. We rode and talked for a couple hours. She was a widow and had two young children at home. I guessed her to be in her mid-thirties, still reasonably slender and attractive, quite young to be widowed. Her husband had been a doctor until he died of cancer two years before, and she was a teacher. I told her I was an aspiring teacher, getting training in Uganda, which seemed to create a bond between us. She said she didn't normally pick up hitchhikers but admitted feeling more comfortable with a man in the car when driving through sparsely-populated areas like these. She told about an incident at the town of Sharpeville, outside Johannesburg, where a protest by some black Africans a couple years before had turned violent and some 69 people were killed, mostly by South African police. I suspect she felt a fear that I noticed among other white South Africans, a fear the black majority population would rise up and take revenge against the whites who had oppressed them for many years.

Eventually she wanted to stop for a snack, saying she was getting tired from the driving. After we ate, I volunteered to drive for a while. She was reluctant but then accepted my offer, so I relieved her for an hour or so. She took over again when we got to a more densely-populated area.

We got to Pretoria about supper time. I guess she'd decided I was OK by then because she offered to put me up for the night. Her children, whom she'd left in the care of her African nanny, greeted her with shouts and hugs, then turned and asked me, "Are you going to be our new daddy?" I must have looked nonplussed because my hostess intervened and laughed, "No, he's just a visitor."

The nanny cooked a quick meal while Ursula put her stuff away. After the meal she invited me to sit on the couch and read while she put the children to bed. Then she returned to me, and we talked for a while longer. About 9:30 she said, "It's been a long day. I'll make up a bed for you."

"Thanks. I hope I'm not causing you too much trouble."

"No, not at all. It won't be too much trouble to make up the bed ... not too much trouble .... not *too* much ..."

I didn't know what to make of that. "Just show me the bedroom and give me the sheets. I can make up my own bed," I said.

"That bedroom hasn't been used for a while. It may be a little dusty."

"Oh, I don't mind."

"The room isn't really comfortable in the warm weather" [it was summer in the southern hemisphere].

I was a little confused. Was I getting some kind of signal here? An invitation? I was twenty-two and still pretty inexperienced and didn't know what to say. Finally I came out with a stupid question: "Do you have a double bed? I mean ... I mean ... I mean, maybe that would save the trouble of making up another bed," feeling extremely awkward.

She looked at me for a long minute, then said, "Well, you're right. It might save some trouble. You can change in there," pointing toward the bathroom.

What the heck is gonna happen? What's she expecting from me?

I put on my pajamas and brushed my teeth. When I emerged from the bathroom, she was wearing a nightgown. She lay down on one side of the bed and gestured to the other side, so I lay down beside her. She murmured something about "time to sleep," then edged slightly over toward me. I reached over and touched her hand, and she edged closer to me, so I drew her hand to my chest, and she sighed.

We made love three times that night.

Next morning I felt awkward, didn't know what to say. But Ursula seemed quite at ease. She cooked me breakfast and then said, "Where do you want to go? Can I drive you someplace?"

"I'm just going to downtown Pretoria," I replied.

We talked about inanities as she drove me to the downtown area and stopped on a street corner. "How's this?"

"Fine. Thanks very much for the ride and for putting me up ... and ... um ... um ..."

"I enjoyed spending the night with you. You're the only one, someone special. I hope you have a wonderful trip in South Africa," and away she drove.

The first thing that struck me as I wandered around Pretoria was the signs on drinking fountains, park benches and other facilities in Afrikaans (the Dutch-based language of the Afrikaners) and English:

```
NIET FUR BLANKES
WHITES ONLY
```

I was told that some facilities had signs in Zulu and other languages reserving those facilities for blacks only, but I never saw any. I was also told that the few facilities for them tended to be run-down and dirty.

To me the most striking tourist site in Pretoria was the Voortrekker Monument, which memorializes the nineteenth-century Great Trek, when bands of *boers* (also called Afrikaners) ventured into the hinterland in covered wagons. In some ways their history resembles American colonial history. Europeans (at first, mostly Dutch), who had started arriving in the seventeenth century, gradually expanded into the interior, sometimes fighting off the original inhabitants, whom they called Bantu, rather like the British and other Europeans who expanded into the interior of North America, sometimes fighting off the 'Indians.' Pretoria was the *boers'* northernmost point of penetration.

The monument is extremely impressive. Set on a hill, 130 feet tall on a base 130 feet square, it dominates the surrounding cityscape. It's surrounded by a circular stone wall with 64 bas-reliefs of oxcarts, symbolizing the covered wagons that brought the Afrikaners to this location. The building itself resembles a cathedral or tomb, with statues of heroic Afrikaner men and their stalwart women. From the outside it's a massive, impressive stone structure, while inside it's a high-ceilinged cavernous space of reverberating echoes. The 'Hall of Heroes' contains a frieze with 27 panels depicting the history of the Great Trek. At its center is a massive stone cenotaph illuminated by a shaft of light streaming through a hole in the ceiling; the light shaft shines on the inscription at 12:00 noon every December 16, commemorating the Battle of Blood River on December 16, 1838, when a band of 470 Afrikaners defeated an army of 10,000 Zulu warriors. The monument is controversial since it is viewed by many as an apotheosis of *apartheid*. All the visitors I saw were white.

> Nelson Mandela, South Africa's first black president, visited the monument in 2002; his visit symbolized the effort to promote reconciliation among the races.

My next destination was Johannesburg, South African's largest city and commercial center. People warned me that it wasn't safe to go out in the streets at night, not primarily because of fear of the blacks, but, interestingly, because of confrontations between gangs of Afrikaans-speaking and English-speaking youths. Nonetheless, I ended up walking in the street one evening after dark. A young guy approached me and spoke in Afrikaans. I kept walking as I said, "You'll have to talk to me in English."

He glared at me for a moment, then asked, "Are you American?"

"Yes."

"I could tell from your accent." Would he have attacked me if I'd been British? "Can you give me some money?" he continued, the only time I ever saw a white beggar in Africa.

By this time I'd gotten close to my hotel and thought I was fairly safe, so I said, "No," and kept walking. He followed for a few seconds, then turned and walked away. Phew!

I'd read about the possibility of visiting a gold mine, but the tourist office said you had to book the tour a month in advance, which didn't accommodate day-to-day tourists like me.

I was intrigued by another possibility: I'd read that foreign visitors could contact the Ministry of Bantu Affairs and get a free tour of a so-called Bantu township, a residential area on the outskirts of the city where blacks who worked in the city could live. Why not? I thought.

The people at the Ministry seemed surprised to see me – I gathered that very few tourists took them up on the offer. Next morning a car, driver and guide picked me up at my (cheap) hotel; the driver was black, while the guide was a middle-aged white man who told me he was a departmental supervisor in the ministry, but he occasionally agreed to take visitors on the tour.

We drove to the township: the notorious Soweto (SOuth WEst TOwnship). It was surrounded by a high chain-link fence; we had to show papers before the guard at the gate allowed us to drive in. Control – the magic word was Control.

Once inside, the first thing I saw was the station for the commuter trains into the city. A group of blacks happened to be boarding a train. Each one had to show a pass to a white guard before he/she was allowed to board the train. Control ...

The township contained rows and rows of tiny brick houses with corrugated-iron roofs standing on cement bases. I was able to glance inside one of the cookie-cutter houses and saw that it consisted of one large room. "These have been constructed for the residents," my guide said with some pride. Well, they might have looked good compared to the mud-and-sticks huts I had seen in East Africa, but I doubted if they were any more comfortable.

I saw women filling jugs with water at an outdoor faucet. "No house is more than 25 meters from a water source," the guide said, again with pride. No running water? – well, at least the faucets were better than having to walk a mile to a river to fill your water-jug, as many people had to do in other parts of the continent.

We stopped in front of one of the few two-story houses. The guide called out, and a black woman appeared. "May we visit your house?"

"Yaas, Baas [yes, boss], of course," she responded. I gathered the guide had brought other visitors to her place.

Inside I saw a living room and a kitchen-dining area with cement-block walls and cement floors. Upstairs were three very small bedrooms with linoleum floors. The house was small and plain, but clean and neat. It had electricity but no running water. "Mrs. Busisiwe's husband is a clerk in an office in Jo'burg," the guide announced.

"You have a very nice place," I said to her.

"Thank you, Baas." She seemed quite proud of the place.

After further pleasantries the guide took me to a store and introduced me to the proprietor, a black man. He had a sort-of local monopoly, one of the few general stores in the township, which doubtless allowed him to charge pretty high prices. He too seemed pleased with his situation.

We drove around the township some more, the guide pointing out various features, and then headed back to my hotel. "I hope you found the tour informative," the guide said. "You can see they lead happy lives."

"Oh, yes, very informative. Thanks so much for taking me," I replied. I didn't add that the whole setup resembled a civilized version of a concentration camp. And privately I thought the government must have been pretty desperate for approval if they were willing to allocate a car, driver and middle-level official for four hours to take a young wayfarer like me on their propaganda tour. And I can't say it was successful since it certainly didn't convince me most black South Africans were happy under *apartheid*.

One of the first acts of the first government headed by black Africans after the end of *apartheid* was to tear down the fences around the townships.

I found myself in the back streets of Jo'burg around 9:00 p.m. It was a white area but not a wealthy one. The streets were sandy with scattered clumps of asphalt rubble. The houses were small and somewhat rundown; many had no foundations except stacks of strategically-placed cement blocks. The residents were friendly, however. I wasn't worried about my safety but was highly concerned about finding a place to sleep.

One middle-aged couple sitting on a slightly-tilting front porch saw me and called out, "Where are you from?"

"I'm an American."

"Where're you heading?"

"Looking for a place to stay."

"Well, come on in." Just like that, invited a stranger off the street into their home.

"Thanks tremendously." I wondered if it reflected a pioneering spirit, a kind of white solidarity, a feeling of 'we've-all-got-to-stick-together-against-the-savages.'

The wife led me to an upstairs bedroom, got out some clean sheets and made up a bed. "Hope you'll be comfortable here," she said. "You can wash up there," pointing to the bathroom.

"Thanks again. Thank you so much!"

In the morning she asked, "How many eggs would you like for breakfast?"

"Oh, just one or two."

"These are very small eggs," she said, holding up a couple. "How about four?"

The smallest chicken eggs I'd ever seen. "Well, wonderful, thanks."

During the meal the husband said he'd been laid off from his job as a carpenter, "but I expect to find something soon."

I was flabbergasted at their hospitality – unemployed, no income, but they opened their home to a complete stranger. Sometimes the poorest people are the most generous.

We talked a little while after breakfast, and then I again expressed my appreciation and said, "I'd better be moving on. Can I pay you for my night's lodging?"

"Oh, no, not at all. We were glad to help you."

"Please, at least let me pay you for the breakfast." I offered them forty pence – about 56 U.S. cents – which they accepted. Then I picked up my suitcase and headed on down the road.

Where to go next?

Well, if I couldn't see a gold mine in Jo'burg, I'd go see a diamond mine in Kimberley. It was about 300 miles on a road through desert-like country, said to be a southern extension of the Kalahari Desert.

I had thought it would be a quick trip, but it turned out to be quite slow because, just like in the U.S., lots of cars passed, but only a few were willing to stop. After several short hops with long waits in between, I hit on the idea of writing "American student" on the side of my suitcase with a piece of chalk. That helped: my rides came quicker, but it still took more than a day to get to Kimberley.

The Kimberley mining museum was reasonably interesting – photos of miners, some old pieces of mining equipment – but nothing spectacular. The mine itself, also known as 'the Big Hole,' was dug out by hand, shovelful by shovelful, to about 800 feet deep, from the 1870's to 1914. It yielded some 6,000 pounds of diamonds over the years. But it had become partly filled with water and wasn't anything special to look at – just a hole in the ground with some water in it. I hitchhiked 300 miles to see *this*?!

On to Cape Town, 500 more miles through an arid region called the Great Karoo.

December 24, 1962: an older Afrikaner and his wife gave me a ride to some small city halfway to Cape Town and invited me to stay for the night. They spoke Afrikaans to each other but switched to English at supper out of courtesy to me. I met their son and daughter-in-law, who had a baby just a few weeks old. I appreciated their hospitality, but the baby cried all night. I didn't get much sleep, which left me feeling out-of-sorts the next morning.

At breakfast I greeted everybody, "Merry Christmas!"

"Oh, yeah, I guess it's Christmas," the older man replied. "Merry Christmas." It obviously wasn't a major holiday to them – no Christmas decorations, no evergreen tree, no exchange of presents.

Well, bright summery morning in the southern hemisphere … I didn't feel especially Christmasy either … but it did affect me, missing my warm family holiday gatherings, seeing all the relatives … Christmas lights shimmering on white snow … turkey dinner with all the trimmings … my first ever Christmas away from home … felt the loneliness … forlornness …

Back out on the road. I have a photo, an old-fashioned Kodachrome slide, that I asked somebody to take of me, standing in shirtsleeves beside my suitcase adorned with the words "AMERICAN STUDENT." It's labeled "Christmas Day 1962, Klein Karoo, South Africa."

Late that evening somebody dropped me on the roadside in the mountains outside of Cape Town. It was after dark, and I felt vulnerable, uneasy, especially since there were rumors of anti-white demonstrations in the townships around the Cape. I stood there for half an hour watching the cars zoom past and wondering how I was going to get out of this mess.

Then somebody stopped, a white M.D. who told me in a disgruntled tone that he was heading into the Cape for a business meeting the next day. "I normally don't pick up hitchhikers, but I decided I might as well take a chance on you. Everything else has gone wrong today, so I might as well take the chance."

Did he expect me to pull a gun on him or something?

Shortly thereafter we rounded a bend, and there, spread out before us, were the lights of the city, a magnificent panorama outlining the curve of the shore to the right and the famed Table Mountain on the left. I thrilled at the sight and exclaimed, "Beautiful! Spectacular! What a magnificent setting for the city!"

"Yes, you're right," he responded slowly. "I'd forgotten how gorgeous the Cape could be. Glad I picked you up. You've reminded me to appreciate the beauty."

We had an interesting conversation after that, comparing medical practice in South Africa to what little I knew about American medicine. I even entertained hopes he might treat me to a meal or invite me into his home, but he stopped in front of a YMCA in Cape Town and said, "How's this?"

"Fine! Wonderful! Thanks for the ride!" Appreciate his hospitality, even if he didn't buy me a meal. At least he got me out of an uncomfortable situation.

The next day, December 26, was a traditional British holiday called Boxing Day, when people put out boxes to collect money and food for the poor. [It's since been renamed Day of Goodwill in South Africa.] Cape Town marked the day with a minstrel parade featuring singers, dancers, musicians, jugglers, stilt-walkers and mummers with gaily-painted faces, white gloves and fancy costumes – a preliminary to the Cape Carnival that takes place on New Year's Day. Many of the participants were Cape Coloureds, people of mixed European and black African descent.

White South Africans and some blacks and coloureds lined the parade route. I carried my suitcase to a spot where I could get a good view and enjoyed the spectacle. It obviously drew inspiration from the Mardi Gras in New Orleans, with floats carrying bands playing Dixieland-style jazz. There must have been twenty or more bands with names like Basin Street Boys, Bourbon Bouncers, Storyville Strutters, Dukes of Dixieland, Bayou Bashers and so on. The mummers and stilt walkers and clowns cavorted down the street showing off their fancy costumes and acrobatic skills. It was quite a show.

While I was watching I noticed a guy and a couple girls about my age standing next to me. I glanced at them, and they glanced at me, and I finally worked up the courage to speak to them with some stupid opening line like "Enjoying the parade?" Fortunately they responded with interest, and we began talking. I figured out one of the girls was the guy's girlfriend and the other was unattached, so naturally I turned my attention to her. She seemed quite interested in talking with me.

After a while we didn't see any more bands or marchers, and the guy said, "I guess that's the end of it. We're gonna go get some lunch. You wanna come with us?"

Well, I wasn't sure the parade was over, and I wanted to be sure I saw everything, so I said, "I oughta wait and see if there's anything more."

"Well, OK," the guy said. "We're leaving now."

I waited and watched another five or ten minutes, and pretty soon the other spectators started drifting away, and it became obvious that the festivities were over. So I looked around for the guy and girls, but they were gone: a missed opportunity. Stupid!

So I picked up my suitcase and ... where to go? what to do? Lonely again ...

STUPID!!!

I don't remember what I did the rest of the day ... probably wandered around Cape Town, looking at the historic waterfront and some picturesque old houses, all the while kicking myself for passing up an opportunity for companionship ... and maybe more ...

STUPID!

———

Next stop: Oudtshoorn, in the semi-desert region called the Klein Karoo, the site of several ostrich farms. Somebody dropped me at one of the farms. I walked in off the road, no advance reservation, no other visitors, but they treated me most cordially. I paid a modest fee and had a personal guided tour, listening attentively as the guide gave a preliminary educational talk: "Ostriches can run forty miles an hour. Their wings are small relative to the size of the animal and don't have feathers. They can't fly." He showed me an egg, which was about six inches long, and said, "It's equivalent to fifteen or twenty hen's eggs." He set it on the grass and invited me to stand on it, and it never broke – amazingly strong shell. Then he led me to a large corral with dozens of ostriches and asked, "Do you want to ride one?"

"I guess so. Is it safe?"

"Pretty safe. You're a young guy. You shouldn't get hurt if you fall off. But if you do fall off, watch out you don't get in the way of his legs. They kick forward and can kick pretty strong. They also bite, so keep your fingers away from his mouth."

Not real reassuring. But an ostrich ride seemed to be part of the package, so what the heck …

He tossed a lasso over the neck of one of them cowboy-style and led it to a fenced-in run maybe a hundred yards long and three yards wide. He instructed, "You sit on his back and put your legs over his wings, sort of like sitting on a horse. Grab hold of his wings, right here, hands next to his body. Don't grab hold of his neck, though; their necks are vulnerable."

He helped me up onto my mount, about five feet above the ground, and jumped aside. The animal took off at a frantic clip down the fenced-in run. I bounced along on his back, holding on for dear life, for maybe ten seconds, and then fell off backwards. I hit the ground pretty hard on my rump and immediately tried to roll to one side, but the bird kept running ahead, so fortunately I didn't have to worry about getting kicked.

"Are you alright?" the guide asked.

"I guess so." But privately I doubted whether it was a good idea to invite people to ride on their backs like that – could have hurt myself pretty badly.

About that time a family of four Afrikaners joined us, father and mother and two school-age kids. We sat on bleachers beside the corral as the guide continued his lecture: "Ostriches are less evolved than other birds. They have fingers at the tips of their wings, vestigial hands, more like lizards or dinosaurs than like other birds," showing us a hand-like structure. "Two of the fingers have claws they can use in fighting."

The Afrikaner father glared suspiciously at the guide and then at me. "Evolution hasn't been proven, you know," he declared.

"No, I suppose not," I replied. No point in arguing with him: I wasn't going to convince him and he wasn't going to convince me. I guessed the family to be among the *verkrampte*, Afrikaners who opposed liberalization of South Africa's racial policies and believed in the literal truth of the Bible. The guide glanced knowingly at me but remained silent.

From Oudtshoorn I headed south to the coast and then along the Garden Route, famed for its Mediterranean climate, lush vegetation, beautiful beaches, and mountains backing up the coastline. I enjoyed the beautiful scenery but had to pass up some interesting tourist sites when I didn't want to give up good rides.

As I was getting out of a car after one ride, I slammed my thumb in the door. The whole thumbnail turned black and blue and smarted with pain.

> I must have damaged the cell structure or something because I continued to suffer agonizing stabs of pain for the next couple months. It wasn't until February that I noticed the thumb wasn't hurting any more. The damage turned out to be permanent: years later the thumb still bears a bluish mark, and the thumbnail has never completely recovered.

I happened to arrive in East London the afternoon of tryouts for an upcoming Formula One auto race. [The track was later deemed too small for Formula One cars.] By the time I got to the raceway the ticket booth had closed, so I was free to walk in and see the last hour of tryouts. I found a comfortable seat with a seat cushion and a curved plastic back and watched the cars maneuver around the curves and accelerate down the straightaways. The comfortable seats were all occupied by whites; the very few blacks in attendance had to sit in bleachers without seat backs. Separate development ...

After the tryouts I briefly visited the city's docks and saw the Union-Castle ship *Winchester Castle*, which was scheduled to sail up the east coast of Africa. I vaguely considered taking it to Dar-es-Salaam or Mombasa but decided it would be too costly. Besides, I wanted to go overland and see as much of Africa as I could.

My next major stop was Durban. I was ready to take a break from hitching, so I found my way to one of the city's famously beautiful beaches, where I saw a sign:

> FOR USE BY WHITE PERSONS
> VIR GEBRUIK DEUR BLANKES

There was a clean, spacious, well-painted beach-house/concession-stand, where I changed clothes and left my suitcase at the counter. The beach was clean and neat and well-maintained. I took a welcome, delightful swim – didn't meet any girls, though.

After the swim and a refreshing shower, I took my suitcase and started walking down the beach. I must have missed the signs, but I obviously crossed some kind of boundary because I suddenly noticed that all the beach patrons were black. I felt conspicuous but not unwelcome or unsafe. A couple of girls with Zulu-style hair braids looked at me and giggled, and other patrons either stared or averted their eyes. The beach here was dirtier and the beach house was rundown and unpainted. Separate development ... ... separate and unequal!...

When I made my way back to the sidewalk, a couple of white girls approached and confronted me: "Why are you walking on the n-----s' beach?"

This wasn't the time or the place to make a stand against *apartheid*, so all I said was, "Oh, I didn't realize. I'm a tourist, an American."

"I mean, prob'ly no harm come of it, but you might not be safe," one of them replied.

"I didn't feel unsafe," I said as I walked on.

I caught a glimpse of the harbor and by chance saw the *Winchester Castle*, the same ship I'd seen in East London. Apparently it was progressing up the African coast at about the same speed as I was progressing up the land route.

In late afternoon I boarded a bus heading back toward the city center, pondering my usual question, "Where'm I gonna sleep tonight?"

After a while I saw a sign, **YMCA** , so I got off and walked into the building. A black man was standing behind the desk. "Can I get a room for the night?" I asked.

"It is against the law of South Africa for you to sleep in this hostel," he replied.

Only then did I realize that I'd stumbled into a facility reserved for non-whites. I responded, "I'm a foreigner, an American."

"I can not and will not check you in. I could be arrested and jailed if I checked you in. You could be arrested and jailed for staying here, although they're not likely to do that to you." Then he took a key out of its box and dropped it on the desk in front of me.

I took this as an invitation and picked up the key – I was willing to take my chances on getting arrested and jailed. I found my way to the room, which was plain but clean. After leaving my suitcase I went back to the clerk and asked, "Is there any place around here where I can get supper?"

"Most of the restaurants around here are reserved for non-whites. ... The Umlakha is down the block to the right. They're not real careful about observing the law."

I walked to the Umlakha and ordered a meal. I was the only white face there. The waiter and other customers glanced at me but then turned away. Nobody bothered me. Tolerable food, cheap.

Next morning I went to the YMCA's dining room and sat at a long table with four or five other men. Again I was the only white face present. The waiter brought me the standard breakfast of toast and jam and a cup of coffee.

One of the men at the table leaned toward me and asked, "Are you visiting Durban on business?"

"No, I'm just a tourist."

After some more introductory talk he asked, "What do you think of the government's *apartheid* policy?"

"It's pretty awful."

This led to a recitation of the non-whites' grievances, which were numerous and well-justified. Eventually my companion began to get a little wild-eyed: "Some day we will all rise up against the whites and kill them all and take our rightful place in this our country."

How do you respond to that? Did he expect to include me among the whites they killed? "How will you all know when the day comes to rise up?"

"Oh, we'll know. We have ways; we'll all know."

I certainly sympathized with their grievances, but this guy was making me uncomfortable, so I excused myself and went to pay for breakfast.

"Breakfast is included in your room cost," the waiter told me.

When I went to check out, a different clerk was behind the desk, but he didn't seem surprised to see me. "I'd like to pay for my room and check out," I told him.

"You were never checked in, so you can't check out."

"I'll pay for the room."

"You were never checked in here, so you can't pay for the room."

"OK, well, thanks."

"Good-bye. Enjoy your visit in Durban."

I would have loved to stay longer in South Africa, which really was a beautiful country. I had found its people of all races very hospitable. Its latitude is approximately the same as the American state of Georgia, warm enough for its sports-crazy citizens to enjoy year-around outdoors activities, but its temperatures moderated by the ocean and mountains. However, I was becoming worried about getting back to Uganda, more than 2,000 miles away over some pretty rough roads, before next semester started, so I headed for the road again.

Just out of Durban a woman about my age in a Volkswagen stopped and called through the open window, "Where're you heading?"

"Pietermaritzburg, Ladysmith, all the way to Uganda if you're going that far."

"Not quite that far, but I can take you a little ways." She leaned over and unlocked the door.

"Thanks."

After I got in, she asked, "You're American? I saw your sign. I heard your accent; I wouldn't have picked you up if you hadn't had an American accent."

"Well, thanks again. Takes a certain courage for a woman to invite a strange man into her car."

"Why'd you mention Uganda?" she asked. I told her about my teaching program, and she responded, "Isn't Uganda pretty primitive?"

I found that somewhat surprising since she must have had plenty of contact with black Africans, living on the African continent herself. But then again, maybe not, given South Africa's policies and its white people's attitudes. But all I said was, "It's not as developed as your beautiful country, but it's nice in its own way. Just got its independence from Britain."

We continued talking about Uganda, and South Africa, and Africa in general, and life in general. Her views were obviously colored by her environment, but she was open to discussion. I was willing to listen to her views, and she to mine.

She told about her job: she was out making sales calls for her company and was heading for Basutoland, then still a British protectorate totally surrounded by South Africa. [Basutoland became the independent country of Lesotho in 1966.]

Somehow we got onto the topic of ethics, and she insisted that she had very ethical attitudes. Then we stopped for gas; the price gauge read 5.50 rand, but she asked the attendant for a receipt for 7 rand. I teased, "Ethical to pad your expense account a bit. Your employer can afford it." She was embarrassed, but laughed.

After a couple hours she pulled over to the side of the road. "This is my turnoff for Basutoland. You're welcome to come with me. We can spend the night together."

She was a little heavy, but still an attractive woman, and we seemed to be compatible. I would have been quite willing to accept her offer but was truly concerned about those 2,000 miles, so I had to answer, "I'd love to stay with you, but I am worried about getting back to my teaching program. They're going to be sending me out to some secondary school for practice teaching in another week or so."

"Well, too bad. Are you sure? Maybe you're not ... not attracted to me ... you think I'm ...?"

"Oh, no, don't think that. I really would like ... I find you plenty attractive, compatible ... enjoyed talking with you, but ... time constraint ..." I leaned over, intending to give her a little kiss, but she thrust her arms around me and turned it into a major smooch. Immediately after she drove away I was kicking myself: how can you pass up an invitation like that?! Fool!

I made it to Ladysmith that evening, which happened to be New Year's Eve. No party for me; I'd just be glad to find a place to sleep. I happened to see the town's police station, so I went in and said, "I've heard that visitors can stay in unoccupied jail cells for free. Is it possible for me to stay here tonight?

"The law of South Africa provides that any white person can spend a night in the jail for free," the (white) desk officer replied, "but I wouldn't advise it, especially not tonight, when we'll be picking up a lot of drunks. It's likely to get pretty smelly."

"Oh. Too bad." Actually I was just as glad: the idea of spending a night in a jail cell had a certain adventurous appeal, but it would have been pretty dirty, and the psychology of being locked up bothered me a little: could I be absolutely sure they would release me next morning? So I asked if he knew a place where I could stay, and he directed me down the road to a rooming house.

The rooming house was pretty rundown. I knocked on the door, and a woman answered and led me to a plain room with a few sticks of furniture including a metal cot with a thin mattress. "I'm not the proprietor," she said, "but the landlord asked me to keep watch over the place."

"Oh, fine with me. Appreciate your help."

After supper I returned to the rooming house, by which time the regular tenants were organizing a little party, which they invited me to join. They had a radio tuned to a pop-music station, a bottle of whisky and a few bottles of beer. There were only eight or ten people, more women than men, middle-aged, obviously not wealthy, not a very exciting crowd, but better than spending the night alone.

I accepted their invitation to a drink but declined a second. The women took turns inviting me to dance: I think I was a special treat to them, a younger man and a foreigner, an American to boot. By midnight they were pretty liquored-up, and one of the women insisted on kissing me to celebrate. Well, alright, why not? Then she started making jokes about sleeping with me – not jokes, really – I'm sure she would have been quite eager if I'd been willing. But she was drunk and middle-aged and kind of fat and frizzle-haired, so I responded to her remarks as humor until I was able to retreat to my own room.

(Should have stayed with the woman in Basutoland.)

In the morning I handed my room key back to the woman who'd let me in, and she said, "If you leave now, you won't have to pay for the night."

"Oh, thanks."

The next couple days were a blur of standing by roadsides, getting rides with drivers-I-don't-remember, sleeping I-don't-remember-where. One ride I do remember was with an old Afrikaaner who took a slight detour through the Orange Free State Province, which had been an independent *boer* republic from 1854 to 1902. "We have a kind of tradition here that no Asian can spend the night in the Free State," he said. "They can drive through, but not stay overnight." I had visions of vigilantes cruising the dark streets with clubs and flaming crosses – frightening!

When I got to the South African border post, I recognized the same official who had given me so much hassle two weeks before. Surprisingly, perhaps, he recognized me too and said, "I hope you had a good visit in South Africa." I could have shot back something unpleasant, but all I said was, "It was alright; it was OK." Shove it up your a--.

My next ride, in Southern Rhodesia, dropped me on the outskirts of some small town. It was turning dusk, and I prayed I'd get a ride into town. Shortly thereafter a fortyish fellow picked me up; after the ten-minute ride into town, he said, "Well, you seem like a nice bloke. You can stay in my home tonight."

That was startlingly quick! Another we're-all-in-this-together-so-we-have-to-help-each-other-out pioneer? Or was he hoping for a little casual sex?

He led me into his house and said, "I have a meeting to go to tonight, should be back after an hour." He opened the fridge and pointed to some items of food: "You can help yourself to some supper." He also lifted a cake-pan lid and invited me to cut myself a piece, and then he left.

Wow, here I am in some stranger's house, feeling extremely awkward. And he's not even at home!?

Messy house, stuff scattered around, dirty dishes in the sink – apparently a bachelor living on his own.

Funny, being in a situation like that made me wonder what I might actually be capable of: whether I might even abscond with some valuables or commit some act of vandalism. But not being an alienated type, I didn't.

I did, however, follow up on his invitation to raid the refrigerator … despite my hesitations … I was hungry … let's see, here's a piece of chicken, and a leftover baked potato, and … well, I guess I'll eat them … not a very appetizing meal, everything cold, but I've eaten worse … use my fingers, don't want to dirty his dishes …. and why not accept his invitation to a piece of cake? … found a knife and cut myself a piece. When I was done, I rinsed off my dishes in cold water, then sat on his couch and read one of my paperbacks.

He returned after an hour. I told him what I'd done, and he said, "Fine, mate!"

As his guest I felt obligated to converse with him, so I said something about Uganda and about my trip to South Africa and my previous few days in Southern Rhodesia, but he wasn't much interested, and we didn't seem to have much in common. So when he suggested it was time for bed, I was happy to retire. Separate bedrooms.

Curious that he would invite a complete stranger into his house, leave me along in the house for an hour, and then be uninterested in conversing …?

Next day I got rides to the Great Zimbabwe ruins in the southeast region of the country: the remains of a stone city, the capital of the prehistoric empire of Zimbabwe.

> When Robert Mugabe became president of Rhodesia in 1980, he officially adopted the country's present name of Zimbabwe from this ancient kingdom.

The major buildings and city walls were constructed by carefully fitting together stones without mortar. The walls are about 820 feet in circumference and reach as high as 36 feet. There are numerous other similar but smaller sites scattered around present-day Zimbabwe and Mozambique. Archeologists have determined that the cities were inhabited from the 12th to 15th centuries A.D. The buildings and walls have stood pretty much intact for as much as 800 years, a tribute to the care and skill with which they were constructed.

Archeologists have found ample evidence that the cities were constructed by Bantu peoples (black Africans), but when the white government ruled Southern Rhodesia, they put pressure on archeologists to say that the sites were not created by blacks. I personally met whites who insisted that indigenous Africans were incapable of constructing such elaborate cities, so they must have been created by Arabs or even Phoenicians.

Unfortunately when I visited the ruins there were only a few placards identifying and describing some of the major structures such as the Stone Tower and the King's Palace, so I didn't learn as much as I would have liked about the history and artifacts of the place.

> The United Nations agency UNESCO designated the ruins as a World Heritage Site in 1986, and more explanatory information has since been made available.

That evening I got a ride with a white Rhodesian who started talking about how the white settlers had made the country into an "outpost of civilization" and a "breadbasket to the world. ... It would be a shame to let the blacks take over this beautiful country and ruin what we've built here. We've been here for several generations, and Africa is our home," he said. (Never mind that the blacks had been there for countless generations before.) Then he admitted that he was worried about the future for whites if black Africans came to dominate the government and that he was thinking of emigrating to South Africa or Australia.

We stopped at a restaurant for supper. My host called a waiter over and, grasping his hand to prevent him from escaping, said, "Look at that black skin, that kinky hair, those thick lips. How can you say he's not inferior?" while I squirmed uncomfortably in my chair. He seemed to regard the waiter more as an object than a person. Fortunately the waiter didn't react; I couldn't tell whether he was cowed into submission or just resigned to the slights.

I reached Salisbury, the capital city [since renamed Harare], the next morning and chanced upon a shipping agency. I went in and learned that the *Winchester Castle* was due into the port of Beira, Mozambique, the next day. The cheapest fare for the three-night trip from Beira to Dar-es-Salaam, Tanganyika, was £10 ($28), beyond my budget but manageable for a few days. The agent said Beira was a little less than 300 miles on a paved road with lots of traffic, so I should to be able to cover it in one day. He cautioned that a band of black Africans had recently started up a movement for independence of Mozambique from Portugal (FRELIMO) and that they had made a few raids in the northern part of the country. He added reassuringly, "Not very likely you'd encounter them, though." Why did he even mention the possibility?

I was getting a little weary of hitchhiking and dreaded the long stretches of seldom-traveled dirt roads in Northern Rhodesia and Tanganyika. Didn't relish the idea of waiting nine hours beside the road again. I also thought taking the ship might be a nice way to relax at the end of my trip, so I decided to try to catch it.

I was concerned I'd be late getting back to the teacher-training program in Uganda and decided to send a telegram to the dean of the university. It was a hassle to find a telegraph office and send the message, but I presumed the supervisors wouldn't penalize me if they understood why I might be late.

The shipping agent was right: I got rides easily, didn't encounter any terrorists, and made it to Beira by nightfall. Next day I booked passage and boarded the ship. My cabin was down in the bowels of the ship but was clean and neat and adequately appointed.

On board I met three guys about my age who were looking for a fourth for bridge. I was eager to improve my skills at the game and was happy to join them. We started playing my first afternoon and played until late that night and most of my second day. Several girls about our age were highly distressed that we shut them out of our intense little world.

We finally tired of bridge on the third day, and I turned my attention to one of the girls. She was willing to talk to me but was so ticked off that she wouldn't dance with me in the evening. Muffed another opportunity?

Our ship was scheduled to land in Dar-es-Salaam on the third day but for some reason was diverted to Zanzibar for a day. I was distressed that the diversion would make my return to Uganda yet another day later but was pleased at the opportunity for a second visit to the island. Several of the guys signed up for escorted tours, but I figured they'd just be put into taxis and be driven around the country a bit, and I thought I could have a more interesting time on my own.

I got rides across the island, passed through pineapple plantations and spice-tree forests, and visited the ruins of an older stone town (Dunga). One of my rides dropped me beside a beach under some palm trees where I watched a group of African workers building a house from local woods and palm leaves. Another ride was with an older Swahili fellow (of mixed African and Arab parentage) driving a rattly old three-wheeled delivery truck. He told me about some ancient Chinese coins that had been discovered on the island, indicating that Zanzibar had traded with China many years before the first Europeans showed up.

Later, as I was walking along the road waiting for my next ride, a taxi pulled alongside, and, lo-and-behold, it was my companions from the ship. "What are you doing way out here? Aren't you afraid you'll get lost or something?" one guy called out.

"Nah, I got a map. We're only ten miles from the harbor," I replied. "See you back at the ship." Granted, they had probably made brief passing visits to more sights than I had, but I felt I had gotten a better sense of the island than they had, felt smugly more worldly.

Next day the ship dropped me in Dar-es-Salaam, some 900 miles from Kampala. I covered the distance in 2½ grueling days, hitching from early morning into late evenings, all a blur to me now. But I got back to the university several days before I was due to be sent out for practice teaching.

In retrospect I probably would have done better to stick to the land route through Northern Rhodesia and western Tanganyika – probably wouldn't have taken any more days and would have seen more of Africa, even if it would have been some pretty remote, boring, arid areas.

Back at the university, the dean called me in, said he'd received my telegram only one day earlier – a week after I'd sent it – a tribute to African inefficiency – and bawled me out for getting back so late. "Where'd you go, anyhow!?" he demanded.

"Cape Town."

"Cape Town!!?" he exclaimed. "How'd you get all the way down there?"

"Hitchhiked."

"Hitchhiked! *Hitchhiked*!!?"

"Yes, sir."

Conclusion: sending the telegram was a tactical blunder. They probably wouldn't even have noticed I was absent if I hadn't alerted them. But the bawling out felt sort of *pro forma*. In spite of it I got the impression the dean secretly admired me for the adventure I'd experienced.

Three days later I started my practice teaching.

CHAPTER 14.
CONGO: A JUNGLE ADVENTURE

After finishing my teacher training at Makerere in March 1963, my first posting was to a secondary school in Tabora, Tanganyika, a pleasant town some five hundred miles up the rail line from the coast. While there I bought a motorcycle, a 150 cc. Honda, which became my basis of transportation, greatly reducing my hitchhiking.

However, I did make one rather spectacular if uncomfortable hitchhiking trip during the school's two-week spring break in June 1963. I decided to head for Congo, a feasible traveling distance from Tabora. The former Belgian Congo, at independence in 1960 it became Congo (Leopoldville) – named after its capital city, to distinguish it from Congo (Brazzaville), a former French colony also bordering on the Congo River. Later it was renamed Congo (Kinshasa), then Zaïre, and still later Democratic Republic of the Congo; in this chapter I'll simply call it Congo.

The papers reported there were only eight college graduates in the whole country at the time of independence, nowhere near enough educated or experienced people to run the government of a large, diverse, grossly underdeveloped land like Congo. Many areas lacked infrastructure – no electricity, no water, only dirt-track roads (if any at all), and few links to the central government, which barely exercised any authority outside of the major cities.

A young leftist, Patrice Lumumba, a secondary-school graduate and former postal clerk who had been taken to jail in Belgium for inciting a riot, was released from prison in January 1960 and returned shortly thereafter to Congo to become its first Prime Minister. However, despite his idealism and that of other early leaders, the country soon became notorious for its poverty, corruption, political strife and armed uprisings. No less than three regions attempted to secede as ambitious regional leaders vied for power and ancient tribal rivalries flared into armed conflicts. There were large-scale massacres and mutilations, including some white missionaries and officials. The Congolese government, unable to restore order, sought the assistance of the United Nations, which sent some 20,000 troops as 'peace keepers' in 1961.

One of the regions that attempted to secede was Haut-Zaïre, in the northeast section of the country; its capital was Stanleyville, a city on the Congo River. [The city was later renamed Kisangani, and Haut-Zaïre became Orientale Province.] Lumumba had attempted to organize rebellions there twice in 1960, but troops loyal to the central government had arrested him and flown him to Leopoldville and then to Katanga (another region that had tried to declare independence), where he was murdered in January 1961, possibly with the complicity of the U.S. and Belgian governments.

> Fighting between the United Nations and Katangese forces continued sporadically in 1963 and 1964, until the U.N. forces were withdrawn in June 1964. There were mutinies in Kisangani in 1966 and 1967, and various wars and rebellions in northeast Congo throughout the rest of the 20th century and into the 21st.

The U.S. State Department issued an advisory against traveling to Congo in 1961 because of 'unsettled conditions' but cancelled it in early 1963 as conditions appeared to stabilize. So, since it was presumably safe to travel there – including hitchhiking? – I decided to set my sights for Stanleyville – rebellion(s) be damned.

The rail line to Tabora ran another couple hundred miles inland (westward) to its termination point in Kigoma, a port town on Lake Tanganyika. It was an overnight train ride, slow and inefficient but safe and comfortable. I had bought a coach-class ticket but found a bed in the sleeper car, and the conductor didn't object when I lay down and slept there.

I had passed through Kigoma on my way from Kampala to South Africa the previous December (Chapter 13 describes how I'd taken a boat south to Northern Rhodesia). This time I got there in time to catch the same boat on its run northward to Bujumbura, the capital of Burundi. (I'd also been in Bujumbura before, when I'd hitched there from Kampala with Phoenecia – Chapter 11).

It was a short hitch across the border to the town of Uvira, where I stayed the night in some local hotel. I needed Congolese francs; I knew there was a huge discount on the black market, but I had no idea what the market rate should be. I also knew it was theoretically illegal to sell foreign currencies on the black market, but I figured the country was so disorganized and corrupt they'd never catch me ... and wouldn't care if they did. I met a Belgian in the hotel who was all too eager to get dollars, and began bargaining with him. I tried to pretend I knew the going rate but felt clearly disadvantaged by my lack of knowledge. Anyhow, he first offered about four times the official exchange rate, and I finally bargained him up to five times. I have no idea if I could have gotten an even better rate if I'd bargained more knowledgeably, but buying francs at an 80% discount from the official exchange rate made it extremely cheap to travel in the country.

From Uvira the map showed a road heading northwestward toward Stanleyville, a dotted line indicating a dirt road passable only during the dry season. It appeared to pass through a vast, undeveloped, sparsely-populated jungle area. This area of northeast Congo has been notorious for strife and instability for decades, ever since Congo got independence in 1960. Tribal wars, army revolts, spillovers of conflicts from Rwanda and Uganda, and several home-grown would-be warlords all wreaked havoc on the area during the 1960's and later. Bandit groups occasionally emerged from the jungle to prey on and sometimes murder villagers and travelers along the road.

This is the road I set out to hitch on.

I lugged my suitcase to the edge of town and stood there ... and stood there ... and stood there ... seeing nary a vehicle passing ...

After a couple hours a truck finally came along and stopped. It was a beat-up dusty old thing that had doubtless plied the jungle roads for many years, a Dodge with running boards and round dented fenders, probably one-and-a-half tons, two tires on each rear wheel, faded from whatever original color to a nondescript gray, with a cab in front and a freight pen in the rear. Three men were crowded into the cab, rapidly dashing any hopes I might have had for a comfortable seat. One of the men gestured to the rear pen, where twenty or thirty people were standing, mostly men but with a few women and children.

I handed my suitcase up to some fellow and clambered up into the rear. The other standees shifted around a bit to make room for me, but we were still wedged in almost shoulder-to-shoulder. I was the only white person on the whole vehicle, but my fellow passengers didn't register any surprise at seeing me.

We started down the road, and red dust billowed out behind us. The road was rutted and bumpy and the truck's shock absorbers long since broken, so the freight pen's steel floor communicated every bump and pothole straight up my legs. Fortunately I managed to get a position standing beside the metal fence enclosing the pen, so I could at least hold onto something as we rattled along; pity the poor standees in the middle of the pen who tried to stabilize themselves against the bumps and lurches without any support. The muffler was rusted out, and the roar of the engine added to our discomfort.

We passed almost no vehicles and very few pedestrians and only a very occasional thatched-roof hut alongside the road. Jungle trees and vines and undergrowth crowded around us, right up to the edge of the road, creating the impression of lurching down a narrow winding corridor. The sun beat down through the opening overhead, making us hot, sweaty and miserable. I was probably the only one to get sunburned, though.

After an hour my legs began to ache. I tried shifting my weight back and forth between legs, but that brought hardly any relief. It got worse and worse as the hours wore on. No room to sit, even if I'd wanted to sit on the hard metal floor. There was nothing I could do unless I wanted to get out and stand by the road surrounded by jungle; I could envision myself standing through the night, plagued by malaria-carrying mosquitoes, fighting off jungle predators and getting miserably hungry and tired.

The dust gradually penetrated into my nose and lungs; I felt like I was dying of thirst. Nagging feelings of hunger began to gnaw at my stomach.

My fellow passengers seemed hospitable enough, but we could hardly communicate, and we were all agonizingly uncomfortable, and nobody felt like talking anyhow. A child vomited on floor. Her mother tried to comfort her but couldn't really do anything to alleviate her misery.

Once we stopped in front of a tiny thatched-roof mud shack, a 'shop' in a small clearing. The women immediately headed to one side of the clearing and squatted down to urinate, while the men headed to the other side and peed into the jungle. I did too, of course.

The 'shop' sold bottles of orange pop and packages of cookies and almost nothing else. I had become uncomfortably thirsty and hungry and figured I'd better take advantage of whatever nourishment the situation offered. I drank three bottles of orange soda, at room temperature; I figured (I *hoped*) it was safe to drink. It was sickeningly sweet and hardly quenched my thirst and made me feel bloated, but at least I figured it would help keep my body hydrated. And the cookies: dry sugary flavorless things, repulsively bland, zero nutritional value, a highly unsatisfactory 'meal.' At least it was cheap.

One of the privileged riders from the cab approached me while we were stopped by the clearing and spoke in English: "The fare is two dollars." I didn't see any other riders making any such payments; maybe that was a 'special fare, just for me'. I suspect the driver spotted me as a way to make some quick cash. Well, he had me over a barrel: if I refused to pay it, they might have abandoned me in the clearing until another vehicle came along, which might have meant waiting for who knows how long, judging from the almost total lack of traffic on the road. I reluctantly handed over the money.

After five or six hours we reached some small market town at a junction with another red-dirt road. The driver said something in a local language, and all the other passengers scrambled down, and so I got off too.

My body ached, my back hurt, my legs were excruciating, my muscles were stabbing with pain, my eyes and nose hurt from the dryness, my skin and hair and clothes were caked with red dust, and I was agonizingly thirsty and hungry. All-in-all, one of the most miserably uncomfortable rides I've ever had.

I had no map and no idea where I was in the jungle vastness, except presumably somewhere on the road to Stanleyville.

Fortunately I found an old woman cooking some kind of pancakes-with-a-bit-of-chicken on a crude charcoal stove under a tree. There were flies buzzing around, but the woman kept brushing them away from the dough. I watched as she poured some batter out of a metal bowl and spread it on a piece of flattened metal that served as a griddle. She pried a few scraps of meat off the carcass of a chicken with her fingernails and flicked them into the batter, making five pancakes. I hoped her fingers were clean and the batter wasn't rancid and the chicken wasn't contaminated. After a couple minutes she flipped the pancakes, and soon after that put them on a piece of brown paper and handed them to me: fifteen cents. At least they'd been cooked, so I had hopes they'd be safe to eat. You take risks when you're desperate. Surprisingly, they were quite tasty.

Then I got lucky: a kindly Congolese man approached me and said in English, "Would you like to visit our missionaries?"

"Oh, yes, please." He led me a short distance down the road and stopped in front of a small house made of wood, a contrast from the surrounding mud huts. He knocked at the door, and a man opened it and immediately invited me in and introduced me to his wife. They were both British; Jack looked about sixty and Fiona about forty. After a brief conversation Fiona asked if I'd like to stay for supper. "Oh, yes, thank you, if it's not too much trouble."

"Not at all," she replied. "We're glad to have some company from the outside world. We're happy to be serving the Lord, but it is rather isolated out here." She may have noticed the reddish grime on my face since she invited me to "freshen up a bit" in their bathroom, which I was only too glad to do.

Their two young daughters, probably about eight and six, joined us at the dinner table. Every so often they joined in the conversation, replying politely when spoken to or contributing a bit when they understood what the adults were talking about; then they headed for bed about 8:00 p.m. What polite, poised, alert, intelligent little girls!, I mused.

We talked into the late evening. Fiona explained, "Jack retired from his job in the civil service seven years ago. He got two years of training from the church, and then we came out here; been here five years."

Jack added, "We're Church of England. The Catholics got here before we did, so most of the Congolese who are Christian are Catholics."

"Well, you've got a challenge," I replied.

"We don't make many converts," Fiona, "but we still feel like we're doing some good. Their needs are so great."

"I'm surprised the church can afford to support you."

Jack responded, "It doesn't really, just a small allowance. I draw a pension from the British government, including a stipend for each of our daughters. They don't know what to make of us: not many old-age pensioners have school-age children."

Fiona added, "We're blessed to have children at our ages. Neither of us had children in our first marriages."

"We know it would be desirable if they had more interaction with white children their own ages," Jack continued, "but they do have some playmates among the Congolese children."

Fiona said, "They speak better Swahili than I do, and also some Lingala" [the most common regional language].

"What about their education?" I asked.

Fiona replied, "We're home-schooling them. The Ministry of Education sends us materials ... when they get here on time, which they don't always. When they're late, the girls read from our own collection of books."

It seemed to me they had a pretty hard life, but I was struck by what a happy family they appeared to be.

Late in the evening Fiona offered, "We don't have an extra bedroom, but you'd be welcome to sleep on our living-room couch." I was glad to accept.

After breakfast the next morning I waited beside the road for several hours and finally got a ride in another truck. This time I was lucky and got to share the front seat with the driver and his assistant. Once again the road was lined with jungle, and the red dust billowed out behind us. The road was so rough we could only make about 25 miles per hour. The road wasn't quite as deserted as the day before; we passed a few vehicles, mostly trucks like ours.

Toward evening we stopped in some settlement, just a clearing in the jungle, a few mud houses with ceilings made of mud-covered sticks. It apparently served as a 'truck stop', although we were the only vehicle there that night.

Out of curiosity I stepped into the jungle, which was so dense I could barely fit my body between the hanging vines and creepers. I walked literally three feet into the overgrowth and could barely see my way back into the clearing; if I'd gone six feet in, I might have gotten lost and conceivably not found my way back – it was that dense.

We ate an evening meal in a tiny mud-brick house – you could hardly call it a 'café' – with a pair of rickety wooden tables and a few chairs. The meal consisted of some kind of tough meat (goat? 'bushmeat'?) and some kind of starch (cassava root?) and more orange pop.

After the meal the driver led me to another mud hut and pointed to a bed made of straw, indicating that I should sleep there for the night. No other choice – had to trust that I wouldn't be robbed or murdered – didn't seem likely in this isolated place anyhow. I hoped the straw didn't harbor bedbugs or other parasites. No mosquito netting, but there was a small smudgy fire outside the huts' doors which fortunately seemed to keep most of the mosquitoes away.

I had heard some sounds coming from the jungle during the day, but nothing especially noticeable. After night fell, however, the cacophony really began: bird songs, insect buzzes, monkey chatter, tree-frog chirping, screams, roars, grunts, growls, howls and on and on. Some sounds were high-pitched, some low-pitched; they covered the whole range of the human ear. Many were repetitive, like frogs or insects, while a few punctuated the night only sporadically (an elephant trumpeting?). Some yowls and screams sounded like animals being tortured, although I suspect they were just normal night-time vocalizations. There was a whole variety of what I believed were bird calls. Some noises sounded like scratching, others like maniacal laughing or an exaggerated version of chickens clucking, still others like whistling or human voices singing, and some were even smooth and almost soothing. There was some kind of scraping sound I couldn't identify, possibly a gorilla 'growl' or maybe the grunting and panting of chimpanzees. There may have even been the low rumble of a jungle elephant.

I presumed – had to trust – that none of the animals would invade our tiny settlement. At first the racket kept me awake, but after a while I got used to it and drifted off to sleep.

I awoke once during the night when some small animal about the size of a rat scampered across my body – rather disconcerting. But nothing I could do about it except lie there and hope he wouldn't bite me. Eventually I drifted off to an uneasy sleep again.

I awoke another time when it started to rain. Fortunately it wasn't a heavy rain, just a slow drip-drip, and the thatched roof of my mud hut kept most of the rain out, although a few drops did filter down through the canopy and splatter on my body. Fortunately again, the air was warm enough that the moisture didn't bother me.

Next morning I reflected: what a night! – mud hut, straw bed, dripping rain, scampering animals, jungle screams. I'm sure it was quite routine to the handful of people who lived in the mud huts, but to me it was spectacular, *really* a night to remember.

It took us another half day to reach Stanleyville. As we approached the city I saw signs to the zoo and thought, why not? So I asked the driver to let me off at the zoo entrance road and carried my suitcase to the ticket window. The ticket seller and another man were sitting in a small room behind the window. I asked if they could watch my suitcase while I went in, just as I'd asked other petty officials to watch it in other situations, and they readily agreed.

But first I wanted to get out my sunglasses. The suitcase was soft-sided and basically impossible to lock; you opened it by unzipping the zipper on the side. I would have preferred not to open it in somebody else's presence, but this situation seemed safe enough. However, my pack of travelers checks fell out: ten $10 travelers checks. One of the Congolese exclaimed, *"L'argent!"* [money].

I responded, *"Ce n'est pas l'argent. C'est des cheques de voyage."* [it's not money; it's travelers checks], but I don't think my words registered with him; he repeated, *"L'argent."* I repeated, *"Cheques de voyage,"* and zipped it shut and went into the zoo.

I had read somewhere that the zoo had at one time been famous for its collection of jungle animals, including a rare pair of okapis, which vaguely resembled small short-necked giraffes with striped legs. They were gone (had died, I'm sure) when I got there, leaving nothing but a forlorn empty enclosure. I did see a pair of mangy fly-plagued jungle lions sprawled on the cement floor of their enclosure. A zookeeper came by as I watched and tossed some repulsive fly-covered red meat into the cage. The lions ignored it completely: no appetite, obviously quite sick. The few other animals that I saw didn't look much better, and there were a lot of empty cages.

Where's your veterinarian? Why don't you take better care of these poor creatures?! And what a shame the zoo had deteriorated so badly since the country got independence ... less than three years ago!! Is this what the end of colonialism was to mean over all of Africa? Or should I blame the deterioration on the former Belgian colonial regime for exploiting the country so ruthlessly and then abandoning it so abruptly?

In such poor conditions the zoo was a depressing place, and I left after wandering around for a while. I retrieved my suitcase, thanked the two guys who'd kept it for me – they seemed somewhat agitated – and caught a ride into the city.

> I unpacked the suitcase after I returned 'home' to Tabora and discovered that one travelers check was missing. It had to have been taken by the Congolese guys. I wrote to American Express, who wrote back that they might not refund my $10 since a couple weeks had elapsed after the theft. Eventually they did refund it, however, indicating that the thieves had never succeeded in cashing it; I doubt if they were even knowledgeable enough to try.

I was immediately struck by how badly the city had deteriorated. Stanleyville had had a reputation under Belgian rule of being surprisingly comfortable and sophisticated for a remote jungle outpost, known for its nightlife and fashion shows, but now plants were growing up through the streets, the buildings were decaying, electrical wires dangled from many of the streetlights, and most of the storefronts were empty.

I found a cheap, decrepit hotel – I mean, something straight out of Somerset Maugham: gray paint peeling off the walls, humidity so high that mold was growing on the woodwork (and don't even think of air-conditioning!), ragged and torn upholstery, bare electric light bulbs in my room flickering erratically on and off – a real end-of-the-earth kind of place.

Later somebody told me it had been, and still was, one of the best hotels in the city.

I spent a day wandering around the city, briefly visiting the old European quarter with its once-fancy homes. The open-air market was one of the largest and smelliest / dirtiest / most rubble-strewn I'd ever seen. It was also one of the most fascinating, especially the meat section, where I saw dead monkeys and parrots, what might have been gorilla feet, and other so-called 'bushmeat', presumably straight from the jungle. The meat was unprotected, and flies swarmed around it.

Another fascinating sight was the Congo River bank, with fishermen standing precariously on a rickety wooden structure and lowering wicker-basket nets into the swiftly-flowing water. Boatmen struggled to pole their long, narrow, hollowed-out-log canoes up the river. I watched as a vastly-overcrowded passenger ferry set out for a trip downriver, swinging out and almost turning around in the swift current, before the pilot got control. No wonder the explorer Henry M. Stanley (for whom the city was named) had such a hard time navigating up the river in the 1870s and 1880s. I'd considered the idea of taking the boat to Leopoldville, but it just looked too perilous, even if I'd had time for it.

In the evening I returned to my hotel, which featured an open-air terrace that at one time had been one of the fanciest watering-places in the city. There were only a few patrons that evening. I nodded to a couple at the next table over, the only other white faces on the terrace, and the husband responded, "What brings you to Stanley? We don't see many non-Africans here." Turned out they were the American consul and his wife. Most foreign-service people were so busy servicing the needs of itinerant business-men and tourists that they didn't have time for casual wayfarers like me, but this couple seemed glad to see me and invited me to join them at their table. I got the distinct impression Stanleyville was a rather lonely outpost and wasn't a top posting for an ambitious Foreign Service Officer.

Later that evening I got into a conversation with a middle-aged Greek businessman who was staying in the hotel while trying to set up some kind of business deal. He shortly turned the conversation to a recent evening when he'd "had a pressing need for sex." He'd asked some Congolese guy to bring him a woman, and the guy'd brought a young woman who spoke only Lingala. Even though they couldn't communicate, "she understood what I needed, and she satisfied it very well." He continued going into some detail about the encounter while watching my reaction. I eventually got the message that he was propositioning *me* for sex and made a hasty retreat.

Next day I saw a couple of white-and-blue vans emblazoned with huge black letters on the sides proclaiming U N O: the United Nations peace-keeping mission. Somebody told me a U.N. plane was leaving for

Leopoldville at 8:00 the next morning. A new challenge popped into my mind: maybe I could talk them into letting me onto that flight. So I found my way to their local headquarters, where I met Mr. Ten Garten, the regional chief of mission. A Dutchman and career U.N. civil servant, he was fully fluent in English. I tried to make up some reason that I had to get to Leopoldville, but the best I could do was claim to be a journalist. Mr. Ten Garten obviously didn't believe my story and refused to grant me permission.

On the morning of the flight I went out to the airport to see if I could talk the pilots into letting me on. It was easy to spot the plane, painted white with U N O emblazoned on its sides. But the pilots were reluctant to let me on without some kind of official orders. Shortly before the plane was due to take off Mr. Ten Garten appeared. He sized up the situation immediately and bawled me out for going behind his back. Embarrassed, I couldn't help but grin foolishly, which only made him angrier. He berated me for several minutes before finally allowing me to slink away.

I couldn't blame him; aside from my effrontery, I'm sure his job in that god-forsaken corner of the world had more than its share of frustrations.

Actually, it was probably good that I didn't get on the plane: how would I have gotten back to Stanleyville, especially since I only had a few days to get back to my teaching job in Tabora?

Back at the open-air dining terrace that evening, I got *really* lucky: met a middle-aged British missionary couple who told me they were driving to Uganda the next day and had room for me.

We left early the next morning, on a major road by Congolese standards but still a rough dirt track. It ran through the northeastern region of the country, which had become even more notorious than the jungle road for bandits who occasionally emerged from the forest to stop cars and rob the passengers at gunpoint. Sometimes they even murdered their victims. Fortunately we didn't encounter any trouble, but we all breathed sighs of relief when we got to the relative safety of Uganda. We made it all the way from Stanleyville to Uganda in one day, a welcome change from the three days it had taken to reach Stanleyville in the trucks. My hosts took me the far northwestern (West Nile) region of Uganda, a couple hundred miles from the capital and lake-port city of Kampala. But even in those far reaches it felt like civilization compared to the Congolese jungles, and riding in their comfortable car had certainly been a welcome contrast from the rattly old trucks of the previous week.

I made it to Kampala the next day, just in time to catch the weekly steamer across Lake Victoria to the port of Mwanza, Tanganyika, only about 150 miles north of Tabora. There was a rail line down to Tabora, but the train ride would have taken twelve hours, so I decided to hitch the distance instead. I made back it to Tabora in four hours, with a good 36 hours to spare before my teaching responsibilities resumed.

CHAPTER 15.
MADAGASCAR:
AN EXPATRIATE CHRISTMAS

After six months in Tabora, I was transferred to Dar-es-Salaam, the capital of Tanzania, a modest-sized city on the Indian Ocean, the east coast of Africa. I taught for a semester, then was granted permission to travel during the Christmas break.

I learned that a ship from the French line Messageries Maritimes was scheduled to sail from Dar to the port of Malajanga (the French called it Majunga) on the northwest coast of Madagascar, in early December and to return to Dar in early January. The timing was just right for me, so I booked a round-trip ticket – third class, of course.

I had hoped to find some compatible young people on the ship, but the passengers turned out to be mostly families of middle-aged parents and young children. Most of them had sailed from southern France, been on the ship for a couple weeks and long since formed their social groupings. They all spoke French to each other – spoke rapidly, idiomatically – effectively excluding me from most social interactions. What's more, I found many people's table manners rude and selfish: always served themselves first and most from the common dishes, talked while chewing with their mouths open, mostly ignored me. For accommodation I was assigned to a double room with a an older French guy who spread his clothes and toiletries all around the cabin, snored at night, and showed no interest in even being polite to me, let alone friendly and conversational. All-in-all, it was one of my least favorite sea voyages.

Malajanga had been the capital of a tribal empire before the time of European colonialism and then an important French administrative center, but by the time I arrived it had faded badly. I saw any number of empty, decaying buildings and even a shipwreck visible from the port. I stayed a night in the Majunga Hotel, which had been the finest hotel in the city at one time but was much decayed. My room was large and fancy, with elegantly-carved white-painted woodwork and a large porcelain washbasin with laminated gold fixtures. The bed was surmounted by a four-poster canopy and covered with a white fringed spread. But the room was un-airconditioned and smelled of musty linen. The hotel provided an electric fan that offered a bit of relief from the heat and humidity, although I still sweated through the night. Cost of a night's lodging: $1.

> Malajanga has recently become an attractive tourist site with beautiful beaches, tours to a few centuries-old shipwrecks on the nearby sea, and restored, picturesque architecture.

I hadn't found a guidebook to Madagascar in Dar, so I suffered the hitchhiker's frequent lament of lack of information about the country I was visiting. So, not knowing what else to do, I set out to hitch south to Antananarivo (Tananarive), the capital city in the central highlands. I got a ride in a nice comfortable Citroen sedan with a government official and his driver. The official was fluent in French and listened patiently as I struggled to construct coherent sentences using my one year of college French; the conversation would have been even better if I could have held up my end of it better.

It was a full day's trip, some 340 miles. The road was paved, unusual in continental Africa at that time, but with surprisingly little traffic. It snaked back and forth across the hilltops, making me carsick as the driver accelerated around each curve. At first the countryside was dry, uncultivated scrub brush, featureless and boring to ride through, but as we got into the highlands, I saw terraced rice paddies along the mountainsides, quite resembling pictures I'd seen of rice cultivation in southeast Asia.

Antananarivo (called Tana for short) was built on a mountain ridge in the center of the island, high enough to be cool and comfortable despite its semi-tropical location. After a night in a cheap hotel I set out to sightsee but soon discovered there was very little tourist information available. I chanced upon the United States Information Service (USIS) library and read that the island of Madagascar drifted apart from the African continent some 135-165 million years ago. Its flora and fauna evolved in isolation, resulting in some of the world's most unique biodiversity. It has more than 50 types of lemurs plus numerous species of chameleons, tortoises, frogs and others found nowhere else in the world. It has, or had, some 250 kinds of birds, about half of which are endemic. Unfortunately some of the most unique animal species have become extinct or are threatened because of hunting and habitat loss.

The people, called the Malagasy (or Malgache in French), are descended from sailors who are believed to have arrived from the Indonesian archipelago by outrigger canoe some 1700 to 2200 years ago. Later they mixed with Bantu immigrants from the African continent and still later with Arab sailors who came down the east coast of Africa as traders and slavers. Portuguese sailors 'discovered' the island in 1500. The British and French began competing for influence in the 17th century. Britain eventually conceded the territory to France, which invaded on a pretext in 1883 and assumed colonial overlordship in 1896. The French granted the country independence in 1960 but remained as the major European influence.

The USIS director was a very pleasant older American named Gabriel. He asked if I was new in town and invited me to his home for dinner, where I met his wife Amanda. They lived in a new-ish stucco house with modern amenities in a prosperous neighborhood also inhabited by many other expatriate Americans.

After dinner Gabriel said, "We're both widowed. This is the second marriage for both of us. We each remember wonderful Christmases with our first spouses and our children, but they're all grown and gone now. We would like you to stay with us for a few days and celebrate a family-style Christmas with us."

What a wonderful invitation! I'd been half-dreading, half-resigned to spending Christmas alone in a crummy hotel someplace, so this was like a call from heaven. I accepted gratefully.

Next evening, December 24, we went to a Christmas party with a couple dozen other Americans, mostly embassy people and some businessmen.
It was a warm, welcoming, wonderful evening. The other guests took an
interest in my East African teaching program, and we all swapped stories
about Christmases back in The States and about our respective travels. We
sang the traditional carols, including a doubtless off-key rendition of O
Tanenbaum ('Oh Christmas Tree') in German by four of us. As expatriates we all appreciated each other's fellowship and the reminders of home.
Unlike other expatriate gatherings I've attended, this group didn't spend
much time complaining about the discomforts of living in Madagascar or
the 'uncivilized' behavior of the host-country citizens. Maybe it was just
due to the holiday glow.

On Christmas Day my hosts gave me a necktie and a package of dried
native Madagascar fruits. I was embarrassed and apologetic that I didn't
have any gifts for them in exchange, but they were very understanding.
[After I returned to Dar I sent them a pair of Makonde figures, considered
the best indigenous carvings of East Africa.]

Next evening my hosts invited me to accompany them to another couple's home for bridge. The men were partnered against the women. I sat
and watched them play for a couple hours, trying to be polite but feeling
impatient and bored. Eventually Amanda invited me to sit in for her. Eager
to show off my prowess at the game, I brashly doubled an opening bid by
Gabriel. This gave him the opportunity to redouble, which he did – with
relish. Afterwards I confided to Amanda that perhaps I was too brazen,
but she assured me that the redoubling was the highlight of her husband's
evening.

On the third day I was ready to strike out on my own again. That
evening I found a cheap hotel and decided after supper to see if there was
any night life in the city. It was a rather cold night at 4,000 feet elevation
– temperature in the 50's – and I shivered in my windbreaker jacket, the
warmest piece of clothing I had with me. I ran across a couple 'night clubs',
forlorn, rundown joints with recorded music and a few men looking over
the available women, but they had no allure for me.

More interesting was a pair of picnic tables in the middle of a city
square with a motley crowd of men and women gathered around. I tried to
strike up a conversation with two Japanese men, but they spoke no English
and very little French. They did manage to communicate that they were

the captain and first mate on a fishing vessel and had been away from their families for two months. One showed me a picture of his wife and children, with an achingly sad expression on his face; he almost wept as he looked at it. Shortly thereafter two young Malgache women – prostitutes – came and joined us. They were obviously well-acquainted with the fishermen and obviously planning to spend the night with them – solace to lonely seamen. But the two nationalities could hardly communicate with each other. Instead, the men sat on one side of the table and talked Japanese together, while the women sat on the other side and gossiped in Malagasy. Well, I figured their evening's activities wouldn't require much verbal communication.

I vaguely considered the idea of linking up with another of the women but immediately thought better of it: unfamiliar city, crummy hotel, the difficulty of communication, the threat of disease, the possibility of being robbed, even some lingering sense of morality, and, frankly, shyness or lack of confidence. So: another night in a lonely rundown hotel room.

Time to move on. The Christmas party acquaintances had suggested the idea of going to Amber Mountain National Park, one of the country's two national parks at that time, where there was a spectacular collection of Madagascar's exotic wildlife. They cautioned me, however, that it was at the island's northern tip, more than 500 miles over rough roads, and so, aware of my limited time, I rejected that idea.

People also suggested two other possibilities: I could head east through the mountains and jungle toward the coast, although the region was pretty underdeveloped, with rough unpaved roads and an oppressively humid, unhealthy coastal area, or I could head down the country's central spine, where the road was mostly paved and there were some towns with colorful markets and picturesque French-colonial architecture. I decided to take the latter route.

At the time of my visit Madagascar hadn't yet started its thrust into environmental protection. As one of the poorest countries on earth and with a population over five million, it was losing by some estimates more than 600 square miles of forest each year due to logging, clearing for coffee planting, mining, subsistence farming and gathering of wood for fuel.

In the late 20th century, by which time the population was approaching *20 million*, government leaders realized that ecotourism could create jobs and generate income while protecting wildlife habitats and preserving the remaining forests. By early 2000's they had established almost fifty national parks, wildlife preserves and 'strict nature reserves,' and they planned to place almost ten percent of the land area under protection.

The road south was mostly paved, but there was surprisingly little traffic, and I often had to wait an hour or two between short rides. Most of the drivers spoke a little French, and we had some rudimentary but interesting conversations. One less-than-satisfactory ride was with a sales rep, a 'route man' for a cigarette company, driving a tiny Citroen *deux chevaux* truck. We poked along at 20 to 25 mph; I could have tolerated that, except that he stopped frequently at small roadside stores and went in to talk to the proprietors, doubtless pushing his brand of cigarettes. After the third such stop I got impatient, thanked him, and went back to the road. When I got a ride an hour later, he was still inside the shop.

I made only about a hundred miles that day and another hundred the second day, ending up in Ambositra the second night. The Christmas-party acquaintances had told me the region was known for its wood carvings, so I agreed to follow when a boy in his mid-teens approached the next morning and offered to guide me to a carvings factory. The factory proprietor greeted me effusively and invited me into the back room, where I saw women and children sitting on the floor half-heartedly poking at pieces of wood with knives. The proprietor said I could ask questions of the workers; when I had none, he invited me into his showroom, which had – of course – carvings of all sizes and subjects and prices. I recognized several different kinds of lemurs and birds endemic to the island. They also included human figurines, some straightforward and some in humorous poses and even a few suggestive of sexual interactions between men and women – something for everybody's tastes. The prices ranged from $1 or $2 up to $50 and more for the large pieces.

"Lesquels font vous aimee?" ("Which ones do you like?") the proprietor asked.

"Ils sont tous jolie" ("They're all nice"), I replied, hoping that would satisfy him.

"Merci. Mais quelles pieces voulez vous?" he insisted.

I noticed the teen-aged boy lingering in the background and divined that he was hoping for a tip from the proprietor. It was then I realized the purpose of the 'factory' was not to produce carvings but to sell them to tourists, who think they're getting them cheaper at the source. I beat a hasty retreat – without buying anything.

I got to Fianarantsoa the third day, where I found a hotel that was actually quite nice, a cut above the ones I'd stayed in the previous three nights, although still only about a dollar a night. I also wandered into a tourist shop, where I saw carvings similar to those in the Ambositra 'factory' at *half of the 'factory's' prices*. You think you're getting a special deal at the 'factory,' but it's really just an elaborate show, a delusion for gullible tourists.

December 31. I hitched to a village a few miles out of the city that somebody had told me was picturesque. And it was – but one more market, a few more once-elegant-but-now-decayed buildings, nothing special. I walked around for a couple hours and got rather tired. Heading back into Fianarantsoa, I watched several colorful wooden oxcarts plod past, pulled by *zebu* cattle, which were related to the Brahman cows of India, with the characteristic fatty hump over their shoulders. Just for kicks I stuck out my thumb, and a cart driver stopped. He was a pleasant fellow, but we could hardly communicate – what do you say to a peasant oxcart driver who barely knows ten words of French? We plodded along at maybe two miles an hour, amusing for a while, but then I got impatient as I watched several cars zoom past and got off and stuck out my thumb for one of those.

New Year's Eve: my third night in the Fianarantsoa hotel. I would have liked to go to a party someplace, but of course I didn't know a soul in the city. Besides, I was tired, so I resigned myself to an uneventful evening and went to bed about 9:00 p.m.

I was jarred awake a little before midnight by noise from below. I realized I wasn't going to fall back asleep, so I got dressed and went downstairs, where a party of riotous Frenchmen and women immediately invited me to join them. Another expatriate celebration, only this time with Frenchmen! I spent the next three hours with them and had a pretty good time: the more alcohol we all consumed, the more fluent in English they became, and the more fluent in French I became.

Interesting – surprising, even – there were no Malgache at the gathering. Even though the country had been independent for more than three years, many French still viewed *les indigenes,* as they called them, with a mixture of condescension and disdain and apparently weren't interested in socializing with them. I got some sense of why the French were still in Madagascar – some were optimistic about the country's future and believed they could help promote its development, while others simply believed they could get higher salaries in *les colonies* (where the French government heavily subsidized them) than they could back home

Around 2:00 a.m. an attractive if quite-inebriated Frenchwoman made moves to kiss me. I was half-willing and half-embarrassed and turned away after the most modest brush of the lips. Thank heaven for the lightness of the touch when I realized that her husband was watching from the next table! Narrowly avoided a disaster!

I awoke around 11:00 the next morning, a little hung over, but suddenly alarmed that I had three days to get back to Malajanga, more than 500 miles to the north, to catch my ship back to Dar. Headed to the road, stuck out my thumb, fortunately had good luck and made it to Tana that same afternoon and to some small town 100 miles short of Malajanga the second day.

On the third day I got a ride with a French guy about my age named Jean-Claude. That was over the boring stretch of the road with the scrub brush, but we were quite compatible and had a good time swapping stories and making jokes in Franglais. He invited me to stay in his apartment in Malajanga that evening, although he could offer me only a lumpy mattress on the floor. It wasn't the most comfortable bed, but after an evening's consumption of wine I had no trouble falling asleep.

I awoke about 8:00 the next morning and remembered with a start that my ship was due to sail at 9:00. Jean-Claude was dressing to go to work. "Could you drive me to the Messageries Maritimes office right now?"

"It will make me late for work," he protested, but added, "I will do it for you."

We got there about 8:45 and dashed into the manager's office.

"I'm sorry I'm late. We were ... uh ... delayed ... uh ... unforeseen difficulties ... My ship's sailing at 9:00! Can you get me on it?!" I begged.

"I can't promise, but we can try," the manager replied; fortunately he was fluent in English.

He drove me to the dock – just in time to see the ship cast its lines and start toward the sea.

What a sinking feeling, standing on the shore watching your ship pull away! I felt overwhelmed with distress, self-blame, self-anger, self-disgust, ...

"Come with me!" the manager exclaimed and dashed down the dock to a patrol boat. "Get in!" He ordered the patrol boat pilot to: *"Suivez cette navire!* (Follow that ship!)" And off we went, bobbing up and down in the passenger ship's wake. Our boat's motor alternately roared and sputtered as the propeller lifted out of the water and plunged back into the waves, and the ocean spray slashed into our faces. We hollered and waved our arms as we pursued the receding ship, which loomed above our heads as we struggled to catch up.

But realistically there was almost no chance anybody on the ship would hear us or notice us, and our pursuit was in vain. The gap between us and the ship inexorably widened even as we watched. Redoubled distress, self-blame, self-anger, self-disgust, ...

Back in the shipping manager's office, I asked, "Messageries is a member of IATA. Could you transfer my ticket over to an airline so I can fly back to Dar-es-Salaam?"

> IATA, the International Air Transport Association, represents airlines' interests. In the 1960's and later it fixed air fares on most major routes. Messageries Maritimes was the only ocean-shipping member.

"I'm afraid not. It wasn't Messageries' fault that you missed the boat," he replied.

I had brought only $200 on this trip and had spent about half of it, so I was suddenly panicked that I wouldn't be able to buy a plane ticket back to Dar – what if I couldn't get back to my job?!

Damn fool!! – cut it too close again, unprepared for contingencies, stupid not to bring a cash cushion, angry at my own immaturity! But again, why should I have expected ... ?

Then, fortunately, the manager must have read the distress in my face because he said, "Hand me your ticket." He stamped something on it and handed it back with another piece of paper. "This will get you on the Air France flight leaving day after tomorrow from Tananarive Airport. Don't miss this one!"

"Thanks!! You saved my life!" I heaved a sigh of relief, doubly appreciating that he had bent the rules to do me a huge favor.

Back out on the road, my third time over the same stretch of scrub brush, this time the boredom exacerbated by the worry that I might not get to the airport in time for the flight. I only made about 100 miles that day, even though I waited by the road until three hours after sunset, seeing almost no cars or trucks passing in the night. Stayed in some cheap local hotel, slept only fitfully.

Out on the road early the next morning, 250 miles to go, but at least getting into the more-populated area. One ride, maybe 50 miles; hour's wait; second ride, 20 miles; third ride, a little better, 100 miles. At least there was beginning to be a little more traffic on this stretch of the road. Mid-afternoon. Belated bite of lunch in a roadside stand, glancing nervously at my watch. Next ride, another 50 miles, getting closer, but where was the airport located ...? 7:00 p.m., night beginning to fall ...

Then, fortunately, a ride with a well-dressed Malgache gentleman, told me the airport was to the north of Tananarive, just off the road we were driving on. Deposited me right at the terminal about 8:00 p.m. Whew, made it!

Only place I could find to sleep in the airport was a large plush chair. Well, anywhere in an emergency. I sprawled in the chair, got a few hours of fitful sleep, arose at 5:00 to catch my 7:00 a.m. flight; arrived in Dar-es-Salaam around 10:00.

> The plane was scheduled to fly on to Nairobi, Addis Ababa, Cairo, Athens and Paris by the end of the day.

I discovered that in my rush to catch my flight, I'd failed to exchange almost $100 worth of Malagasy currency back into dollars. I took the currency to the Dar-es-Salaam bank that had sold it to me, but they were unwilling to buy it back. Rats! – a lot of un-spendable money to get stuck with.

Well, the Messageries ship was due in port that afternoon. Maybe they'd take it. So I went down to the ship and, sure enough, the bartender was willing to buy it from me, at a price a little over $100, a better rate than the amount I'd paid for it – made a slight profit on it! I vaguely considered the idea of going back to the Dar-es-Salaam bank, buying more Malagasy currency, and selling it to the bartender. In economics they call that currency arbitrage, buying in one market and selling in another. But it would have taken a couple hours, would have been only a small profit, and would have run the risk that maybe the bartender would run out of dollars and be unwilling to buy any more Malagasy money from me. Better leave currency arbitrage to the banks.

———

Looking back now, I regret not having taken better advantage of the opportunities Madagascar offered. If I'd had more money, I could have seen some of the exotic wildlife and scenery, even though the country didn't yet have adequate facilities to support such sightseeing.

On the other hand, my primary purpose on this trip, as on most of my others, was not to maximize the amount of sightseeing I did, but rather to maximize the variety of experiences. By travelling on the cheap I was able to go more places and meet a greater variety of people than if I'd paid more and traveled more comfortably.

And I was still putting aside savings for future adventures.

CHAPTER 16.
SOMALIA: BAR GIRLS AND AN EVIL SPIRIT

The headmistress of my school in Dar-es-Salaam granted me leave to travel during our two-week mid-semester break in April. I learned that an Italian freighter was scheduled to put into Dar at the start of the break, then continue up the African coast. The timing was perfect for me to take this ship to Mogadishu, Somalia, fly to Nairobi, and hitch back to Dar, so I booked a ticket.

I boarded the freighter early one afternoon. My African girlfriend Honore came to see me off, but the ship's captain wouldn't allow her to come on board, so I had to bid her farewell on shore. "He thinks all African women are prostitutes," she fumed.

The freighter trip was interesting enough: meals in the ship's officers' dining room, conversations with some other adventurous travelers, star-gazing at night in the wind on the top deck.

Our first port of call was Mombasa, Kenya. We arrived about noon one day and were scheduled to depart the next afternoon, giving me a little over twenty-four hours shore leave. I had visited Mombasa the previous year and seen its few sights, so I decided to hitch out of town on a road along the north coast. The road was mostly sand, which made slow going, but I made it to the town of Malindi by late afternoon.

I ran into a young British woman teacher who invited me to come to dinner with her and her housemate. They were among the few Europeans living in the town and were glad to have the company of another white face. Indeed, they readily invited me to sleep on their couch for the evening. We played poker for an hour, and I happened to win a couple pounds. At the end of the game I insisted on giving back my winnings, saying I didn't feel right about taking their money when I was accepting their hospitality.

Early the next morning I headed back toward Mombasa. My first ride dropped me in some small settlement with maybe two dozen mud huts. I had to urinate, so I stepped off the road into what I thought was a private spot and relieved myself. When I was done, I glanced around and discovered half-a-dozen African kids watching me. They never said a word, never smiled or frowned, just stared at me in silence. Was it such a novelty to watch a *muzungu* (European) pee?

Then an African guy appeared with a pre-nubile girl in tow, whom I guessed to be about twelve or thirteen. I assumed she was his daughter until he offered to sell her to me. The poor girl looked half-miserable, half-hopeful: slump-shouldered but trying to smile. I could have had her for two pounds – about $5.60. I actually vaguely considered buying her and taking her to Mombasa and freeing her – abandoning her – but quickly realized that that would have been an even worse fate than leaving her in the care of a man who didn't want her. She would have had to turn to begging and, doubtless, prostitution as soon as she reached puberty. And I obviously couldn't take her on the ship with me, even if I'd been willing to take on the responsibility of caring for her.

I made it to Mombasa with a half-hour to spare before my ship sailed.

We hit Mogadishu two days later. It was another candidate for my list of Most Unimpressive National Capitals. Most of the buildings seemed to be made of mud bricks, and its business district was a sprawl of small shops and street peddlers. It had a small contingent of Europeans and Americans: a white woman came up to me in the street and commented, "You're new here, aren't you?" She turned out to be the wife of the American ambassador. She invited me to join her family at the beach and for dinner afterwards. She offered to contact a young male Foreign Service Officer named Chris who lived in his own small house to see if he could put me up.

I ended up staying with Chris three nights. He said he spoke three Scandinavian languages and had served four years in Copenhagen. He lamented being sent to "this God-forsaken corner of the world" after such an idyllic posting, but said it was Foreign Service policy to move its officers around every four years. We discussed the relative merits of Scandinavian and African women. He noted, "Somali women have big butts and small breasts, but they're enthusiastic in bed."

In those days Somalia was ruled by a king, who may have been old, infirm, incompetent and corrupt, but at least the country was stable and the city streets relatively safe. There wasn't much to see or do in Mogadishu and only a few roads out of town, so my second day there, I decided out of boredom to hitch to the nearby town of Balcad, twenty miles into the interior. The road was all sand, and Balcad turned out to be a collection of low mud buildings with absolutely nothing of interest. I considered venturing further inland, but several people cautioned me against it, saying there were tribesmen who would think nothing of killing me for whatever money and clothing I had. As a white-skinned foreigner I would be an especially inviting target.

Back in Mogadishu I met an older American and a Spanish guy about my age who spoke a little English. The American had built a fairly large but crude sailboat out of wood in Mombasa and had sailed it northwards along the African coast until he ran into a storm that damaged the boat and washed it onto the shore. He'd been living in Mogadishu for several months while trying to design a winch to get the boat back into the sea. He'd enlisted the help of the Spanish guy, who had deserted from the French Foreign Legion. The latter told about the hardships in the Legion: lousy pay, lousy food, lousy uncomfortable barracks, hardship postings in isolated desert stations, sadistic officers, cruel and inhuman punishments for slight infractions, fellow soldiers who were fleeing from the law, and so on. He said the standard punishment for desertion was death by firing squad. He was trying to get back to Spain while avoiding French soil. Sure destroyed any illusions I might have had about the romance of the Foreign Legion.

I didn't want to overstay my welcome with Chris. Fortunately I met an American marine who told me about a bar where a lot of locals and foreigners hung out. So I lugged my suitcase about a mile and walked into the place about 7:00 p.m. It was a fairly large room with a goodly number of Somalis and a few Caucasians. I approached some white guys sitting with Somali women and asked, "Can I join you guys?" (Takes courage – effrontery? – to invite yourself to join a group of strangers, even if they were fellow countrymen.) They looked me over for a minute, and then one said, "Sure, siddown," gesturing to an empty seat.

They turned out to be marines assigned to guard the American embassy. One of them was nicknamed "Gunny," an appropriate name for a marine, I thought. He was the sergeant, in command of the small contingent posted there. Most of the Somali women spoke a sort of knockabout English, ungrammatical but serviceable, that they'd probably learned from the marines. Gunny began negotiating with one of them. They agreed on a price for the night, and then he said, "I'm gonna stay here and drink with my buddies for a while. When I'm ready to leave, I'll signal you like this" – giving his head a jerk – "and you come with me." She agreed, but as soon as he walked away, she said, "I don't like Gunny." They didn't like him, but they were willing to f--- him and take his money.

I got into a conversation with a woman named Kedijah, who soon invited me to go home with her. I didn't feel entirely comfortable about going with a pick-up in a strange city and unfamiliar culture – was it unsafe? dirty? did she have a disease? – but I decided if the marines could do it, I could too. We took a taxi back to her place, a room with white-washed mud-brick walls and a few sticks of furniture in a one-story mud-brick building. I carried my suitcase into the room, hoping it wouldn't be stolen during the night. There was a double bed where a woman and a child were sleeping. Kedijah woke them and spoke to them, apparently telling them to leave, which they did, reluctantly. She gestured for me to lie down on the bed, which I did, reluctantly, feeling guilty about evicting the woman and child – where would they have to sleep? I was coming to feel that I didn't especially like Kedijah, but I'd gotten myself into this situation and didn't have any practical alternative except to spend the night with her. I had sex with her – once – and then fell into an uncomfortable sleep.

Next morning my suitcase was still there. I gave Kedijah fifteen shillings – about $2 – and left as soon as I could.

That evening I went back to the bar – what else can you do when you're alone in a strange city? – and it was a friendly place, very welcome to a lonely wayfarer. The marines weren't there, but several of the women were, including Kedijah. I acknowledged her presence but didn't engage her in conversation. Instead, I starting talking with Amina, who also invited me to spend the night. I wasn't eager to repeat my previous night's experience, but Amina seemed somehow nicer than Kedijah, and so I half-reluctantly decided to go home with her. Kedijah watched us leave but didn't seem particularly upset.

Amina's place turned out to be quite nice: third (top) floor of a house, half open-air, half roofed. She had a kitchen, living room, bedroom with a double bed, and an indoor oriental-style toilet. I stayed with her three days. We quickly developed a sort of quasi-domestic lifestyle: she prepared meals, which we ate family-style, sitting at her table. I went grocery-shopping with her (paid for the groceries), helped her clean the apartment, relaxed and read or listened to music with her in the evenings. We even brushed our teeth together, me with a toothbrush and she with a twig from a tree: she chewed on the end to soften it up a bit, then polished it up and down on each tooth. Well, who's to say whether a toothbrush or a twig is better?

I guessed she was in her early twenties. She was surprisingly fluent in English and obviously not stupid, even though she'd had only three years of formal schooling, and we had several quite interesting conversations. She was married, the fourth and youngest wife of a much older tribal chieftain who had paid a substantial bride-price to her father. She hadn't had any choice in the matter – was forced into the arranged marriage – and said her husband was tyrannical. Eventually she'd fled him and come to Mogadishu, where she'd found a job in the bar. She had had a long-term relationship with an American Peace Corps volunteer – "He want to marry me" – but hadn't wanted to leave her own country. I never learned if he was black or white.

On the first afternoon we went out, she covered the mirror with a cloth. I looked at her questioningly, and she said, "That's so Jinn can't get out." I knew Somalis believed Jinn was an evil spirit who dwelt in mirrors and liked to come out and wreak havoc when nobody was home. Sometimes you could catch a glimpse of him if you turned suddenly and stared into the mirror. She immediately looked embarrassed, however, possibly fearing I would make fun of her superstition. She refused to discuss it any further and didn't cover the mirror the next time we went out.

She wore a bra and blouse when we went out but took them off and went bare-breasted around the house. She had beautiful breasts, round and firm and dusky-colored with almost-black nipples, and seemed to enjoy having me caress them, which I did frequently. We had sex two or three times a day. Sometimes she put a spoonful of sugar into her mouth, then turned to kiss me, making a very sweet kiss, if somewhat over-salivated. She liked to have a pretend-struggle before the sex act, in which I was supposed to overwhelm her and quasi-rape her. But that didn't work too well for me – I didn't feel comfortable even pretending to rape someone and didn't always get erections during this play.

On the morning I left we had sex one more time. I gave her 100 shillings – $14 – I considered it my contribution to the rent. That actually exceeded my three-dollar-a-day budget, although I got the impression the marines might have given her even more.

I hitched to the airport and flew to Nairobi, where Grace, an African woman I'd dated in Dar-es-Salaam, met me. This one was a true long-term girlfriend, and indeed she'd eagerly tried to persuade me to marry her. We'd had an intense romance in Dar, and then she'd given up and moved to Nairobi. I was feeling slightly guilty about my sojourn with Amina, temporary though it was, until I learned that Grace had found an English boyfriend named Michael in my absence. Grace introduced me to him and seemed quite comfortable that each of us knew she was sleeping with the other; indeed, she told me, "He's very lustful." He was quite entranced with her – she was quite an intriguing woman – and wanted to marry her. She even persuaded him to loan me his car one evening so she and I could go out dancing. She spent the next couple nights with me and then, after I left, went back to Michael.

So it goes in Africa.

———

I still had to get back to Dar, some 400 miles distant. I got a slow start out of Nairobi and only made it to Moshi, Tanzania, on the slopes of Mount Kilimanjaro, about 150 miles, the first day. No problem: I figured I'd go stay with a fellow TEAer named Dave Court, an English fellow I'd gotten to know during our teacher training in Uganda. He'd been posted to Moshi Boys School after we finished the training. He lived in a modest cement-block cottage on the school grounds at the edge of town on the slopes of Mount Kilimanjaro, similar to the cement-block house I'd been allocated in Dar.

We didn't have telephones in those days, so I couldn't call in advance. But no problem: we were accustomed to dropping in on one another unannounced – it was quite acceptable in the less-developed conditions of Africa. I knocked on his door, but nobody answered, so I went around back to see if there was a servant's quarters. Most expatriates had a domestic servant, usually male, called a 'houseboy,' who cooked, cleaned and did the laundry. (The term sounds demeaning today, but it was customary among both Europeans and indigenous Africans in those post-colonial days.) And sure enough, there was a small house, also made of cement blocks, where Dave's houseboy lived with a wife and small child.

The houseboy greeted me in Swahili, and I understood enough to reply that I was a friend of Dave's and was hoping to visit him that night. The houseboy accepted me unquestioningly; he said Dave wasn't there – was traveling somewhere – but he (houseboy) had a key and could open the door so I could stay there that evening. (Like many expatriates, we TEA'ers entrusted our houseboys with keys to our houses.) He even offered to cook a meal and make up a bed for me, which I accepted. It felt a little strange to be making myself at home in somebody else's house without him there, but this was Africa …

I was just settling down to eat the meal when Dave came in. He didn't seem surprised to see me – turned out he'd driven to Dar over the weekend and had stayed in my place! My houseboy wasn't there – he lived across town since there were no servants' dwellings accompanying the expatriates' houses in my subdivision – but Dave had asked the next-door neighbors to let him into my place and had slept there for two nights. So it went with TEA hospitality …! He'd had to drive into town for his evening meals, though.

Dave assured me I was welcome to stay in his place as long as I liked, but he wanted to go spend the night with his girlfriend, an African woman who taught at the girls' school a couple miles away. So I spent the night alone in his place.

Dave later married the girlfriend and stayed in East Africa working for an international agency for several more years.

Next morning I tipped the houseboy five shillings (as per standard etiquette) and set out to hitch the rest of the way to Dar. The road southeast out of Moshi was one of the few roads paved with asphalt; most of the other roads were rough gravel. An African fellow about my age named Humphrey picked me up on the outskirts of Moshi. He was a university graduate and had a salaried job, which immediately put him into the ranks of the privileged elite, and he had a late-model car.

We breezed along at 50 miles an hour discussing Tanzania's prospects for development. Pretty soon we came upon an old grey-ish school-type bus parked on the road, which was a common practice since the traffic was so light. Women wearing colorful cotton-print dresses were lifting bundles off the tops of their heads, and men dressed in ragged shirts and pants were loading them onto the top of the bus, a typical scene in Africa. I thought we should slow down since there were so many people milling around, but Humphrey maintained his 50 mph. I wondered if he considered his status so important that he didn't have to slow down for these uneducated countrymen.

Unfortunately an old fellow came out from behind the bus and stepped into our path. Humphrey hit the brakes, but it was too late, and we hit him. Humphrey then stopped. I went over to the old fellow, who was lying on the ground. I could see his right leg was broken; the ragged edge of his calf-bone was pressing up against the skin. He must have been in quite a bit of pain, but he didn't wince or complain. I knew virtually nothing about first aid but had read that anybody who suffers trauma like this would most likely be in shock and should be kept warm. So I borrowed somebody's jacket and covered the injured man. Very soon he began to sweat profusely in the morning heat, so I took the jacket back off.

Nobody else seemed to have any better idea what to do; they just stood around watching. The few people who said anything were speaking a local language, so neither Humphrey or I could communicate with them. The idea of trying to set the broken leg even passed fleetingly through my mind, but I knew that would be disastrous. I did remember reading that you shouldn't move an accident victim but should wait for an ambulance corpsman or other knowledgeable person to do so. In the U.S. somebody would have tried to alert a highway patrolman and an ambulance, but such resources didn't exist on African roadways. The injured man was left to the mercy of his fellow citizens

As a product of the litigation-prone U.S.A., I immediately began speculating about a lawsuit and liability, but that too was obviously way beyond the scope of an unsophisticated country with a rudimentary court system.

Humphrey was beginning to get impatient as we fussed around. I thought the decent thing would at least be to take the injured man to the nearest hospital and meekly suggested we do so, but Humphrey didn't seem inclined to. I was only a hitchhiker dependent on his hospitality, so I didn't feel comfortable urging him.

About that time a rickety old three-wheeled truck came rattling along. Apparently the other people prevailed upon the driver to take the injured man to a hospital. The last thing I remember as Humphrey and I pulled away was some men helping lift the injured man into the truck's rear freight pen. Poor old guy, almost certainly doomed to spend the rest of his life as a cripple ... through no fault of his own.

Humphrey got me back to Dar by nightfall without further incident.

———

My contract with the Teachers for East Africa program ended in December 1964. Everybody else on the program got on planes and flew home, but I wasn't especially homesick and wasn't tired of the discomforts of low-end living in Third World countries. I was still eager for the excitement and the learning I could get from further travels.

Granted, I had wasted a lot of time standing beside roadsides with my thumb stuck out, but my kind of travel-on-the-cheap allowed me to go more places, spend more time and see more things than if I'd paid more money and traveled in more conventional ways. It was right for me, even if it wouldn't have been right for most people.

The experiences of living and traveling in so many foreign countries afforded me a certain kind of education, which, hopefully, could be augmented by work experience and/or book-learning and could eventually form the basis for a career. I thought about trying for the Foreign Service, but the prospect of starting in an entry-level position and working my way up through the bureaucracy didn't appeal to me. Maybe I could build a career in international business, finance, law or consulting, but again the nature of the everyday work didn't appeal to me. Also, it was highly questionable how much help the international experiences would be in any of those jobs – I was aware that the travel adventures might turn out to be a pleasant and personally rewarding interval in my life, but with no direct relevance to my future career.

Another possibility would be an academic career. I'd been a teacher for two years, thought I'd done pretty well at it, and had quite enjoyed it. This route would involve a lot of book learning – several years of grinding away in graduate school and then the rat race to get tenure in some college or university.

I actually considered the idea of continuing to travel – becoming an itinerant (a bum) – and supporting myself at whatever jobs I could find. However, this life style might have been OK in my twenties, but not in my forties.

Maybe the best compromise would be to spend another year traveling and postpone the career decision until I returned to the U.S.

On to new adventures!

HITCHHIKE THE WORLD
BOOK II: MIDDLE EAST AND ASIA
BY WILLIAM A. STOEVER